GUIDES

SARDINIA

www.insightguides.com/Italy

⊙ Walking Eye App

Your Insight Guide now includes a free app and eBook, dedicated to your chosen destination, all included for the same great price as before. They are available to download from the free Walking Eye container app in the App Store and Google Play. Simply download the Walking Eye container app to access the eBook and app dedicated to your purchased book. The app features an up-to-date A to Z of travel tips, information on shops, activities and destination highlights, as well as hotel, restaurant and bar listings. See below for more information and how to download.

MULTIPLE DESTINATIONS AVAILABLE

Now that you've bought this book you can download the accompanying destination app and eBook for free. Inside the Walking Eye container app, you'll also find a whole range of other Insight Guides destination apps and eBooks, all available for purchase.

DEDICATED SEARCH OPTIONS

Use the different sections to browse the places of interest by category or region, or simply use the 'Around me' function to find places of interest nearby. You can then save your selected restaurants, bars and activities to your Favourites or share them with friends using email, Twitter and Facebook.

FREQUENTLY UPDATED LISTINGS

Restaurants, bars and hotels change all the time. To ensure you get the most out of your guide, the app features all of our favourites, as well as the latest openings, and is updated regularly. Simply update your app when you receive a notification to access the most current listings available.

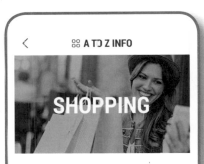

Shopping in Oman still revolves around the traditional souks that can be found in every town in the country – most famously at Mutrah in Muscat, Salalah and Nizwa, which serve as showcases of traditional Omani craftsmanship and produce ranging from antique khanjars and Bedu jewellery to halwa, rose-water and frankincense. Muscat also boasts a number of modern malls, although these are rare elsewhere in the country.

TRAVEL TIPS & DESTINATION OVERVIEWS

The app also includes a complete A to Z of handy travel tips on everything from visa regulations to local etiquette. Plus, you'll find destination overviews on shopping, sport, local events, health, children's activities and more.

HOW TO DOWNLOAD THE WALKING EYE

Available on purchase of this guide only.
1. Visit our website: www.insightguides.com/walkingeye
2. Download the Walking Eye container app to your smartphone (this will give you access to both the destination app and the eBook)
3. Select the scanning module in the Walking Eye container app
4. Scan the QR code on this page – you will be asked to enter a verification word from the book as proof of purchase
5. Download your free destination app* and eBook for travel information on the go

* Other destination apps and eBooks are available for purchase separately or are free with the purchase of the Insight Guide book

Contents

THE BEST OF SARDINIA: TOP ATTRACTIONS

From wild landscapes, beautiful beaches and rocky coves to fine old towns rich in history, here are the island's most spectacular attractions.

△ **Cagliari.** The citadel district of Castello reeks of history and power, and is dominated by the Pisan-Romanesque cathedral. Set on a hill with spectacular views over the city, Castello is also home to aristocratic mansions, ancient defensive walls and excellent museums. See page 101.

▽ **Nuraghic relics.** More than 7,000 Bronze Age towers called nuraghi pepper the Sardinian landscape, each providing intriguing glimpses of a mysterious civilisation.

△ **Costa Verde.** Miles and miles of unspoilt golden beaches backed by rolling sand dunes and lush *màcchia* vegetation make the southwestern Green Coast a playground for sunbathers, beachcombers and horse riders. See page 192.

△ **Grotta di Nettuno.** Set sail to Capo Caccia for a journey into the otherworldly wonders of this marine cave, including eerie chambers filled with ancient stalactites, stalagmites and simmering pools. See page 163.

△ **Trekking in the Sopramonte and Ogliastra.** Get kitted out in your best outdoor gear for trekking adventures in Sardinia's wild mountains, which include Europe's deepest gorge, Gola di Gorroppu, and one of its most challenging routes, Il Selvaggio Blu. See page 217.

△ **Bosa.** Up and down medieval alleyways to the castle of Malaspina, there are captivating glimpses of Bosa's Pisan and Catalan-ruled past through its crafts, architecture and food. See page 178.

◁ **The Sinis Peninsula.** Head west to the southernmost tip of the Sinis peninsula to journey back in time to the Punic-Roman town of Tharros; wander around atmospheric architectural fragments and unspoilt beaches. See page 177.

▷ **Trenino Verde.** The "little green train" rattles over a narrow-gauge railway (dating from 1888) which penetrates deep inside Sardinia's wild interior; this is the way to see the lush gorges and rocky peaks of the Gennargentu national park. See page 120.

▽ **Alghero.** Catalan Culture, cuisine and Alguerès dialect still reign supreme amid the cobbled lanes, fortifications and bustling eateries of this beguiling seaside town. See page 159.

△ **Golfo di Orosei.** Charter a speedboat and explore 40km (25 miles) of wild coastline, where dizzying limestone cliffs tower over marine grottoes, isolated pebble beaches and enchanting bays in everchanging blue-green hues. See page 122.

THE BEST OF SARDINIA: EDITOR'S CHOICE

Most memorable boat trips, best museums and galleries, freshest seafood, stunning beaches and outdoor activities galore... here, at a glance, are our recommendations.

MOST MEMORABLE BOAT TRIPS

Capo Caccia. Frolic with dolphins on the Andrea Jensen sailing boat while cutting through the azure waters around Capo Caccia and Grotta di Nettuno. A bountiful lunch is served and there are plenty of stops for snorkelling. See page 163.

Isola di San Pietro. Explore the volcanic rocky coastline of this island in the southwest where you can spot Eleonora's falcon, and sample Carloforte's curious Tunsian-Ligurian culture and cuisine. See page 188.

Golfo di Orosei. Hop on a speedboat from Arbatax or Cala Gorone and let the Golfo di Orosei's limestone wonders – marine caves, hidden coves and towering cliffs – unfold. See page 123.

Isola Tavolara and Isola Molara. Head to stunning beaches below Isola Tavolara's dramatic 6km (4 mile) limestone ridge and the granite sculptural folds of Isola Molara, off the Gallura coast. See page 131.

Arcipelago della Maddalena. Escape Costa Smeralda's uber-rich crowd by taking a boat from Palau to navigate pristine waters around the national park of the Maddalena archipelago. Here you'll spot abundant birdlife, including cormorants and peregrine falcons, and absorb the untouched beauty. See page 141.

Pescaturismo at Teulada. Fishermen take groups and families around their favourite bays; after helping haul in the nets, and splashing about in limpid waters, there's the freshest *pescato del giorno* (catch of the day) for lunch. See page 242.

Su Nuraxi, one of the finest examples of Nuraghic civilisation.

BEST MUSEUMS AND GALLERIES

Cittadella dei Musei. Cagliari's citadel and former arsenal is home to a 1960s-built museum complex which contains mesmerising archaeological finds, artworks and Siamese treasures. See page 101.

Galleria Comunale d'Arte, Cagliari. Stunning 20th-century art including haunting sculptures by Francesco Ciusa housed within a gunpowder store turned neoclassical palazzo. See page 107.

MAN, Nuoro. The Museo d'Arte di Nuoro has works by Sardinia's brooding artistic luminaries Biasi, Ciusa and Nivola alongside temporary shows. See page 215.

Museo Nazionale G.A. Sanna, Sassari. Dig deep into the island's prehistoric and ancient civilisations, discovering 3,000-year-old *bronzetti* as well as Etruscan, Greek and Roman artefacts. See page 153.

Su Nuraxi. One of Sardinia's most famous museums and a Unesco World Heritage site, Su Nuraxi consists of an impressive Nuraghic fortress dating from the 13th to the 6th century BC, surrounding a 15th-century BC defensive tower with a well. See page 193.

For the best views, take a boat trip.

FRESHEST SEAFOOD

Seafood is a highlight.

Lillicu, Cagliari. Amid the marble tables and open kitchen of this long-time favourite, enjoy the ebb and flow of lively banter, delicious seafood and good wine. See page 228.
Rifugio dei Peccatori, La Maddalena. This rural osteria is a perfect

place to try simply prepared authentic Sardinian specialities. See page 232.
Da Ugo, Castelsardo. Pick your pesce then examine its fresh lustre before tasting the fishy delights at Castelsardo's best eatery. See page 232.
Nicolo, Carloforte. The Pomata family mix Carloforte's Sardinian, Ligurian and Arabic influences at this renowned *ristorante*. Luigi Pomata in Cagliari echoes these sublime culinary creations. See page 234.
Peschiera San Giovanni, Tortolí. Run by a fishermen's cooperative, this no-frills place serves excellent sea bass, bream, red mullet, shellfish and *bottarga* (cured fish roe). See page 230.

Kitesurfing at San Giovanni de Sinis, Oristano.

STUNNING BEACHES

La Pelosa. Fine white sand and transparent waters give this sheltered beach at Capo del Falcone a tropical feel. See page 146.
Chia. The long golden sands of Spiaggia Campana and Spiaggia Su Giudeu have a wild backdrop of sand dunes and broom-covered granite outcrops. See page 185.
Cala Goloritzè. Plunge into the azure waters that lap some of the smoothest white limestone pebbles on the Golfo di Orosei. See page 123.
Spiaggia di Tavolara. A curvy promontory of dunes and pebbles

makes for a spectacular bathing spot below Tavolara's awe-inspiring cliffs. See page 131.
Spiaggia Rosa, Maddalena Isola. Budelli's famous pink beach with its sparkly, rosy complexion is due to the pebbly remains of protozoan organisms. See page 142.
Is Arutas and Sa Mesa Longa. The Sinis peninsula has stunning beaches and surging surf – Is Arutas has sparkling quartz sand, while Sa Mesa Longa has a long table-like rocky platform that forms a marine pool – perfect for families. See page 177.

The sculpted granite silhouette of Isola di Tavolara.

BEST SPORTS AND OUTDOOR ACTIVITIES

Treks in the Supramonte di Baunei. Scramble around the limestone pinnacles and caves above the Golfo di Orosei then plunge down to the isolated beach (*spiaggia*) of Goloritzè. See pages 122 and 242.
Canyoning in the Barbagia. Get acquainted with nature's power by following the course of a river, clambering over sculpted rocks and dangling over dizzying chasms. See page 241.

Canoeing and kayaking. Glide and paddle along the river Coghinas, in the far north near Castelsardo, exploring banks covered in *màcchia*, lakes and canyons rich in birdlife. See page 241.
Diving, windsurfing and kitesurfing near Palau. Set off for the Maddalena archipelago's fabulous dive sites off the northeast coast, or tackle the wind-whipped waves at L'Isuledda Porto Pollo. See page 241.

Enjoying a family meal in Cagliari.

Country track leading to the simple church of San Pietro di Golgo in the Altopiano del Golgo.

THE RUGGED JEWEL

With its rich history, rugged coastline and fabulous beaches – some of the best in the Mediterranean – the island of Sardinia has universal appeal.

Alfresco lunch on Piazza Costituzione in Cagliari.

Sardinia is the second-largest island in the Mediterranean after Sicily. Its geographic position prompted D.H. Lawrence to write that the island was "lost between Europe and Africa and belonging to nowhere". This isolation has worked both for and against the island, producing the unique character of its people and flora and fauna but also attracting a succession of foreign rulers eager to exploit its strategic position and fertile land.

Phoenicians and Romans, Arabs and Spaniards, Savoyards and Italians have all left their mark on the cultural, artistic and architectural life of the island. Historically mingling these influences with their own has produced a rich and varied Sardinian identity, which is difficult to grasp at first. Although Sardinia has been part of Italy since 1861, even today many islanders wish it were not.

Fonni, Barbagia.

There remain striking differences between the island and the mainland. Sardinia's individual regions are completely different from one another, and villages which may lie only a few kilometres from each other will often seem worlds apart, so much so that the island can appear to be a miniature continent.

Sardinia's beaches have attracted many visitors and some unfortunate overdevelopment. The expansion of the tourist industry has seen the growth of watersports facilities, and dive centres have been set up to explore the island's thriving marine life. Birds of prey can be found swooping over the mountains of the interior and flamingos rest during their winter migration in the coastal marshes and lagoons. The Barbagia region in the interior offers opportunities for hiking, rock climbing and speleology. Horse trekking has also become very popular with the development of *agriturismo* (farm holidays) in the provinces of Oristano and Sassari. The cities of Cagliari and Sassari have renewed vibrancy through their student and artistic populations, while recent civic plans are aimed at improving facilities and enhancing cultural life.

A local character.

THE SARDINIAN CHARACTER

Loyal but wary of outsiders, witty, stoical and brave, this diverse group of islanders has evolved a tough and independent spirit shaped as much by geography as by the successive waves of invaders.

To some Italians on the mainland, the jokey view of a Sardinian is a proud, sturdy shepherd who lives a rustic, old-fashioned existence. A similar stereotype was even transposed onto Willie, the feisty Scots groundskeeper, who gets a Sardinian accent in the Italian version of *The Simpsons*. The reality is somewhat more complicated of course, although independence, stoical strength, bravery, loyalty, warmth and occasional bouts of dour mien laced with sardonic wit are descriptions you could ascribe to Sardinians.

Sardità, or Sardinian-ness, has been shaped firstly by environment – the sea and mountains that have contributed to intermittent invasion and isolation. Its diverse dialects and the character of its people reflect a mixed-up and compelling history characterised by foreign domination and cultural assimilation. A succession of foreign interlopers has left its mark, leaving deep impressions on *Sardità*.

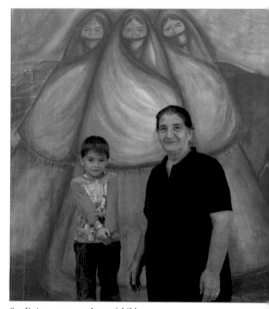

Sardinian nonna and grandchild.

> The Sardi are proudly attached to their own piece of *terra sarda*, expressed through festivals, crafts and hearty cuisine, all of which vary from village to village.

Periods of relative peace and natural barriers have allowed for its myriad close-knit communities to grow independently. And therefore every Sardinian town and village has a different story to tell. *L'isola delle storie*, the "island of stories", they call it, and a literary festival in Gavoi, in the once impenetrable mountains of the Barbagia, celebrates this storytelling tradition.

Breaking away

Around 60 million years ago some colossal rocks which would become Sardinia and Corsica were chipped off the European landmass and drifted southwards as an archipelago. After much upheaval, sea incursion and erosion they ended up marooned halfway between the Italian mainland and North Africa. Although part of Italy, Sardinia is something apart from the mainland peninsula. *Quasi un continente*: almost a continent, as a saying-turned-slogan to lure visitors across the Tyrrhenian Sea would have it.

Neolithic peoples were the first to inhabit Sardinia 8,000 years ago. It wouldn't be too fanciful to suggest that Sardinian traits of self-reliance, togetherness and ingenuity derive from these prehistoric Sardi. Natural resources including obsidian – volcanic glass used to make arrowheads and tools – made them some of the wealthiest people

> Sardinia's strategic location meant it was fought over by African, Middle Eastern and European powers, and each trading partner, invader and ally left its mark on the inhabitants.

once in a circle of friends they warm up and are extremely loyal. So where did this social conservatism come from? *Sardità* is an island mentality like no other. Sardinia's strategic position meant that it became a pawn in the battle for western Mediterranean supremacy, fought over by African, Middle Eastern and European powers. First it was the Phoenicians who began coastal settlements in 1000 BC and brought Greek, Etruscan and North African influences: writing, crafts and new building methods. A happy coexistence between the Punic settlers and the tribes

The Sardinians are understandably proud of their cheeses.

The island of San Pietro.

on the planet back in the Stone Age. Trade flourished in this black gold, and Sardinian Neolithic culture peaked with the Ozieri civilisation (3500–2700 BC), who built the curious *domus de janas* tombs ("fairy houses") to honour their dead.

A succession of invaders

One of the island's best-known maxims is *"Furat chi benit dae su mare"* (Whoever comes by sea comes to rob us). Sardinians are said to be wary of outsiders (unsurprising when you consider their history) and are generally less animated than other Italians. Foreigners who come to the island often comment that it is hard to strike easy friendships, but

lasted until the 7th century BC. Carthaginians took over, enslaving the locals and stripping away the Nuraghic past. Sardinians were now colonial subjects. Romans came during the Punic Wars, but the ferocious mountain people, the Barbarie (from the Barbagia) put up a fight. The Sardi Pelliti (Hairy Sardinians) wore animal skins and fought heroically to preserve their land and culture. The Romans brought infrastructure and Latin – from which Sardinia's language, Sardo, derives. In the end the Byzantines and monastic orders spread Christianity on the island, but facets of the polytheist past survived, as witnessed in today's rich and often strange folk traditions.

A rich heritage

Subsequent landlords, the naval powers Pisa and Genoa, then Aragonese Spain, the Savoyards and a unified Italian state divvied up the island and its people, introducing new blood and culture. Present-day Alghero, Iglesias and Oristano all have evidence of Catalonia in their architecture, dialect and ceremonial exuberance. Carloforte's residents speak Tabarkino, an 18th-century Genoese dialect, and blend Tunisian and Ligurian cuisines, eating couscous and tuna. In the north, the purest form of Sardo – Lugodorese – is spoken,

influences, but many possess an innate independent spirit, stoical determination and moral fibre. Historical figures like Arborea's Mariano IV and Eleonora fought for independence against the Aragonese. In the 14th century Eleonora penned the Carta de Logu, a set of progressive laws that introduced new concepts like female suffrage and servant citizenship. During the Italian Risorgimento's resurgence of liberal ideas, Sardinia hosted inspirational leader Giuseppe Garibaldi on Caprera – debates over the benefits of being part of Italy still rage on, though. After World

Local man from Abbasanta with his horse.

while down south Campidanese is coloured by Pisan traits. In the Barbagia mountains the people survived off the land and largely turned their backs on the sea, which generally brought nothing but trouble. Their struggle against poverty and wariness of outsiders is embodied in strange, solemn processions that combine pagan fertility rites and exorcism of evil spirits with Catholic iconography. Those strange masked and fur-clad carnival dresses of *Sos Mamuthones* and *Issohadores* conjure images of pagan festivities.

Independent spirit

Sardinians may have assimilated a hotchpotch of overseas cultural and linguistic

SARDITÀ VERSUS ITALIA

Sardinia is the only region of Italy whose native peoples are recognised as an ethnically distinct group, related to the island's original inhabitants. Even though the island has been part of Italy since 1861, not all Sardinians are happy with the alliance. There is a feeling that the Italian state uses the island's space and resources to the detriment of Sardinians.

NATO has numerous Sardinian bases, and it's easy to find examples of natural resources plundered, profits siphoned off and indigenous culture tainted. The Aga Khan's Costa Smeralda has brought tourism to the island, but at what cost?

War I, the Sardinian unit Brigata Sassari were hailed as fearless heroes renowned for their united spirit. Their wartime experiences and interaction with mainland Italians led to the establishment of the Partidu Sardu (Partito

> A few villages in central Sardinia have some of the world's highest concentration of male centenarians. Ten times as many men celebrate their 100th birthday here than the world's average.

Berlusconi-backed Ugo Cappellacci. The new administration reversed taxes on super yachts and curbs to coastline development. Modifying Soru's landscape plan, it also scrapped the futuristic museum building project in Cagliari. In 2014, Cappellacci was succeeded by centre-left Francesco Pigliaru.

Disillusioned with both Sardinian and Italian politics, a group of activists called Canton Marittimo are calling for Sardinia to become the 27th canton of Switzerland. They argue that this is the way for landlocked Switzerland to get miles of amazing coastline, and for

Vibrant, colourful youth.

Sardo d'Azione), which aimed at furthering Sardinian independence. Italian Fascism largely absorbed and contained these political tendencies.

Disillusioned Sardinia

Despite misgivings towards Italy's use of the island, the movement for more autonomy is splintered, mired in the nepotism of Italian politics and short-term alliances. However, in recent years there has been renewed vigour to protect the islanders' interests. Entrepreneur Renato Soru's Progetto Sardegna Party introduced measures to limit development near coastlines and encouraged local industry in the interior. In 2009 Soru was replaced by

Sardinia to benefit from administrative efficiency and economic wealth. "The madness does not lie in putting forward this kind of suggestion," Andrea Caruso, co-founder of the Canton Marittimo said. "The madness lies in how things are now."

As Italy continues to struggle with recession, one of the more serious suggestions put forward to boost the island's economy has been to turn Sardinia into a tax haven. Indeed since 2013 Porto Scuso has been the island's first free-trade zone Although it's unlikely that this scheme will expand to include the whole island, one cannot underestimate the exceptional Sardinian instinct for survival and indomitable spirit, which may turn this dream into a reality.

The Sardinian Language

Sardinian, made up of several dialects, has never been standardised. Many fear that, unless this happens, it will be overwhelmed by Italian.

Sardinian is an old Romance language with a highly original and, in some cases, extremely archaic vocabulary. It is linked to Italian and all other Romance languages by the Latin of Roman times. During the Roman conquest of the island, Latin took over all the existing languages introduced by the Phoenicians and the Carthaginians. In addition to its Latin skeleton, the vocabulary of Sardinian reflects the entire history of the island.

A rich mix

Place names, in particular, retain roots from the Phoenician, Etruscan and Byzantine periods. By the 14th century, Sardinian had developed from vulgar Latin.

For the next 400 years, first Catalan and then Castilian were the official languages; in Alghero, people speak a variation of Spanish Catalan introduced in the 14th century, and there are traces of Spanish in all the island's dialects infused from Spain's 300-year colonisation of the island.

More dialects

During the 13th and 14th centuries a quasi-official Sardinian language also established itself through the promulgation of laws in Sardinian by the ruler-kings of Arborea. The dialects spoken in Sassari and Gallura to the north reveal close links with the languages of Tuscany and Corsica due to waves of migration during the course of the 17th century.

On the isle of San Pietro, off the southeast coast of Sardinia, a strong Piedmontese dialect is spoken, mixed with an ancient Genoan dialect dating back to the 18th century.

Today, the rich and complex language is an amalgam of the island's many dialects: Logudoro in the northern central region, Campidano in the south, and a number of ancient dialects in the mountainous region around Nuoro.

Lingua Sarda

All the regions are bilingua, and it is only recently that Sardinian has taken second place to "standard Italian". In general, people use their dialect in informal situations only.

The issue of standardising the Sardinian dialect remains unresolved, although there were attempts made during the 1970s to identify the main body of the language and to introduce it to the media and literature.

This fragmentation of Sardinian is a major problem for the island's writers and poets. All the great Sardinian writers, including Sebastiano Satta,

Proud Sardinian, Oristano.

Grazia Deledda, Giuseppe Dessì and Gavino Ledda, have felt obliged to write in Italian. During the 1970s the Partito Sardo d'Azione launched a series of campaigns in order to persuade the regional authorities to put Sardinian on an equal footing with Italian.

What next for Sardo?

Nowadays, the main threat to the survival of the Sardinian language is undoubtedly posed by the Italian media. More than a million Sardinians (which represents approximately 80 percent of the population) speak a form of Sardinian, which makes it the largest linguistic minority in Italy. In 1996 a law was passed to encourage the study of Sardo.

The ruins of Phoenician columns
at Nora.

DECISIVE DATES

350,000 BC
First traces of human presence found.

6000 BC
Trade in obsidian with Corsica and south of France.

4000–2700 BC
Archaeological finds at Bonu Ighinu and Ozieri.

1800–500 BC
Period of the nuraghe, squat, cone-shaped stone buildings used as forts and citadels.

1000 BC
The earliest Phoenician traders arrive in Sardinia.

500 BC
Carthage controls the Sardinian economy.

264–238 BC
The First Punic War between Rome and Carthage. Rome

Palaeochristian fresco in Sant'Andrea Priu

annexes Sardinia but unrest continues in the island.

1st century BC–5th century AD
Period of Roman rule in Sardinia.

5th–8th centuries AD
Roman empire collapses as barbarian tribes invade Western Europe.

AD 711
Arab raids on Sardinia.

815–27
Arab conquest of Sicily cuts off Sardinia's links with Christian powers, affecting the economy.

1015–16
Victory by combined Genoese and Pisan navies over an Arab fleet from Mallorca. Rivalry between Genoa and Pisa for control of Sardinia. Island divided into four *giudicati*.

1130
Comita d'Arborea, *giudice* of Oristano, tries to seize control of the island with Genoese backing.

12th century
Supported by Emperor Frederick Barbarossa, Barisone d'Arborea is crowned King of Sardinia. Monastic orders improve Sardinia's agriculture.

1190–1200
Pisa in firm control of Sardinia.

1284
Genoa becomes the dominant power in the north-western Mediterranean.

1297
Pope Boniface VIII names James II of Aragon as regent of Sardinia, in an effort to end the Pisan-Genoese rivalry.

1323
Defeated at Santa Gilla, Pisa renounces its claims to Sardinia, which becomes part of the Kingdom of Aragon.

14th century
Sardinia is subdivided into 376 fiefs, many awarded to Spanish noblemen, after an Aragonese viceroy.

1392
Eleonora Doria publishes the *Carta de Logu*, a constitution of common law written in the Sardinian language.

1417
The *giudicato* system ends: direct rule by Aragon.

15th century
Plague and famine reduce Sardinia's population from 340,000 to 150,000. Catalan immigrants and Jewish settlers arrive.

1469
King Ferdinand of Aragon marries Isabella, Queen of Castille, creating the Kingdom of Spain.

1708
During the War of the Spanish Succession English and Austrian forces seize Sardinia from King Philip V of Spain.

1718
Briefly reassigned to Spain, Sardinia is then given to the Dukes of Savoy by terms of the Treaty of London.

1730
The Duke of Savoy, Charles Emmanuel III, becomes King of Piedmont and Sardinia, and remains king until his death in 1773.

1793
French troops attempt to invade Sardinia but fail.

1839
Abolition of the Sardinian feudal system.

1861
Victor Emmanuel II proclaims himself King of Italy.

1870–1904
Banditry increases as nomadic sheep-farming revives. Growth of mining and tragedy at Buggerru.

1915–18
13,000 Sardinians die in World War I.

Nuraghic sacred well.

1924
Fascist "Law of the Milliard" against Sardinian unrest.

1926
Grazia Deledda (1871–1936) wins the Nobel Prize for Literature.

1940
Italy enters World War II.

1946
Italy becomes a republic.

1948
Sardinia established as autonomous region.

1962
Heavy industry and business sectors are stimulated. The Aga Khan creates the Costa Smeralda syndicate and tourism opers up.

1995
Mining industry in crisis.

2001
An ancient fleet of Roman cargo ships s unearthed in the Bay of Olbia.

2004
Renato Soru, the owner of Tiscali, is elected president of Sardinia; encourages foreign investment and limits coastal developments.

2009
Soru replaced by Berlusconi-backed Ugo Cappellacci, who reverses curbs on coastline construction and taxes on super yachts.

2013
Cyclone Cleopatra hits the island; 18 people perish and and 3,000 are made homeless.

2014
Francesco Pigliaru of the centre-left Democratic Party becomes president of Sardinia.

2015
Serving his second term, Italian president Giorgio Napolitano retires and is replaced by Sergio Mattarella.

Giuseppe Garibaldi (1807–82).

FROM PREHISTORY TO THE 12TH CENTURY

From the earliest times, Sardinia's island status has protected its distinct culture. Yet its natural wealth and strategic location were coveted by successive imperial powers.

The first Sardinians probably came from the European mainland, but who they were and when the island was first settled is less certain. Fairly precise dating has attributed human and animal bones found in the Grotta Corbeddu – a cave near Oliena – to the late Palaeolithic era, 13,000 years ago. During glacial periods the sea level dropped and Sardinia and Corsica formed one large island, separated from the coast of Tuscany by a relatively narrow strip of water. After this, though, Sardinia remained cut off from the continent for thousands of years. It was not until the beginning of the Neolithic era that a completely different race of men appeared on the island.

> Hard, black obsidian was ideal for the manufacture of tools and weapons, and trade in this prized raw material helped establish a high level of civilisation in Sardinia during the Neolithic era.

These new inhabitants had clearly reached a more advanced stage of civilisation than their predecessors. To them, Sardinia must have been like the proverbial happy land, with its dense forests filled with game, broad lagoons with an inexhaustible supply of fish and shellfish, fertile plains and rolling hills for arable farming, excellent conditions for cattle raising, and – above all – obsidian, their "black gold". By the 4th millennium BC, they had achieved a considerable degree of cultural independence. Their customs and conventions were further developed and refined over the centuries, in two principal periods which archaeologists have named after the sites at which signs of life were first discovered:

Nuraghic sacred well at Santa Cristina, Paulilatino.

the Bonu Ighinu culture (c.4000–3500 BC) and the Ozieri culture (3500–2700 BC).

Artistic artefacts

The discoveries from these cultures include relatively sophisticated pottery, frequently decorated with pictorial and geometric forms, engraved or scratched before firing and sometimes filled out in colour. Limestone was used to make perfectly formed stone vessels and female cult statues.

The most noteworthy relics left, however, are over 1,000 burial chambers, hewn from solid rock with stone chisels. The simplest of these, dating to the Bonu Ighinu period, consist of a hidden vertical entrance shaft and a small chamber usually large enough for only one body. These were known as *forredus* ("ovens") because of their spherical shape. In later years several such chambers were linked together to form underground burial apartments with a common antechamber and an entry corridor. The Sardinians called the tombs *domus de janas*. According to local superstition, the powerful but not always benevolent *janas* (fairies) are tiny female creatures who live in these houses (*domus*). There are particularly impressive examples in Sant'Andrea Priu near Bonorva, and Montessu near Santadi, where several dozen linked tombs form a town of the dead.

The Neolithic era was followed by a transitional period of approximately 1,000 years, often known as the Copper Stone Age. Then new influences brought Western Megalithic culture to the island: dolmens, obelisks, stone circles, rows of menhirs and even well-developed menhir statues hitherto only found in northern Italy and southern France. This cultural heritage gave birth to Sardinia's great Bronze Age civilisation.

The Nuraghic civilisation

The Nuraghic civilisation lasted from around 1800 BC to 500 BC. Sometime during the first

Horn reliefs in a burial niche at Montessu.

THE GREEK CLAIM

The Greeks were so impressed by Sardinia, they claimed Nuraghic accomplishments were the product of Greek ingenuity. They refer to the "magnificent buildings" of Sardinia as *daidaleia* – attributing them to Daedalus, the legendary Athenian architect/inventor who built the labyrinth for King Minos of Crete before fashioning wings for himself and his son, Icarus, by which they could escape imprisonment. Daedalus fled to Sicily, whence he travelled on to Sardinia. Evidence has been found of trading links between the Mycenaeans and the Nuraghic from the 14th century BC, but the golden age of the Nuraghic civilisation was clearly the cause of this contact.

half of the 2nd millennium BC the first nuraghi appeared, circular towers dotted across the Sardinian countryside like giant upturned buckets. The largest and technically most perfect Megalithic buildings in Europe, they are found only in Sardinia, in awe-inspiring profusion – today some 7,000 are registered as historic monuments.

The basic form of a nuraghe is a blunt-topped cone. An entrance corridor at ground level leads to the interior, a more or less concentric circular room with a domed vaulted roof. This classic design is similar to the famous "Treasury of Atreus" near Mycenae in the Peloponnese. Both the Mycenaeans and the Nuraghic built these structures from about the 16th century BC, although the basic principles differed. In addition to the solitary towers, there are hundreds of nuraghi settlements of all sizes, some full-size fortresses. The largest and most interesting are the Nuraghe Santu Antine near Torralba, the Nuraghe Losa near Paulilatino, the Nuraghe Su Nuraxi near Barumini and the

Domus de janas means "house of the fairies". More than 1,000 of these tombs can be found in Sardinia, often carved into rocks and mountains, with reliefs decorating the walls.

usually covered by a more carelessly constructed burial mound that, from the outside, resembles the hull of an upturned boat. On each side of the entrance, at right angles to the main chamber of the grave, a pair of walls was added. They demarcate a semi-circular forecourt 10–20 metres (32–65ft) wide. The imposing facade thus formed gave the graves an appropriately monumental and possibly mournful and private ambience.

The forecourt contains a fireplace and often an encircling stone platform used as a seat or table for sacrificial offerings. This was the setting for both funeral rites and commemorative cer-

Interior of a prehistoric tomb (domus de janas) at Sant'Andrea Priu decorated with a fresco.

Nuraghe Arrubiu near Orroli. The function of these strongholds was probably similar to that of medieval castles: in peacetime they may have served as the official residences of tribal chiefs and centres of a wide range of communal activities, and in war as a refuge for the inhabitants of the surrounding villages, as is evident from their numerous defensive strategic features.

Graves and temples

The tombs of the men who built the nuraghi are as monumental as the towers themselves. Sardinians call these burial places *tumbas de sos zigantes* (in Italian, *tombe di giganti*). Like the nuraghi, they have no parallel on the mainland. They were built from well-matched stones and

emonies in honour of the dead. The members of a tribal group, clan or village met to pay their respects to the dead, who were buried by the community with no consideration for rank or privilege, and without funeral gifts of any value. The graves of the giants constructed by the Nuraghic should be seen rather as charnel houses, in which the bones of the dead were piled up after skeletonisation was complete. Some graves contain as many as 100 to 200 skeletons.

The most elaborate structures from this era, however, are water temples, built on the site of natural springs. The heart of a water temple is the Nuraghic domed vault, in which the sacred spring water was collected. A staircase linked this pump room with the temple antechamber at ground level. The antechamber was ringed by small stone benches upon which votive gifts or cult objects were placed. There was also often a sacrificial stone with a small gully; this seems to point to blood sacrifices or specific rites involving the use of what was believed to be holy water.

Some particularly fine temple complexes, such as Predio Canopoli in Perfugas, Su Tempiesu near Orune, Santa Cristina near Paulilatino and Santa Vittoria near Serri, were thought to date from the 8th to 6th centuries BC. More recent finds, however, have led archaeologists to believe that the temples are several centuries

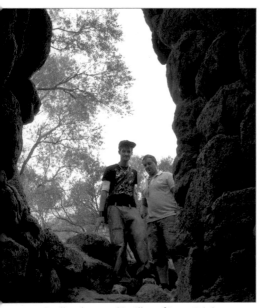

Sacred well at the Nuraghic village of Santa Cristina at Paulilatino.

older than this, reaching back into the time of close contact with the late Mycenaean kingdom in Greece and Cyprus.

The mysterious Sardana

Recent theories support the notion that the Nuraghic of Sardinia may have been the mysterious people known as the Sardana, mentioned in 14th-century BC Egyptian texts. Certainly by this time there was a remarkable increase in Nuraghic communications with eastern Mediterranean societies, especially Cyprus – even after the 12th century BC when, following the Trojan Wars and the eclipse of the royal house of Mycenae, Greece entered a dark age which was to last many centuries.

It was thanks to its trading links that Sardinia continued to flourish culturally. This is confirmed by remarkable artefacts such as the statues of warriors found in 1974 on Monte Prama. They are exact copies of Nuraghic votive statuettes, but are almost 3 metres (10ft) tall and carved in stone. If, as has been suggested by archaeologists, the first large Nuraghic sculptures were created in the 8th century BC, they predated even the oldest Greek sculptures. These statues are among the signs that, in some places, Nuraghic life was moving towards a city-based social structure. Archaeologists have no doubt that the reason for this development was the arrival at this time of the first Phoenician settlements on the Sardinian coast.

Phoenicians and Carthaginians

The first Phoenician traders probably arrived in about 1000 BC. During the 9th and 8th centuries BC, they built their first urban colonies around the principal harbours on the Sardinian coast: Karali (Cagliari), Nora and Bithia (both near Pula), Sulki (Sant'Antioco), Tharros (near Oristano), possibly Bosa and others. Scarcely 100 years after they founded the city of Sulki, the colonists had succeeded in conquering the entire fertile hinterland and the access routes to the lucrative mining areas, securing their conquests with smaller outposts and fortified towns.

In the 6th century BC the Nuraghic banded together to mount a counterattack. In 540 BC Carthage sent an army of reinforcements to its Phoenician sister cities, but the expedition ended in disaster, and the army was routed. In Carthage, the shock of this defeat gave rise to a reform of political and military institutions, and well-organised armies of mercenaries were despatched to Sardinia. The island was soon so firmly under Carthaginian rule that, in 509 BC, the Romans were compelled to sign a contract recognising that all trading with Sardinia was subject to Carthaginian control.

By the 5th century BC the Carthaginians occupied two-thirds of the island. They founded towns such as Macopsisa (Macomer), built numerous forts, including those on the northern boundary of the Campidano high plains and in the northern Giara region of Gesturi. Hand in hand with a vigorous policy of deforestation, farming land was criss-crossed by an amazingly dense network of paths and farmsteads: the island was being transformed into the granary of Carthage.

Outside the museums traces of this period are not so accessible, since the Romans destroyed virtually everything, but Monte Sirai and Tharros are well worth a visit.

Monte Sirai is an excellent example of a self-sufficient garrison town complete with necropolis and its own sacrificial altar for burnt offerings. Tharros is situated on a narrow promontory about 2km (1.25 miles) long, with two hills: one for the town, one for the necropolis. It is a classic example of a Phoenician coastal town: it has a safe harbour, an easily defended single narrow land approach, shallow lakes with copious stocks of fish nearby and an extensive, fertile hinterland.

> *Phoenician art blended styles from trading partners with its own aesthetic traditions to create highly individual works. As well as burial gifts, these include frightening masks to keep evil spirits away from the dead.*

Sign to Santa Cristina.

LITTLE BRONZE STATUES

Of the countless votive presents that visitors to the water temples would leave behind, a number of little bronze statues have survived, now housed in the archaeological museums in Sassari and Cagliari. These statues take the form of household items, farming implements, tools, weapons and boats, but also exquisitely naturalistic representations of wild and domestic animals and, above all, people. With a little imagination we can glimpse their different activities and recognise the social strata: shepherds, farmers, musicians, worshippers, the sick, mourners, priests, aristocrats and soldiers, some of whom, armed with assorted weapons, bear the terrifying countenance of demons.

It has proved impossible to date the figures with any precision, although recently support has been won for the theory that some Nuraghic bronze art is much older than comparable artefacts found in the western Mediterranean – in contrast with the accepted picture of the Nuraghic civilisation as one of the relatively unimportant fringe cultures of the Mediterranean. According to experts, the island's rich ore deposits, especially its lead and copper, played a key role, and the Nuraghic golden age coincided with an upsurge in metalworking. It seems likely that the bronze boom and the resulting trade with the eastern Mediterranean gave the island a cultural impetus not shared by anyone else.

Allies against Rome

In 238 BC, three years after the First Punic War, Roman troops annexed Sardinia without encountering much resistance. In the course of the Second Punic War (218–201 BC), the Carthaginians on Sardinia, supported by the local mountain dwellers, made several unsuccessful attempts to overthrow them. As the war dragged on, the citizens of Rome started to view the island as an unnecessary burden. In 54 BC, when Cicero took on the defence of a certain Scaurus, a man who had acquired excessive wealth during his time as governor of Sardinia,

the lawyer's plea for his client echoed the popular mood: Sardinia was a Roman province but not a single town was friendly towards Rome; and the Sardinians as a race were the descendants of the nefarious Carthaginians.

As the Roman republic approached its last days, Sardinia was the only one of more than 30 Roman provinces without a single city whose inhabitants were entitled to Roman citizenship. Cicero was basically right in his depiction of Sardinians' provenance. The year of Sardinia's annexation was of purely political significance; in cultural terms, the Carthaginian influence on

Bronze Nuraghic sculpture from around 800 BC.

CHILD SACRIFICES

A little-understood Phoenician custom was the sacrifice of children by fire to the deity Baal, or later to the Carthaginian goddess Tanit. The sacrificial altars, referred to as *tephatim* in the Bible, were erected outside towns. The first was found not in the Middle East but near Nora in Sardinia. Here, and on half a dozen other *tephatim* discovered on the island, archaeologists found thousands of clay urns filled with charcoal and human remains. Some urns contain remains of substitute animal sacrifices, and it is also evident that children who died of natural causes were cremated in the *tophet*.

Sardinia remained evident for many centuries after Carthage had been destroyed by Rome.

The general situation on the island improved during the reign of the emperor Augustus. The residents of many towns were awarded the right of Roman citizenship, and a dramatic upsurge in the amount of building testifies to increasing prosperity. By now even the mountain folk had accepted Roman rule and the occupiers could restrict their supervisory activities to mediating in the feuds between sheep-farming tribes and Sardinian peasants on Roman estates. But to the Romans the island was doomed to remain a much-hated imperial doormat, not least because the dreaded malaria was found to be prevalent there.

The Arabs

Arabs first ventured ashore on Sardinia in AD 711, capturing the town of Cagliari and occupying various regions along the coast. Their visit was short-lived, and they perished in a storm during the journey home. This mishap did little to discourage the Arabs, who resumed their raids, terrorising the Sardinian coast, stealing food and kidnapping the natives. The initial, ill-fated raid on Sardinia was followed by others in 722, 735–6 and 752–3. Despite some unexpected naval victories, by 815 the Sardinians were in desperate need of liberation. They

became progressively more depressing, large stretches of the previously fertile coastal margin regressed into malarial swampland.

The Arab prince known to the Italians as "Museto" had already conquered the Balearic Islands and Denia in Spain when he set sail

> Dorgali, on the Bay of Orosei, was founded in about 900 by Saracen pirate Drugal. Its people display characteristics distinguishing them from other islanders.

Marble carving of Roman emperor Caligula in Cagliari's archaeological museum.

Engraving showing Louis the Pious (778–840), emperor and king of the Franks from 813.

sent a plea for assistance to Emperor Louis the Pious, to no avail: in 816 and again the following year, Cagliari was destroyed.

The occupation of Sicily by the Arabs in 827 cut off Sardinia's links with Byzantium and forced the island to rely on its own resources. Countless raids by a succession of new invaders followed: many of the seaside towns and villages were destroyed or left to decay. Since the Sardinians believed even then that danger invariably came from across the sea, many left the fertile coastal regions in order to make new homes in the interior. They paid dearly for the security thus acquired: whilst life in the new settlements was marked by hardship and

from Mallorca with a fleet of 120 ships. He had recognised the strategic importance of Sardinia and now sought to subjugate the island once and for all. The states bordering the Tyrrhenian Sea were roused from their lethargy by the fact that en route the Saracens had raided some Tuscan coastal towns. They also feared that the invaders might revive their former ambitions of empire and use Sardinia as a base from which to conquer Italy and the rest of Europe.

Pope Benedict VIII felt particularly threatened and used his influence over Pisa and Genoa to persuade them to unite in the common cause against the Arabs on Sardinia. In 1015–16 the fleets of Genoa and Pisa duly put to sea and routed the Saracens, aided by the armies of the Sardinian *giudici*, with whom they then established lively trading links.

The Genoese and the Pisans

The fierce rivalry between the two maritime republics soon affected Sardinia. At the beginning, Pisa had the upper hand, not only in military success but also in its archbishop, who was the metropolitan of two Sardinian dioceses. After AD 1130 Genoa decided to support the *giudice* of Oristano, Comita d'Arborea, in his attempt to unite the entire island under the

Pope Benedict VIII, pope from 1012–24.

aegis of the d'Arborea family. There was vigorous opposition to this plan from the other three *giudici*; in 1146 a provisional peace treaty was concluded, but a few years later Barisone d'Arborea took up the struggle once more. The troops of the *giudicato* of Torres supported the Pisans; together, they besieged Barisone in his castle in Cabras. With Genoese help the latter broke the siege, then appealed to Emperor Frederick Barbarossa to proclaim him King of Sardinia. This was duly done and he was crowned on 10 August 1164.

Even this success was not enough to satisfy Genoa, which took the precaution of ensuring the benevolence of the Papal States and then persuaded all four *giudici* to sign a number of treaties which declared them to be virtually the vassals of Genoa. This was a severe blow for Pisa, but again Emperor Frederick intervened, dividing the island into two separate dependent territories; Lugudoro and Campidano were subject to Genoa, and Gallura to Pisa. From this time onwards, wealthy Ligurian and Tuscan families with a long tradition of seafaring and trading brought increased prosperity to the island's economy. Both Genoa and Pisa sent monks from a number of orders to convert the islanders to Catholicism, building abbeys and churches the length and breadth of the island.

At the end of 1190, following a complicated dispute over the succession, the governor's throne in Cuglieri (Cagliari) was occupied for the first time by a man from the mainland, Oberto di Massa, who adopted a policy favouring Pisa. In 1215 the death of his successor, Guglielmo di Massa, revived the power struggle between the

GIUDICI AND GIUDICATI

Sardinia was divided into four provinces, called *giudicati* – Torres, Gallura, Oristano and Cagliari – each of which had its own jurisdiction and social order. The ruler of the *giudicato* was known as the *giudice*; he lived with his family and an armed bodyguard in a castle. He was responsible for the administration of justice and the government of affairs of state. He was aided by the clergy and a secular civil service, as well as by the *curatores,* each of which governed in his name a *curatoria* consisting of a number of villages and estates. The individual communities were run by the *majori*, men who enjoyed the trust of the *curatores.*

The social hierarchy was divided into estates into which one was born: freemen – ranging from wealthy and powerful owners of large estates to the poor – and peasants and serfs.

The latter were further subdivided into three groups, depending on how many days per week they were required to work for one or more masters. The *integri* had to work the whole day for their master, the *laterati* owed him half a day's work and the *pedati* worked for him for a quarter of the day. On their time off the *laterati* and *pedati* could work on their own plot of land – if they possessed one – or could undertake other work.

two seafaring republics, but this time the first families of Sardinia were also involved.

By the middle of the 13th century, a complicated policy of arranged marriages brought virtually the entire island under Pisa's sway, although, supported by various Ligurian families, the *giudicato* Logudoro attempted to organise resistance to the Pisans. The majority of Sardinians, most of them being too involved with the everyday problems of town life, took no part in the affair.

Thus came the end of a highly promising golden age in which culture, religion, the arts

as seigneur in perpetuity over the islands of Sardinia and Corsica. At first this change of regency had little effect on the island, but during the early years of the 14th century James II saw his opportunity to take an active part in the affairs of the land. On 28 February 1323,

> The monasteries attracted local labourers and farmers anxious to learn the agricultural methods that the monks had brought with them from mainland Europe.

Holy Roman Emperor Frederick I (1123–90), known as Barbarossa or "Redbeard".

Portrait of Charles Albert, King of Sardinia, by Horace Vernet (1789–1863).

and the economy had all flourished, without giving rise to any local political or economic power that could take overall control of the country's future.

Pisa loses control

Between 1250 and 1260 the *giudice* Ghiano di Massa drove the Pisans from Cagliari, and towards the end of the 13th century, against the backdrop of the bitter feud between the Guelphs and the Ghibellines, the position of the factions in Pisa itself deteriorated; it was not long before the effects spread to Sardinia too. In 1297 the Papal States intervened again. Pope Boniface VIII named James II of Aragon

the armed forces of Aragon and Pisa met at the Santa Gilla Lagoon, just outside Cagliari. Pisa suffered defeat; later that same year, on 19 June, a peace treaty was signed in which the vanquished state abandoned its claim to almost all of its rights associated with towns and estates on the island. Only one section of the fortress at Cagliari and the harbour remained in their possession, and that only for one more year.

This marked the beginning of the suzerainty of the Kingdom of Aragon, which was followed over four centuries by the kings of Spain in an institution which – as if by some irony of fate – came to be known as the *Regnum Sardiniae*.

S. rapaira · longofando

olbia

farcon

tilium

gallia · turris libisonis
olim nunc eorom
toloma · roxan

· S.
paulus

· C·mnali

forcoli

aleguora

marar=
gio
recius

orgamer · bolla

Sardonitos
olim nunc
Sardinia uo
catur

Sancta luria

pizanco

salme

Caput
Sancti
Marti

cedrus flug

maler
mieteu

SARDINIA

arestam

tufis · flg

aquilastno · F· lancto

neapolis
portus

alba bassara

Longitudo istius isule expte
orientis · CLXXXVIII · M·P· &
Exparte occidentis · CLXXXV
et exparte meridie · LXXVII · &
Latitudo septetrionali · CXXII
Ambitus totius isule · S· LXV

storgeto

Sanctus · theseus

Argentera

facer flg

Sulso

petri

Callari

qia

facito

Salme

porto bote

mar
sram

tauo
lar

Carbona
ra

Carolitanus
promontoriu

THE STRUGGLE FOR IDENTITY

Oppressed by the Spanish, misruled by Savoy and
exploited under the new Kingdom of Italy, Sardinian
national consciousness survived against the odds.

Once James II had appeased Sardinia, the island was placed under the regency of a viceroy from the Kingdom of Aragon. Half of the land was awarded to Spanish noblemen, whose one aim was to increase their fortunes at the expense of their Sardinian estates. The underpopulated, impoverished, malarial island was entirely at the mercy of foreign interests; its fate was decided in faraway Zaragoza, over the heads of the local citizens.

Of Sardinia's former masters, only the rulers of Arborea had been able to maintain their previous position. In order to destroy their power the Spanish encouraged discord between the two sons of the *giudice* Hugo II by favouring the younger son, Giovanni, rather than his elder brother Mariano. However, Mariano came to power and decided to fight with the Genoese Doria clan against the Spanish. He received valuable assistance from one of the Dorias, named Brancaleone, "The Lion-Catcher". In order to confirm the latter's allegiance, Mariano agreed in 1367 that Bran-

Peter IV, King of Aragon and Sardinia, being visited by Guillaume-Raymond Moncada.

On his 1535 visit, Charles V lifted the ruling whereby all Sardinians had to leave the Castello quarter of Cagliari by sunset. Previously, anyone disobeying the cry "Foras los Sards" ("Sardinians out!") was thrown over the wall.

caleone should marry his daughter Eleonora. Subsequently known as the Giudicessa, Eleonora is still remembered by Sardinians today as a symbol of the island's independence.

Mariano was succeeded not by Eleonora but by her brother, Hugo III. He ruled harshly and strictly, imposing a high tax burden and rigid military conscription, for he was obsessed with the aim of freeing his country from the hated Aragonese. His approach, however, was too dictatorial; on 6 March 1383 he and his daughter were assassinated during an uprising in Oristano. Three days later Brancaleone appeared at the court of the King of Aragon in Zaragoza and proposed that his son Frederick should succeed Hugo, with his wife Eleonora as regent.

Eleonora brought the country under control within a few months. Her popularity increased when, in 1392, she published the *Carta de Logu*, a written constitution of common law on which her predecessors and their legal advisers had worked for half a century, and which was to remain in operation until the beginning of the 19th century. Though this legal code contained no innovations, it was written in the Sardinian language and thus became one of the cornerstones of Sardinian national consciousness.

Eleonora died in 1404, followed by her son in 1407 and Brancaleone soon afterwards. Margrave William III of Narbonne, a distant cousin of Eleonora, took over the post of ruler in the *giudicato* of Arborea. He found himself having to face Aragon in battle shortly after arriving on the island. He and an army of 20,000 Sardinians were defeated by the King of Sicily, Martin of Aragon, whose force was smaller but possessed better strategy and weapons. William fled from Sardinia; King Martin died of malaria shortly afterwards, whereupon William III returned, leaving the island for the last time in 1417 and abdicating his rights in return for adequate compensation some three years later. One hundred years after its first military invasion, the Kingdom of Aragon finally had the entire island under its control.

Statue of Giudicessa Eleonora di Arborea in the square of the same name, Oristano.

THE INQUISITION

In 1469, with the marriage of King Ferdinand of Aragon and Isabella of Castile, the linking of the two crowns created a unified Spanish kingdom. In order to be able to deal "appropriately" with the large numbers of Arabs and Jews in their land, the two monarchs – who were highly praised for their Christian virtues – asked the Pope to reintroduce the Inquisition, requesting the right to appoint the Inquisitors themselves. The long arm of the Inquisition reached as far as Sardinia. Here, however, influential people were able to avoid its grasp thanks to their powerful protectors; those who landed in its net were "small fry".

Immigration

Epidemics of plague, failed harvests and famine followed, and the population declined drastically; at the beginning of the 14th century there were 340,000 inhabitants; by 1483 this figure was reduced to 150,000. To provide compensation for this decline and to increase the Spanish element on the island, settlers from the Iberian peninsula were transported to Sardinia. During the 14th century the town of Alghero was resettled with Catalan immigrants, after the native population had been driven away in retaliation for an attempted coup against the Aragonese rulers.

Jewish immigrants also reached Sardinia at about the same time as the Catalan settlers.

They established themselves in Alghero and Cagliari as money-changers, traders and doctors; however, in spite of their contribution to the otherwise stagnant local cultural life, they were driven out towards the end of the 15th

> During the 400 years of Spanish colonial rule strict censorship was imposed, even in the cultural sphere. Catalan Gothic and Spanish Baroque styles were permitted, but the Italian Renaissance was banned.

fully occupied by his wars against King François I of France and problems caused by the spread of the Reformation. Sardinia was no more than a pebble on the beach of his world empire.

Yet in 1535 and 1541, Charles V passed through Sardinia with Andrea Doria, a Genoese mercenary leader, on a joint expedition against the buccaneers of Algiers. On the second visit, during his brief stay in Alghero, the emperor described the local inhabitants as *todos caballeros* – "all gentlemen" – in a speech thanking the citizens for supplying food for the mercenary forces while their ships lay in the bay.

A Spanish fort (no longer standing) in Sassari.

century. The few who preferred conversion to Christianity were forced to face the Spanish Inquisition. Suspects were expropriated and sentenced to large fines – if they escaped being burnt at the stake.

Forgotten island

Ferdinand and Isabella now ruled over an expanded united kingdom. In 1492, following the discovery of America, their interest was diverted towards the more promising territories in the New World, and Sardinia slipped into oblivion. Nor could the Sardinians expect a greater share of the attention of Charles V, the grandson of Ferdinand and Isabella and heir of the Habsburg Emperor Maximilian; he was

In the turbulent years of the 16th century, Sardinia's totally inadequate system of coastal defences lay in the hands of 86 men, who stood watch over the island from hilltops near the coast. Instead of sending troops, the colonial rulers supplied the Sardinians with weapons. Since the latter were required to pay for the arquebuses and lances they received, the cost to the Spanish crown was actually nil. An equally neat solution was found in the case of the coastal watchtowers, which Philip II, who had succeeded Charles V, had constructed towards the end of the 16th century. A survey indicated that to provide real protection against enemy attack, Sardinia would have needed 132 "Saracen towers", standing at 15km (9-mile) intervals along the coast. In fact, only 66 were built, financed by the barons or the town councils on whose property they stood.

A detailed map of Sardinia entitled *Description de la Isla y Reyno de Sardena*, printed during the 17th century under Philip II, shows illustrations of these coastal towers. The map also depicts the coat of arms of the Kingdom of Sardinia: a shield with a red cross and four Moors' heads bearing a headband as a sign of their royal status. Across the centuries, the band slipped down, representing their complete defeat. Since the 19th century the Moors'

nobles and merchants would only lend them money at exorbitant rates of interest, and the Spanish monarchy commandeered soldiers, horses, grain and vegetables.

This blatant injustice sowed the seeds of Sardinian banditry. Lacking protection, the poor resorted to self-defence. A particular problem was posed between 1610 and 1612 by the 20-strong band of robbers under Manuzio Flore from Bono. He incited the populace to refuse to pay its taxes, and, like a Sardinian Robin Hood, directed his attacks against all officials who were "poor when they assumed office and rich when they retired".

Portrait of Charles V, c. 1520, by Bernaert van Orley.

Victor Amadeus II, king of Sardinia 1718–30.

heads with the blindfolded eyes have remained symbols of the Sardinian claim to the self-determination denied them for so long.

Decline and fall

To keep close tabs on the better-educated classes, in the middle of the 16th century Jesuits were sent to the island, founding colleges in Cagliari and Sassari. They were also responsible for imposing Castilian (i.e. Spanish) as the official language. The country people, though, spoke exclusively Sardinian: in these times, in which they had been robbed of almost all they possessed, it represented their only wealth. The towns demanded their grain at cut-throat prices, the Church demanded its tithes, the

Towards the end of the century, the attention of the major powers in Europe was directed towards the declining Iberian monarchy. Charles II, the last Spanish Habsburg king, had no male heir. In 1708 the Spanish were forced to surrender to the English and the Austrians on Sardinia. In 1714 the island was ceded to Austria, and in 1718, as part of the Treaty of London, Sardinia was passed to the Dukes of Savoy in exchange for Sicily. Victor Amadeus II therefore became king of Sardinia until 1730.

The Savoy mismatch

Sardinia was not a country to which Savoy had aspired. They could muster little interest in the island, nor could they make themselves understood there. The natives spoke Sardinian and the educated classes Castilian and Catalan; the rulers of Savoy-Piedmont, however, spoke French. During the first years of their rule the Piedmontese observed and detailed weekly reports to Turin. Their aim was to get to know this new, unknown European country and to assist it towards more order and discipline by means of administrative reform. Unfortunately, in doing so they tried to make the Sardinians fit a Piedmontese mould.

Apart from their concern at the poverty of the island, the Piedmontese were troubled by the unrest and lawlessness. In some regions the bandits had formed armies. Signore de Rivarolo, a former governor of the Savoy prisons who served as Viceroy of Sardinia from 1735 to 1738, tried to eradicate banditry with military expeditions, accelerated trials and harsh punishments. During his three years in office he had 432 people executed and over 3,000 condemned to severe punishments. His deterrents brought few results.

Reform, riot and revolution

Count Giovanni Battista Bogino, who was appointed Minister of State of the Piedmont in 1759, began to introduce a reform programme, concentrating on encouraging agriculture by the distribution of seed and loans for farmers. Not all reforms met with success, but the Piedmontese were unable or unwilling to grasp the situation. In April 1780, the starving peasants in Sassari rioted, plundering the granaries and storming the town hall. The revolt was quelled not by force of arms, but by holding up a portrait of the king, whereupon the mob reverently doffed their hats and fell down on their knees, calling out *Viva il re!* (Long live the king!).

During the last years of the 18th century the riots increased in frequency due to the presumptuousness of the feudal lords. When French troops invaded Sardinia in 1793, believing they had discovered a "revolutionary" land, they were defeated by a 4,000-man Sardinian regiment. As a reward for their courageous defence of their native land, the Sardinians requested the king in Turin to appoint Sardinian natives to all public positions, and to grant them direct involvement in all governmental affairs. Their wishes were

denied; in response, on 7 May 1794 the Sardinians arrested 541 Piedmontese officials and shipped them back to the mainland. For the first time in 500 years, Sardinia was under Sardinian rule – but the royal standard still fluttered from all public buildings, and protestations of loyalty to the monarchy could be heard from all quarters.

Property problems

The Piedmontese had still not succeeded in giving the necessary impetus to Sardinian agriculture. All their attempts in this direction

Count Giovanni Battista Bogino.

BAD REPORT

The regular reports sent from Sardinia to the capital, Turin, by the Baron de Saint-Rémy – the first Viceroy of the Piedmont – did not sound encouraging: "The nobles are poor, the country itself miserable and depopulated, its citizens idle and without any sort of trade – and the air is most unhealthy." Further on, he claimed: "The vices to which these people are most inclined are theft, murder and cheating." Nor do the 400 years of Spanish indifference seem to have been good for the clergy: the priests showed so little respect in their personal appearance "that they wear a peasant's cap and greatcoat in public, even at church during celebration of the Mass".

failed because there was no private ownership of land: one year a field would be available to the peasants for agricultural purposes, and the next to the shepherds as pasture. With the "Olive Tree Enactment" of 1806, a peasant who planted olive trees was granted the right to enclose his land; planting more than 4,000 trees gained him a title. In 1829 an Enclosures Act was introduced to put an end to the perpetual conflict between peasants and shepherds by providing a clear distinction between agricultural land and pasture. Once again, however, it was the wealthy who gained

Giuseppe Garibaldi (1807–82), Italian military and nationalist leader, c.1870, by Vincenzo Cabianca.

In 1848 Frederico Fenu stated: "The attempt to transfer mainland laws to Sardinia... can be compared to an attempt to make adult clothes fit a child or to dress a man in a woman's skirt."

the upper hand: with more labour at their disposal and more skill at cutting through the bureaucratic jungle, they were able to lay claim to larger areas of land.

Once again, riots broke out. In the first instance the Piedmontese were ruthless in quashing the unrest; in 1833, however, they

were forced to repeal the edict. Six years were to pass before the enclosure of land was permitted again, as part of a large-scale reorganisation of property laws following the abolition of the feudal system. Sardinia thus took an important and irreversible step forward into the modern world. But the traditional equilibrium within island society had been destroyed for ever.

"Fusion with the Motherland"

The islanders could see only one way out of this economic catastrophe: the incorporation of Sardinia into Piedmont, in order to guarantee the same treatment as the much wealthier mainland state. In November 1847, a delegation of Sardinia's leading citizens made the journey to Turin, where they requested the island's "perfect fusion with the Motherland". Unification with Piedmont was proclaimed on 30 November.

Thus with trusting enthusiasm Sardinia became part of the embryonic state of Italy, which was being formed by a Piedmontese politician, Count Camillo Cavour (1810–61), fought for by the leader of a volunteer army, Giuseppe Garibaldi (1807–82), and ruled over by the House of Savoy. The islanders had high hopes that the Italian Risorgimento would pave the way for a second resurgence in their own neglected homeland. However, instead of the hoped-for improvements, the Sardinians found themselves faced with still more disadvantages: nomadic sheep farming was banned, entire forests were felled, and the mines were exploited by foreign companies.

Conditions on Sardinia were deplorable. Despite the exorbitant taxes levied, communities received nothing in return. In addition, there was enmity between the north and south of the island, especially between Sassari and Cagliari. The Piedmontese, expelled from Cagliari by the local citizens in 1794, would have been pleased to transfer the capital to Sassari, where most inhabitants were immigrants from the mainland. Carlo Baudi di Vesme, a Piedmontese nobleman, proposed a solution: in administrative and religious affairs (except in sermons), the Sardinian dialect should be banned and the use of Italian obligatory. "Unity of language would lead to a closer unity of spirit... thus overcoming the deep-rooted differences between the inhabitants of the various regions." In other words, since no one really knew what to do with the island as it was at the time, the plan was to destroy its national identity.

However, in 1860 a rumour began to circulate on the island that Piedmont was hatching

The poems of Sebastiano Satta, like the novels of Grazia Deledda, attracted the attention of Italian intellectuals to Sardinia's archaic language and folklore, which retain many traces of pagan influence.

production in agriculture and the management of pastureland defied all attempts at progress.

Sardinia's mines could have brought the island prosperity, but too small a percentage of the profits was reinvested. The miners began to voice demands for better conditions, and in 1900 went on strike, following in the footsteps of the ferry crews of Carloforte and the printers of Sassari. The wave of strikes reached a tragic climax in 1904 in Buggerru, when three men were killed during violent clashes with the army. But repression didn't change anything. The entire working popula-

Workers pose for a photograph during construction of the railroad from Tirso to Chilivani via Ozieri.

plans to cede Sardinia to France. Giuseppe Garibaldi, who had settled on the nearby island of Caprera, intervened, and Sardinia remained a part of Piedmont. On 17 March 1861 it became part of the new unified Italian state. Victor Emmanuel II proclaimed himself King of Italy, and Sardinia ceased to be the kingdom in its own right which it had been for the previous 650 years.

Exploitation

Despite high property taxes, a rising cost of living, starvation and revolt, Italy started to improve conditions on Sardinia. The road network was completed in 1862 and the first railway in 1880. But the antiquated methods of

tion of Sardinia was in a state of unrest, and a new political awareness was dawning.

During World War I, thousands of Sardinians laid down their lives for their country. The dauntless men of the Brigata Sassari were mentioned in four military dispatches, and more than 13,000 of them died brutal deaths on the battlefield. Disenchantment with the government, which again failed to keep its promises, embittered the ranks of returning troops. Within the next few years they united to form the Partito Sardo d'Azione, the Action Party of Sardinia. At long last, after centuries of inaction, Sardinians were once more sufficiently conscious of their national identity to take their fate into their own hands.

MARZO
APRILE
1914

THE SHAPING OF SARDINIA TODAY

The shift from sheep rearing to tourism in the last century has had profound effects on the island's economic structure and population.

The events of World War I were to provide the main impetus for Sardinia to abandon its insular existence and enter the modern world. This transition was marked by success and failure in equal measure.

The number of Sardinians who took part in the war was unusually high. So, too, was the number of casualties. Almost one-eighth of the entire population, approximately 100,000 soldiers, saw active service; 13,602 of these never returned. Following the war, many Sardinians realised for the first time that Italy and Sardinia shared a common heritage; and that they must also accept joint responsibility for the fate of Italy as a whole. They fought for a country which they hoped would not forget their valour once the war was over, and which would help them end the reign of misery on their native shores. Italy certainly acknowledged Sardinia's soldiers, in particular the legendary Brigata Sassari. Qualities of bravery and mutual cooperation between officers and men made the Brigata a symbol of the indomitable spirit of the Sardinians.

Putting food in the oven, Tratalias, c.1925.

In World War I, Sardinians met people whose culture and history were different from their own. These encounters were to leave a lasting impression on the islanders.

Post-war confidence

Sardinian feelings of ethnic unity intensified during the post-war years. The encounter with other people who had already profited from economic progress and whose standard of living was much better than their own was bound to make the demobilised Sardinian soldiers

ponder their lot and draw unfavourable comparisons. Many ex-soldiers joined together to form a *Movimento Combattentistico*, a movement of front-line fighters. They held their first congress in May 1919 in Nuoro. A few months later, three members of the party were elected to the Italian Parliament. Many cherished the secret hope that they would finally be allowed to carry the island's economy and society forward into the 20th century on an independent footing.

The Sardinian Action Party

For Antonio Gramsci from Cagliari (1891–1937), the movement was 'the first people's country party, above all in central and southern Italy'. Although Gramsci was about to turn his back on the socialists in order to found the Italian Communist Party, in 1921 the Sardinian front-line fighters, foremost among them Camillo Bellieni and Emilio Lussu, decided at their congress in Oristano to form the Sardinian Action Party, the Partito Sardo d'Azione. The central elements of the party programme were a varied array of demands directed towards Rome, plus the concept of self-determination for Sardinia.

In the wake of Fascism

In 1923 Paolo Pili, the leader of the wing with Fascist sympathies, brought about a split in the party when he and fellow-sympathisers left to join the PNF, the Partito Nazionale Fascista, the Fascist Party. Pili was skilful in taking advantage of Fascist policies as well as part of the cooperative programme of the Sardinian Independence Movement in order to further his own cause, until he fell from favour and was expelled from the PNF.

The declared political aim, that of "providing a new framework for some aspects of the Partito Sardo d'Azione within the Fascist Party", was never achieved. In the 1924 elections the Sardinian Action Party did less well than the

Rural workers at the end of the 19th century.

FROM RURAL TO POLITICAL

One of the prime achievements of the Movimento and later of the Partito Sardo d'Azione was their encouragement of an active political awareness in large numbers of young people and peasants who were tired of the old liberal democratic order.

As the population became more politically active, so their representatives put into practice with greater fervour the views acquired in the trenches, that a unified Sardinia was a powerful regional entity. And so, for the first time, Sardinia possessed a strong people's party. Even the rural population gathered together, lured out of their exile from political and social life.

Fascist unified list of candidates, but it was still represented – much to the chagrin of the Fascists. Thanks to the influence of Emilio Lussu and Camillo Bellieni, the Sardinian Independence Movement became more popular and more anti-Fascist in tone.

After the assassination of the socialist Giacomo Matteotti, Lussu withdrew from the government and hardened his anti-Fascist stance, one of the most radical in Italy.

Water shortages and dams

From 1924 the Fascist Party laid great emphasis on including in their own programme some of the characteristic demands of the Sardinian Independence Movement, such as the abolition of unemployment and an increase in productivity. The state of the island at the time was in many respects truly wretched. In two-thirds of the communities there was no running water; only seven communities had their own sewage system. In 1925, the Inspectorate of Public Works was established to give priority to the Sardinian "renaissance". Several swamps were reclaimed around the island and agrarian communities founded, mainly in the area of Oristano, where the village of Mussolinia (now called Arborea) was located, and in the Nurra, where the town of Fertilia sprang up.

Efforts were made to overcome the island's chronic water shortage: in 1923 the king officially commissioned the Tirso Dam, while in 1926 the Coghinas Dam was put into operation and construction work began on the hydraulic station on the Flumendosa.

Mussolini's Sardinian policy

Following Mussolini's declaration of absolute rule, exploitation of the metal and coal mines on the island was intensified, especially in the Sulcis Basin, where the town of Carbónia was founded in 1938. From here coal was exported via the port of Sant'Antioco. The settlement grew rapidly, acting as a magnet for Sardinia's unemployed as well as for workers, peasants and shepherds from all over the island. The development naturally led to the rapid formation of a working class – the first in the country.

Nuoro became the provincial capital in 1926, but failed to develop to meet expectations and requirements. In the interior of the island things remained as they had always been: the inhabitants eked out a meagre existence as labourers and shepherds, while many of the more august leading citizens discovered an unexpected taste for Fascism, using their position as head of the district council or as mayor to promote their own interests. Corruption was rife.

The Fascists failed utterly in the most remote country areas, where the population continued to adhere to traditional working methods and social norms. However, in the most densely populated towns they attracted more active support. Between 1921 and 1931 the population of Cagliari almost doubled, reaching a total of almost 100,000. During the same period Sassari topped the 50,000 mark,

and smaller towns – Olbia, Alghero, Oristano, Tempio, Iglesias and Carbonia – also gained in significance.

War against bandits

The inhabitants of the interior devoted themselves exclusively to their own problems rather than to national politics. Orgosolo was the scene of a bloody feud; between 1925 and 1935 there was further unrest. This was the heyday of the legendary bandits, who were soon translated by folk tales and popular song into resolute, philanthropic heroes. The best-known of

Nineteenth-century photo of children playing cards.

In the 1930s Sardinia was dominated by the Fascists, who took the wind out of the sails of independence movements such as the Sardinian Action Party, which had arisen after World War I.

these Sardinian Robin Hoods were undoubtedly Samuele Stocchino from Arzana and the Pintore brothers from Bitti. Mussolini's representatives fought with particular determination against the *banditismo*. All suspects were utterly at the mercy of the prefect, commander of the *carabinieri* or chief of the militia. Even a hint of suspicion was sufficient to put someone behind bars; informers flourished and old feuds were revived – but went unreported by the heavily censored press.

Land reforms of the 1930s

Italy exhibited a diminished concern for the island's problems for a number of years, but showed a revived interest during the years leading up to World War II. The 1933 Land Reform Ordinance for the whole of Sardinia had the ambitious aim of developing one-quarter of the entire island. This was intended to bring about improved crop production and an increase

Sardinian autonomy

At the end of World War II, the worst effects of which the island was largely spared, Sardinia felt itself more isolated than ever from the political and economic situation of main-

> In the years leading up to World War II Sardinia acquired strategic importance, both as a military base and supplier of raw materials, which fuelled Mussolini's dreams of an all-powerful Italy.

Coal boats on Iglesiente beach, 19th century.

in the population, which had stagnated. New crops were introduced, such as the cultivation of rice near Arborea. By 1938 only about 10 percent of the target had been developed.

Shortage of labour

During the years leading up to World War II, the Ethiopia Campaign and the Spanish Civil War led large numbers of Sardinians to join the armed forces for a second time. There was a shortage of male labour in all areas of industry; many projects begun by the Fascists were never completed, and the lack of men to work on the land made farming even less productive than it had been. Furthermore, a fresh malaria epidemic on Sardinia took a heavy toll of victims.

land Italy, so hopes became concentrated on autonomy, universally considered to be the only way of tackling the province's numerous unresolved problems.

In 1944, the government in Rome appointed a High Commissioner to supervise the running of the island. A regional assembly was created to advise him, with two main aims: to produce a draft statute of autonomy, and to submit plans to improve the island's economy and the health of its people. The Sardinian Statute, which became law in 1948, stated that Sardinia and its islands were an autonomous region, which could lay claim to their own legal responsibility within the framework of the Republic of Italy.

This autonomy has contributed to the remarkable economic progress Sardinia has made since World War II. In the 1950s the Rockefeller Foundation supplied the DDT needed to drain the coastal marshes and finally eradicate malaria, freeing more land for agricultural development. Investment from mainland Italy also transformed the production of Sardinia's famous pecorino cheese, opening up export markets and increasing profits. In the 1960s the Cassa per il Mezzogiorno (Southern Italy Development Fund) bankrolled the building of huge industrial concerns run by state-run

friends. Copy-cat resorts sprung up in the following decades. Businessmen were attracted to the island, and a full-scale tourist industry blossomed, enthusiastically transforming previously uninhabited or uninhabitable regions to attract foreign investment.

Booming tourism, industrialisation and the rapid transition from agriculture to the service industries, combined with the introduction of universal education and new transport systems, have altered Sardinia's countenance more profoundly during the past 50 years than the previous two centuries had done.

The matanza, when hundreds of tuna are caught.

organisations such as ITALSIDER (steel), ENI (chemicals) and EGAM (mining). The oil crisis of the 1970s hit Sardinia's oil refineries particularly badly, and migration from rural provinces to the bigger cities and mainland Italy peaked between 1955 and 1975. During this period, Italy was a battleground of Cold War politics which, combined with Sardinia's tradition of banditry, produced kidnappings and Red Brigade terrorist bombings.

Post-war trends

In the early 1960s the tourism industry kicked off when the Aga Khan invested huge amounts of money in the Costa Smeralda, the Emerald Coast, creating an exclusive resort for close

FACTS ABOUT SARDINIA

Since 1945 Sardinia's population has risen from 1.27 million to a most 1.7 million.

Nearly 70 percent of Sardinia's visitors arrive from June–August. Recently the tourism industry has tried to enccurage tourists to visit at other times of the year. Eco-tourism and cultural tourism are attracting more visitors outside the peak months. Still, the coastline remains the biggest draw.

Sardinia has 24 NATO bases – that is more per square kilometre than anywhere else on earth. It also has a heavy Italian military presence.

In 1999 the Sardinian language was given the same official status as Italian.

However, these developments appeared to benefit non-Sardinians and spurred the re-emergence of the Sardinian separatist movement: the Sardinian Action Party (Partito Sardo d'Azione) re-entered the political fray and grew more vociferous in the 1990s. This, combined with a revival of kidnapping, posed a threat to the burgeoning tourist industry. On occasions, extra police have been drafted in to protect holiday homes on the Costa Smeralda belonging to such high-profile people as the clothing magnate Luciano Benetton and former Prime Minister Silvio Berlusconi. Angelo Caria, who

was elected president of the Sardinia region in 2004, and many applauded his left-wing measures – such as banning development within 2km (1.25 miles) of the shoreline and taxing super yachts and second homes. The grip of the economic crisis and disarray within the centre-left coalition favoured a shift in politics and the centre-right candidate Ugo Cappellacci won the 2009 election. One of Cappellacci's first acts was to repeal the tax on luxury yachts. In 2014, Francesco Pigliaru of the Democratic Party became the new president of Sardinia.

Mussolini inspects a model of the city of Carbónia.

was the leader of the Partito Sardo d'Azione, accused such "colonialists" from the mainland of illegally installing barriers on footpaths and public land next to the beaches, preventing access to the land by local people.

> Sardinian separatist spirit assumes a new shape as Sardinians want Italy to sell their island to the Swiss. This "proposal" was put forward in 2014 by the Canton Marittimo.

Controversies in the 21st century

The entrepreneur Renato Soru, owner of Sardinia's successful internet provider Tiscali,

Profound changes

There seems little doubt that the lifestyle and character of the Sardinian population have undergone profound changes – unfortunately not always for the better. Particularly in the remote regions of the interior, they have precipitated a crisis in the native culture and behaviour patterns based on traditions reaching back over thousands of years. The adjustment to new ways of life will take time and will not be a smooth ride. The fortunes of many of the island's industries seem increasingly precarious. While there has been some growth in Sardinia's service and technology sectors – including the success of the internet service provider Tiscali and the Sardegna Ricerche science and technology centre – many industries have gone into meltdown. One sector to buck the economic trend is tourism.

Gripped by the economic downturn, Sardinia faces new socio-economic problems, experiencing industrial-relations unrest and spiralling poverty in some parts of the country. To make things worse, in 2013 torrential rains and a cyclone hit the island causing floods which took 18 lives and made thousands homeless.

Continued instability and *clientalismo* in Italian politics, combined with a fragile economy, have triggered the emergence of the small-scale Canton Marittimo movement, which in the run-up to the regional elections in 2014 provocatively suggested that Sardinia should be sold to Switzerland. Sardinians would also like the whole island free of custom duties, including VAT and fuel excise. Although it's unlikely to happen, in 2013 a free trade zone was indeed established in the town of Porto Scuso. Still, Sardinians will have to wait for the fulfilment of their long-cherished dream of independence and self-reliance.

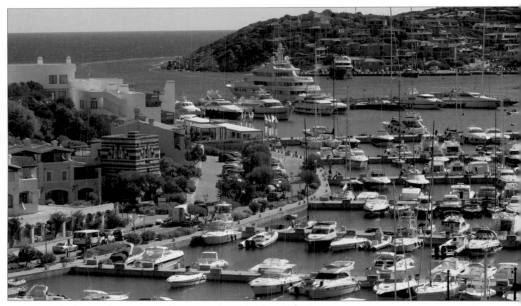

Porto Cervo's harbour on the Costa Smeralda, a resort designed exclusively for the very rich.

THE SARDINIAN STATUTE

The Sardinian statute lists areas which the region is entitled to administer independently from central government:

the organisation of offices and administrative bodies within the region, including the legal position and pecuniary situation of its employees;
the local districts;
the local community or town police force and the regional police force;
agriculture and forestry, small development measures and projects aimed at increased yields or soil quality improvement;

public works affecting only the region;
building construction and town planning;
public transport by bus or tram;
thermal springs and medicinal spas;
hunting and fishing;
the right of administration of public waterways as if they were public property;
the right of administration of mines, quarries and salt works as if they were public property;
customs and morals;
crafts;
tourism and gastronomy;
local-authority libraries and museums.

The wild coast at Is Arutas.

A WILD LANDSCAPE

Sardinia's diverse array of striking geological features, natural wonders and indigenous wildlife is the main attraction of the island to many visitors.

Sardinia's wildlife and vegetation are genuinely unique – the island's detached location in the middle of the Mediterranean has presented something of a natural barrier to migration and cross-pollination. The land and climate help to provide the ideal habitat for species found only in Sardinia, some parts of the neighbouring island of Corsica and certain regions in North Africa.

Travel west from the millionaires' paradise known as the Costa Smeralda, with its secluded beaches, cliffs and caves, and you will find forests and vineyards surrounding the city of Sassari. The forests here are dominated by cork oak, for years a source of income. Head into the central hinterland and you will proba-

> Two main factors have contributed to Sardinia's diverse wildlife; its isolation and its variety of terrains, ranging from rugged mountains to wind-eroded plains.

bly get lost in the infamously wild and hostile hills, mountains and plateaux of the Barbagia. Descend southwards from the Barbagia and you enter the fertile plain of the Campidano, at either end of which are lagoons and reservoirs. The plains are bordered by the geologically fascinating high inland cliffs and table-like plateaux.

The island's habitat can be broken down into the following categories: coastal lagoons and wetlands, including some of the island's, and indeed Europe's, most important wildlife parks; *màcchia* (scrubland); plains and plateaux; coasts and beaches; mountains and woodland/forest; and finally, caves.

A purple gallinule one of many species which attract birdwatchers to Sardinia.

Coastal lagoons and wetlands

Sardinia enjoys a reputation for having some of the most sublime beaches in Europe, typically featuring powdery white sands and limpid waters framed by dramatic rock formations. At key points the coastline also features lagoons, reservoirs and marshes, some of them spread over vast expanses. The most notable of these are the *stagni* (lagoons) of Cagliari.

It was the Phoenicians who initiated the industry of drawing salt from the marshes east of Cagliari about 10,000 years ago. The name of these marshes originates from *sumolenti* ("little donkey"), the reference being to the donkeys on whose backs the sacks of salt were carried.

Cagliari (and its sister town Quartu Sant'Elena) expanded around the waterlands.

The largest of the lagoons is Santa Gilla, west of Cagliari. This stretches over 4,000 hectares (9,800 acres) and incorporates the salt flats of Macchiareddu – the only area of active salt production remaining today. The land that at one time supported salt flats has been transformed into nature reserves.

These reserves are inhabited by an incredible 200 species of birds, that is, one-third of the number of species found in Europe. The bird population of Cagliari's reserves is esti-

The purple gallinule (swamp hen) was once hunted to the verge of extinction until it became legally protected. It is now fairly common in Sardinia.

of bushes resistant to strong sunlight and able to survive with little rainfall and poor soil. This scrubland, or *màcchia mediterranea* (Mediteranean maquis), flourishes in Sardinia where once there were forests. Centuries ago Sardinia was renowned for the wood gleaned from its

Flamingos can now be observed year-round in Sardinia.

mated to be in excess of 100,000. This figure can be attributed to the fact that the sea-feeding bird population is attracted to the *stagni* by the abundance of shrimps *(Artemia salina)* that thrive in these waters. Some of the most noteworthy species are: avocets, black-winged stilts, cormorants, pintail ducks, teals and purple gallinule *(Porphyrio porphyrio)*. Purple gallinule are also often seen around freshwater irrigation canals rich in vegetation near the towns of Oristano and Cabras.

Scrubland and *màcchia*

Rising inland beyond the beaches and cliffs of Sardinia's coastline, the terrain consists of rocky slopes overrun by coarse scrub, that is, species

extensive forests. But invaders and colonists, not least the ancient Romans, ransacked the forests to the point of depletion.

The denuded land gave way to erosion and a terrain insufficiently fertile for natural reforestation. In place of the once abundant trees the maquis flourished. Still today, when fires ravage the remaining forests – a regular occurrence every year – the maquis springs up. The maquis is itself vulnerable to wildfires, thus presenting the authorities with a constant hazard.

Typically the *màcchia* consists of a tangled, heavily scented and richly colourful array of plants including juniper, lentisk, myrtle and the strawberry tree *(arbutus)*, or *corbezzolo* in Italian. Rosemary, heather, yellow-flowering broom and gorse, and both the pink- and white-flowered varieties of the cistus are all common.

From the SS 125 main road, also known as the Orientale sarda, a three-hour walk down the Codula di Luna, from Teletotem near the Supramonte to the sea, takes you to Cala Luna. This is one of the island's most beautiful and secluded beaches. The path describes a deep valley that follows the river bed, passing through aromatic maquis scrub. The surrounding land is dotted with shepherds' huts and entrances to caves.

The vegetation in the Codula di Luna valley, one of the island's wildest canyons, is quite beautiful; the oleander amid the thick Mediterranean maquis is particularly colourful. In summer, the song of the "gru-gru" bee-eaters can be heard throughout the day and the night. In the Sinis peninsula, on the coast between San Giovanni di Sinis and Punta Is Arutas, are more than 100 hectares (250 acres) of sandy coast with dunes covered by vegetation punctuated by cliffs and caves.

Behind the sandy dunes grows a thick Mediterranean scrub with rosemary, dwarf palm and even an Aleppo pine wood. Declared a nature reserve in 1981, this parkland is inhabited by numerous species of birds, such as the peregrine falcon and kestrel, that nest in the cliffs, and the rare Sardinian partridge.

The plateaux

The steeply inclining areas known as the *giare* comprise large, dark basalt plateaux formed by the lava that flowed from violent volcanic eruptions. The *giare* now appear as unique tablelands, utterly flat and supported by sheer walls of dark basalt.

The *giare* of Siddi, Serri, and especially the *giara* of Gesturi, are particularly noteworthy. They are 16km (10 miles) long and up to 6km (4 miles) wide. A stretch of cork forest, where the trees are all blown by the ever-present mistral wind, covers the plateau, with the exception of a few depressions called *pauli*. These *giare* are home to pony-sized horses called *achettas* that graze in fenced-off pastures.

Coasts and beaches

Sardinia's coastline and beaches are among the Mediterranean's most beautiful. Clear waves

Pedra Menralza, a volcanic outcrop in the province of Sassari.

IL FENICOTTERO ROSA – THE PINK FLAMINGO

Pink flamingos *(Phoenicopterus ruber roseus)* are one of a number of once-migratory birds that have settled permanently in Sardinia, and can be observed all year round, nesting and breeding in the lagoons. In a fascinating evolutionary development, they are no longer instinctively drawn to continue their seasonal passage between North Africa and Southern Europe.

The flamingo population, which now totals more than 4,000, sprung from an original colony of 1,000. The first arrivals nested in the Molentargius marshes of Cagliari in the spring of 1993, having flown from the winter-feeding grounds of the Camargue in France. These birds are a delight to observe, especially as they are easily accessible at relatively close quarters, and have become an attraction which draws birdwatchers from all over the world.

Of the other lagoons, the Stagno di Sale Porcus in the centre of the Sinis peninsula (in Oristano province) was so named because in the past the lagoon incorporated a small salt flat from which salt was extracted to conserve pork meat. Now a wildlife area protected by the Italian League for the Protection of Birds (LIPU), it is home to 10,000 pink flamingos, thousands of cranes, wild geese, cormorants and mallards. There is even a small museum dedicated to the pink flamingo: the Museo del Fenicottero.

lap shorelines whose small coves alternate with rocky ravines in which the sea changes colour from emerald green through light turquoise to a sparkling azure. The beaches are of fine golden sand; the cliffs have been smoothed

> With its high limestone cliff, its grottoes and isolated beaches, the Golfo di Orosei combines sheer beauty with drama. Clear waters in various shades of blue and green make it a favourite for boat trips.

The Roman town of Nora sits on a peninsula in the southwest of the island.

and transformed into huge sculptures by the wind. The island's various coasts all have their own particular beauty. On the western corner of the province of Sassari, the Alghero features beaches and the limestone reef of Capo Caccia. La Pelosa beach, 2km (1 mile) from Stintino, the island's northwestern point, is one of Sardinia's loveliest beaches. White sand gradually descends into the sea, its colour giving the water some magnificent turquoise hues.

From here you can join an excursion to the Asinara island, once a prison and now a national park. Following some 100 years of isolation, Asinara remains a mysterious island that is home to 500 mouflons (wild sheep), wild boars, hares,

weasels and white (albini) donkeys. Of the bird populations, there are coarse seagulls, crested cormorants, magpies and the Sardinian partridge. In the migrating season the royal seagull stops here, too. The western coasts have long rocky tracts that lead north towards Bosa and Cuglieri. In the south, near the Sinis peninsula, Is Arutas beach features white quartz crystals that give the water its turquoise colour. The quartz at the nearby Mari Ermi beach is pink.

Further south, in the province of Cagliari, there is the Costa Verde, and in particular Piscinas, a beach of high dunes perfumed by junipers. Here, where the mistral can be quite severe, the sand gives on to an immediately deep sea. Continuing south, Cala Domestica is a narrow fjord of transparent waters set between steeply rising rocks covered in thick Mediterranean maquis.

Of the two sister islands you will find here, Sant'Antioco has a beautiful beach that is 18km (11 miles) long and 8km (5 miles) wide; San Pietro is the home of the falcon *(Falco eleonorae)* that nests among the rocks every summer. Today there are more than 100 of these magnificent predatory birds, named after Queen Eleonora d'Arborea who, in 1400, declared the island's falcons to be a protected species.

The southwestern coast has an uninterrupted series of beaches. Here natural shade is provided by the pine trees of Santa Margherita di Pula. These culminate in the stunning Chia beach, near the location of the Punic city of Bithia. The city of Bithia was founded around 720 BC at the foot of the Torre di Chia promontory. The ruins of the temple of Bes and the remains of the necropolis can be found here. Baia Chia is known as "the Pearl of the South", and features emerald-coloured water and pink granite sand, courtesy of dunes that reach heights of 65 metres (213ft) where the ancient gnarled junipers grow.

The eastern coast has its own beautiful and uncontaminated beaches: San Teodoro e Budoni, then Posada and Siniscola e Orosei, where the wildest terrain starts. The Gulf of Orosei at Cala Gonone-Dorgali is interesting because one of Europe's last coastal forests grows here, right on the seafront.

Further south, the stretch of coastline between Muravera and Villasimius offers a number of delightful spots. These include the promontory of Capo Ferrato, the wild beach of Costa Rei and the fascinating inlet of Cala Sinzias. At Villasimius a very extensive and wide beach, Porto Giunco, almost gives the impression of being an African desert. The sandy shore of Capo Carbonara is so wide that one can relish the feeling of being absolutely alone. The whole region is characterised by a wild and weird natural environment. Small rocky islands here, such as Isola dei Cavoli and Isola di Serpentara, are populated by rabbits and seagulls.

Finally we reach Cagliari. The Poetto beach starts in the capital, and it is easy to reach from the city centre. The beach continues for 13km (8 miles) to Quartu St Elena, the island's third-biggest city. It is one of Sardinia's liveliest sea-

The deep, green woodlands, one of the most enchanting Sardinian features, form a heritage of great environmental value. The Gennargentu National Park (including a 25 sq km/10 sq mile forest that is one of the island's most beautiful), eight regional parks and several oases of flora and fauna form a network of protected areas measuring more than 59,102 hectares (146,000 acres). The mountainous landscape dominates the central part of the island. The highest point is Punta La Marmora on the Gennargentu massif, at 1,830 metres (6,000ft).

Sand dunes on the Costa Verde, west coast.

side stretches, from morning when families and young people meet for an hour's sun and swimming, to the evenings when the bars along the beach organise concerts, cabaret and cinema.

Mountains and woodland

Sardinia's 24,000 sq km (9,250 sq miles) are, the plain of the Campidano notwithstanding, made up largely of massifs. These were formed in the Palaeozoic age, and thus predate the Alps and the Appennines. The predominant rock is granite which, as a result of wind and other forms of erosion, has often come to resemble all sorts of things in people's imagination. Locals and tourists alike have spotted the bear, the tortoise, the elephant, the mushroom and the dinosaur among the rocks.

WILD PONIES AND PRICKLY PEARS

The mystery that shrouds the origins of Sardinia's wild ponies is obscured further by the isolation of the plateaux where they are found. Many believe they are descendants of Arabian and Barb horses, with some Spanish equine blood thrown in.

The wild plateau is also home to the prickly-pear fig *(sa figu morisca)*. This cactus, probably introduced by Arabs, has for centuries marked the rural landscape, often demarcating the borders of landowners' territory while enriching the farms of the poor with lush fruit. The thorns mean it's best to buy the fruit rather than pick it.

Serious trekkers can enjoy walks from the Supramonte di Oliena to the dense oak and chestnut forests along the old railway line near Belvi. The rough and inhospitable Supramonte is riddled with precipices and caves, many of them unexplored. It is covered by maquis, and springs gush from a myriad of underground watercourses. The Supramonte, which is really the heart of Sardinia, features one of the most spectacular gorges in Italy – Su Gorroppu, with walls 400 metres (1,300ft) high and the famous source of the Cologone.

The name Gennargentu derives from the Latin *janua argenti* (silver door), which refers to snow-capped peaks or the legend of silver in these mountains, according to whom you believe. This inaccessible area is well preserved and contains a 25 sq km (10 sq mile) ancient holm oak forest. Near Sassari the well-kept Foresta di Burgos features oak, cedar and chestnut trees.

The Natural Reserve of Monte Arcosu–Monte Latias is a World Wildlife Fund area that climbs 1,000 metres (3,200ft) from the sea. It includes an ancient, 3,600-hectare (8,900-acre) forest of holm oak and cork oak that is the largest green forest in the Mediterranean. Here live

Fonni, one of the highest towns in Sardinia, nestles on a wintry Mount Spada in the Barbagia.

GORGEOUS BEACHES AND RED ROCKS

Among the many delightful spots on the Golfo di Orosei is the stunning beach of Cala Luna, with six enormous caves and an oleander wood, especially impressive in summer and early autumn when the trees are in bloom. The combination of amazing rocky landscapes and the clear transparency of the Tyrrhenian Sea is compelling: sheer cliffs rise from the sea, wooded slopes are inhabited by an interesting array of wildlife, and enchanting beaches can be found in such spectacular bays as Cala Sisine, Cala Biriola, Cala Marioulu and Cala Coloritzè. The entire gulf is part of the Gennargentu national park, which was created in order to safeguard the flora and fauna of this part of Sardinia. One of the region's most picturesque stretches is around Arbatax, which is dominated by the maquis-covered Capo Bellavista. Much of the island's coast is formed by dark granite or limestone, but the rocks of Arbatax (whose name exemplifies the Arabic influence in Sardinia) are an exception. Composed of red granite porphyry, the rocks' astonishing rosy colours flare up when reflecting the slanting rays of the sun. From this point the topography changes somewhat. The terrain is dotted with wild oleaster, the *oleastru* after which the Ogliastra region is named.

wildcats, Sardinian deer, hawks, kestrels, buzzards and golden eagles. Horse-riding tours, excursions and summer camps take place here.

The dark-coated Sardinian deer is the island's biggest wild mammal, though it is smaller than the mainland deer. Another difference from its larger cousin is that its mating season arrives a month earlier, around the middle of August. The Sardinian deer's favourite habitat is the thick maquis near the forest. It became almost extinct in the 1960s, when its numbers were reduced to 50 animals, but it survived with the help of WWF protection.

Rare peonies such as this one grow in the Montarbu forest.

Mountain forest

The Sette Fratelli Mountain, named after the seven peaks that can be seen from Cagliari, is a gigantic granite massif with wild gorges, high cliffs and fast streams shaped over the centuries by the wind. The multifarious forms of terrain found here play a contributory role in the mountain's sense of mystery.

The mountain forest covers an area of 4,000 hectares (nearly 10,000 acres), making it one of the largest as well as one of the best-preserved sclerophyll (woody plants characterised by small, leathery, evergreen leaves) forests of the Mediterranean Basin. Replanted with pine, eucalyptus and cypress trees, the forest reaches an altitude of over 1,000 metres (3,300ft). It is one of the few remaining areas inhabited by the now almost extinct Sardinian deer.

Along the streams there is much interesting vegetation, including wild oleander, ferns, willows and alder trees. This used to be the location of royal eagle hunts and the habitat of the goshawk. The area also features the wood of Tuviois, near the Serpeddi Mount. In the torrents lives the amphibious urodele the tritone sardo *(Euproetus platycephalus)*. Among the reptiles there is the rare lizard of Bedriaga, present only in the north of Sardinia, and the del Cetti snake. The real symbol of the area is the Sardinian deer, of which there are at least 700. Another distinctive animal, now protected against the threat of extinction to the extent that it thrives all over the island, is the mouflon.

The Montarbu forest in the middle of the island is particularly rich in plant species: in addition to the holm oak, you can find yews, holly, strawberry trees, phyllireas, hawthorns, alders and the rare peony, which is also known as the "rose of Gennargentu".

Caves

Hidden in the mountainous landscape above the town of Ulassai, amid rocky outcrops and deep ravines, is the cave of Su Marmuri, one of the most impressive caves in Europe. It has huge 50-metre (165ft) high ceilings and imposing, natural limestone towers whose white peaks stand out among the dark green vegetation.

To the south of Dorgali, the Grotta del Bue Marino is named after the now-vanished monk seal, which has lost all but a few of its Western Mediterranean habitats, where it dives to depths of almost 20 metres (65ft) in its quest for fish and octopus. Also in the Dorgali area is the impressive cave of Ispinigoli. Here one can admire a 38-metre (125ft) high stalagmite and, at the rear, the Abyss of the Virgin chasm, where human sacrifices were made in prehistoric times. Along the Codula di Luna river is the entrance to one of the island's biggest and most extensive caves, the Su Palu, which was discovered in 1980.

In the Capo Caccia area the caves include the Grotta di Nettuno, which has 2km (1 mile) of chambers and small lakes and can be reached by hired boat. Other caves in the area that are worth exploring are the Grotta Verde and the Grotta dei Ricami. The former is so called due to the moss which covers its stalactites and stalagmites. There is a small lake where examples of ancient "graffiti" have been discovered.

SARDINIAN WILDLIFE

Sardinia's island ecology has given rise to some unique species of wildlife, which are now protected in popular reserves and national parks.

In recent years marine and wildlife reserves have been set up to protect Sardinia's unique habitats. Being on the migration route for birds between Africa and Europe, the island is particularly rich in birdlife. The best time to see some of the 170 species of birds identified here is between August and March, which is also when the flamingos arrive.

Flamingos and other migratory birds can also be seen at the Sale Porcus Reserve on the Sinis peninsula, while the best place to spot Eleonora's falcon is on the island of San Pietro. Other habitats for rare animals include the sand dunes at Piscinas, where loggerhead turtles come to lay their eggs. The shy and rare Sardinian deer is often glimpsed on the slopes of Arcosu in the Sulcis region and in the Gennargentu national park on the east coast.

Marine life is best observed in the clean, warm waters of one of Sardinia's marine reserves, including Tavolara. Dive trips go to the islands and to the coasts of Asinara and Gallura and the Golfo di Orosei. Dolphins can be spotted off the Maddalena archipelago and many bird species can be seen on the Golfo di Orosei.

Cinghiali (wild boar) can be found all over the island but favour woodland areas.

The Sardinian tree frog, or Tyrrhenian tree frog (Hyla sarda), is found in Corsica, Sardinia and the Tuscan Archipelago.

Fallow deer (Dama dama), seen here in Oglistra, prefer shrub areas and open woodland.

Trees growing on a mountain in the Gennargentu national park.

THE GENNARGENTU NATIONAL PARK

The Gennargentu national park in the province of Nuoro covers 59,100 hectares (146,000 acres) and includes Punta La Marmora, the island's highest peak, and the prehistoric village of Tiscali. In the valleys and lower mountain slopes are holm oak forests. Further up, maple and bay oak trees can be found, with clusters of juniper, holly and yew trees towards the summit. On the mountain tops are plum trees and Corsican junipers. At springtime peonies flower, and in summer oleanders carpet even the most barren of places. Mouflon, marten, wild boar and foxes inhabit the mountains in large numbers. In the woods are wildcats, hares, partridges, sparrow hawks and goshawks, while buzzards and kestrels hunt in stretches of open space. The rare monk seal may have disappeared from the park's coastline, but you can still spot the Corsican seagull and Eleonora's falcon.

On the island of San Pietro, colonies of the rare Eleonora's falcon can be seen.

The ocellated skink (Chalcides ocellatus) inhabits coastal areas in particular.

Pink flamingos winter in the lagoons of Cagliari and Oristano during their migration to Africa. A small colony of birds now nest in Sardinia permanently.

FESTIVALS, FOLKLORE AND MUSIC

Sardinians are especially proud of their music, folk roots and festivals. These are celebrated and preserved island-wide by all generations.

At the end of the 18th century, Sardinia was known as an *India de por acá*, an "India in the midst of the Western World". And thus, strictly speaking, it was to remain, at least until the end of World War I, an exotic culture about which virtually nothing was known, even by the few visitors whose spirit of adventure drove them to explore the island. Sardinia fitted into no specific category except perhaps that of "living antiquity", a place in which time had stopped dead.

Early visitors

It wasn't until D.H. Lawrence visited the island in 1921 with his wife and wrote *Sea and Sardinia* that it was brought to the attention of the English-reading world. Many, including the novelist and critic Anthony Burgess, have felt that Lawrence managed in six days what others had failed to do in years: "A single week's visit was enough for him to extract the very essence of the island and its people." But Lawrence's conclusions were in part grounded in the

A musician plays a launeddas, a type of flute found only in Sardinia.

Grazia Deladda, born 1871 in Nuoro, rejected the traditional role of women in Sardinian society and wrote many books in an earthy, realist style about the island and its people.

inscrutability of the island and islanders that had confounded others. "Lost between Europe and Africa and belonging to nowhere… as if it never really had a fate. No fate. Left outside of time and history," he pronounced.

The geographic and cultural character of the island, noted by Lawrence, has not lost its poignancy some 80 years later. The interior of Sardinia, with its harsh, sun-drenched terrains reminiscent of North Africa, still presents an aspect of inhospitability. The lives of its inhabitants have for centuries been marked by drudgery and privation.

In addition, a diffidence towards visitors from outside these tight-knit communities completes this picture. However, do not be mistaken: this is Europe, and a region of one of the world's richest, most industrialised nations. Yet, even so, a haunting paradox as to Sardinia's fate and destiny persists. Sardinians jealously guard the autonomous nature and character of their culture, while remaining, on the whole, committed Italians.

Sardinia is, after all, both geographically and culturally separate from mainland Italy. And Sardo is a distinct and recognised language, as opposed to one of Italy's myriad of dialects. It is not surprising, therefore, that you may still hear mainland Italy referred to by Sardinians as *il continente*.

Folk roots

Traditional folklore and culture, tied as it is in Sardinia to the land and agriculture, is under threat of disappearing, as elsewhere in the developed world. What remains will inevitably lose something of its authentic value, being a celebration of the past, rather than the rituals and festivities that express the average Sardinian's real-life activities and way of living. That said, as an expression of regional pride modern generations of Sardinians (often now part of the modern urban population) have striven to keep the historic traditions of past generations alive and to preserve distinctive characteristics of the indigenous culture.

Genuine folklore and its essential links with the island's traditions are a colourful and complex aspect of the Sardinian national heritage.

Folkloric band in traditional costume.

INSPIRING ARTISTS

Writers such as Sebastiano Satta, Nobel Prize-winner Grazia Deledda and Giuseppe Dessì all wrote about their native land, while artists like Antonio Ballero, Giuseppe Biasi and Filippo Figari painted it. The 19th and 20th centuries were characterised by an exceptional degree of artistic creativity for the island. Alan Ross, in *Bandit on the Billiard Table – a Journey through Sardinia*, said of Deledda's novels: "They are local in the best sense, touching off on almost every page illuminating truths about the Nuorese peasantry, their customs, ideas, ways of feeling… [They] are the best substitute for Sardinian landscape painting."

They are, however, all related to each other, as well as being inextricably interwoven with both the civilisation and the legal, economic and social structures of the country. It would thus be wrong simply to dismiss Sardinian folklore as a mere cultural phenomenon, which developed among the lower social classes of the community and is of concern only to them.

To a much greater extent than in many other societies, the roots of Sardinia's cultural heritage lie in both folk culture and the customs of the so-called upper classes. Modern research has confirmed that all strata of society proudly see the cultural heritage as their common inheritance.

This is reflected in Sardinia's writers and artists. No other folkloric tradition has been so lovingly immortalised by the literature and art of its own area, whilst at the same time exerting such a profound influence on its native artists.

The shepherd's role

All classes of society see the shepherd as a symbol of their cultural heritage. The historian Manlio Brigaglia makes an interesting observation in this respect. He reports that, shortly after World War I, the artist Mario Delitala had suggested that the Sardinian coat of arms should

a thief). Historically there is some justification for this attitude. Through the centuries Sardinia has been occupied (at times in total, at others in part) by a series of foreign invaders who have exploited its natural resources.

The Land of Poetry

One typical characteristic of Sardinian folklore is its penchant for pointed remarks. It would be no exaggeration to claim that language is the second, secret master of the island. From everyday encounters to special occasions, every event is accompanied, underlined and explained by a

Mosaic depicting shepherd life in Dorgali.

be changed. He proposed that the four blindfolded Moors, dating from the time when Sardinia was ruled by the house of Aragon, should be replaced by motifs representing the island's "four traditional occupations" – a shepherd, a farmer, a mountain-dweller and a fisherman. The idea found little support on the island and a consensus was not found for the change. So the "imported" coat of arms remained, while the figure of the shepherd is seen as being truly symbolic of Sardinia.

Intriguingly, as the figures of the Moors are blindfolded, it contrasts with one of the island's best-known local proverbs originating from the shepherd communities: *Furat chi benit dae su mare* (He who comes from across the sea is

THE LAMENT FOR THE DEAD

The lament for the dead, the *attitidu*, is often unmistakably aggressive in tone. Usually the chant of the *attitadoras* (the wailing women who perform a similar function to the *voceratrici* of Corsica, but who in Sardinia are usually related to the deceased) is a tribute, complimenting the virtues of the deceased and their ancestors and imagining the deeds they would have accomplished had death not snatched them away. In some villages, like Samugheo, *attitadoras* still practise "waking the dead", mourning all night beside the body, singing dirges, surrounded by the family, even tearing their own hair out and scratching their faces.

verbal commentary. Few peoples possess such a broad palette of set phrases and such an extensive and colourful vocabulary as the Sardinians. Significantly enough, another Sardinian expression describes the island as being the *Terra di Poesia* (The Land of Poetry).

It is unsurprising, then, that folkloric poetry, existing in a wide variety of genres, is such a vital part of the island's culture. A rigid metricity is particularly noticeable, even in simple incantations, curses, excommunications and *berbos* (teasing rhymes), in *ninnias* (lullabies), *attitidus* (lamentations for the dead) or *Gosos*

Revenge

In Sardinia, when someone dies and was the victim of a vendetta, the job of the *attitadoras* (wailing women) is to stir up feelings of hatred and vengeance (*attizzare*, to stir up/ to fan, may well explain the origins of the word). J.W.W. Tyndale, a 19th-century traveller in Sardinia, noted how "the feelings of the relatives are appealed to with the utmost earnestness by the Prefiche, who enumerate the murdered members of each family, recapitulate the wrongs and injuries, appeal to God, honour, and duty, and use every argument for

Performing the ballu tundu.

(eulogies of the saints). It extends to elaborate forms of love poetry such as the *mutos*, the miniature variations of which are called *muttettus* or *battorinas*. The rhythmical pattern of the *mutu* resembles that of the *strambotti* and *stornelli* of Tuscany (short traditional love songs written in the 17th century). It consists of two parts: the *isterria* (exposition) and the *torrada* (response). The finest *mutos* possess "a note of fantasy"; they resound with "poetic intelligence", an expression of "a higher plane and great sensitivity" which moved Italian film director Pier Paolo Pasolini (1922–75) to describe them as a "female" lyric form of poetry which he said "knows neither brute force nor Orgosolo".

revenge". As long ago as the mid-19th century the government was trying to prohibit these emotional incitements to avenge the death of a loved one, but the ceremony of the *attitidu*, which forms part of the *sarja* (wake), continues to be practised, particularly in some of the more remote regions of the Barbagia. Nonetheless, persistent pressure by the Church has resulted in the reluctant abandoning of the most violent curses in favour of a "quieter, more sorrowful, almost liturgical" lamentation (Gino Bottiglioni).

Max Leopold Wagner saw the *mutu* as an expression of the Sardinian tendency to melancholy, which assumes concrete form in the "grim solemnity" of the nuraghi, the ancient towers dating from the 2nd millennium BC that are dotted all over the island. Not every visitor, however, is of the opinion that the Sardinians are a melancholy people – although it is a trait which somehow seems in keeping with the rugged desolation of much of the countryside. Some observers maintain that the islanders are fundamentally a cheerful and outgoing race. Many would say both attitudes are correct, for the soul of the typical Sardinian – who celebrates with such gusto, who is so full of vitality and who organises horse shows and poetry competi-

anaesthetic, numbing the painful consciousness of their tragic existence – and not because they regard them as a means of amusement. If a Sardinian actually laughs then more often than not it is the proverbial *ghigno Sardonico* – a sardonic, spiteful laughter which is neither amusing nor an expression of joie de vivre.

Their tragedy, some maintain, is expressed by the scary masks of the *Mamuthones* and those of their companions, the *Issocadores*, both of which can be seen in the village of Mamoiada in the Barbagia, the heart of traditional Sardinia. (In Ottana and other villages in the same region

A political mural in Nuoro.

tions between the shrewdest *improvisatori* – is remarkably contradictory.

> Respected 20th-century Sardinian artists Mario Delitala, Stanis Dessy and Carmelo Floris have all painted symbolic representations of the ballu tundu.

In a work which is in essence an essay on the nature of the Sardinian, published under the meaningful title *Miele Amaro* (Bitter Honey), the writer Salvatore Cambosu maintains that the Sardinians do indeed enjoy festivals, but only because such celebrations act as an

the carnival processions are mostly dominated by the presence of *Boes* or *Merdùles*, wearing masks based on an ox's head.)

The wild, cumbersome *Mamuthones* (who also wear sheep fleeces and huge bells on their backs), according to anthropologists, are caught by the *laccio or soca* (lasso) of the nimble, mocking *Issohadores*, who are nothing less than images of the island's countless foreign conquerors. Francesco Masala, one of the principal writers of Sardinia's so-called *Ideology of the Vanquished*, believes this to be the case.

The *ballu tundu*

Another remarkable manifestation of the contradictory combination of sadness and mirth is the *ballu*, the dance – a traditional form of expression held in high esteem by the Sardinians and still popular on high days and holidays. Though similar to the national dances of Greece and Romania, the Sardinian version is usually executed more solemnly.

Traditionally, only men and women who were betrothed or married were allowed to link fingers or touch palms – though J.W.W. Tyndale noticed that this rule was not respected in the village of Osidda in the province of Nuoro, where "whether by uniform usage, or by a peculiar dispensation from the patron saint of the day, the greater part danced with their hands round waists".

Here, too, the observations of travellers and researchers are in blatant contradiction with each other. It is perhaps interesting to note that the comments of the "Interpreters" of Sardinia, to adopt the phrase coined by the cultural anthropologist Alberto M. Cirese, fall into two distinct categories: calumny or eulogy. Some writers – like Baldessare Luciano – regarded the *ballu tundu*, the "national dance" of Sardinia, as lascivious; others, such as Pater Bresciani, insisted that it was on the

Flower-bedecked carts called traccas take pride of place in the festival of Saint Efisio in early May.

FESTA DI SANT'EFISIO

The island's most famous festival, dating from 1656, is that of Sant'Efisio, the martyr and patron saint of Cagliari. On 1 May, in a grandiose procession, his statue is borne high on an ox cart from the capital to Pula, the place where he was executed. Local residents in traditional costume join his train, which is accompanied by the music of *launeddas*. The festival is an annual highlight in the lives of many of Cagliari's citizens. Sardinia's festivals are like many of the islanders themselves – frequently sombre, rarely to be taken lightly. They are fiercely Christian, but often their traditions make reference to pagan roots.

contrary dignified, serious and solemn, despite the occasional interludes of frivolity. Recently the semiologist Leonardo Sole drew attention to what he called the significant "mythical silence" which still surrounds the *ballu tundu*, and which bears a certain resemblance to a "sacred chorus". Ethnographer Francesco Alziator, who has made a study of the age of the *ballu tundu*, wrote: "Two basic features of this round dance support the theory that it is very ancient: firstly the *launeddas* [flutes], which traditionally accompany the dance throughout almost a quarter of the island, and secondly the association of the dance with fire. For in the olden days there was almost always a fire in the centre of the circle of dancers." It is easy enough to imagine the scene; all one needs to do is to study the paintings by Mario Delitala, Stanis Dessy, Carmelo Floris or one of the other 20th-century Sardinian artists. All the painters mentioned have frequently found inspiration in the symbolic representation of the *ballu tundu*.

> Although tourism has popularised Sardinia's festivals, there is no better way of gaining an insight into the character and moods of the island than by taking part in one.

The art historian Carlo Aru has discovered what may be the earliest portrayal of the Sardinian *ballu tundu* in an interesting painting that hangs in the medieval chapel of San Pietro di Zuri, which was built in 1291 by Anselmo da Como (the ruins of the adjoining historic village are now completely submerged beneath a reservoir). Aru remarks that "On the outermost right-hand pillar, on the apse side, is a painting of people dancing: tiny figures holding hands; on their heads they are wearing the *berretta* [the traditional beret of Sardinia]".

The *launeddas*, the musical instruments which provide the accompaniment for the *ballu tundu*, are thought to be very ancient indeed, possibly dating from as long ago as the time of the Nuraghi. They are a type of flute, but quite unique, occurring only on Sardinia.

Music and culture

In a detailed study of the *launedda*, distinguished ethno-musicologists Giulio Fara and Gavino Gabriel speculate that this "triple-piped" instrument, which looks like a bagpipe without the sound bladder, might in fact be closely related to the shepherd's flute with pipes of varying length which is described by Virgil.

Tyndale worried that the "great exertion required to blow the *launedda* has considerable effect upon the health of the musicians, who frequently play for hours together". In his remarkable summary of the island's cultural heritage, a work which has assumed the form of an ethnographic stream of consciousness, Salvatore Cambosu attributes more sinister qualities to the sound of the *launedda* than the amiable Tyndale does, defining it as an existential metaphor for a "historic illness".

All of a sudden we see again before us the terrifying, grim expression of the Sardinian with the evil eye, whose character has supposedly left its ugly mark so irrevocably on the island's history. During the 20th century the cohesive strength of Sardinian culture – which is so introverted that it has earned the nicknames "Culture of Stone" and "Culture of Loneliness" – has suffered a damaging blow which threatens to destroy utterly an entire folkloric tradition.

This transformation has happened within the framework of changes that have taken

A couple marry in traditional Sardinian costume.

place in Sardinia this century, and is, according to the ethnologist Giulio Angioni, the result of two "conspicuous historic turning points" on Sardinia: the abolition of the feudal system at the beginning of the 19th century and the monopolisation of cheese production by the large cheese-making companies on the Italian mainland during the last century. These two events challenged the basis of island society and its foundation in the pastoral culture. In an alarming, tangible way cork and plastic – the incompatible symbols of two extremely different cultures – simultaneously determined everyday life and manufacturing techniques on the island in the 1960s.

Sardinia's festivals

Nowadays, Sardinia's great folkloric traditions are virtually restricted to the most important religious *sagre* (folk festivals), such as the processions of the *Redentore* (Saviour) in Nuoro in August, the *Candelieri* (Festival of Candles) in Sassari in August and *Sant'Efisio* (the biggest festival on the entire island, held in Cagliari each May), or the principal feudal tournaments such as the *Sa Sartiglia*, which takes place every spring in Oristano.

These are festivals in which sacred and profane elements coexist. Tourism may have commercialised the festivals, but their effect is still powerful.

Cow bells of the Mamuthones of Mamoiada.

Nostalgic, religious and full of contradictions, they provide an ideal starting point for an exploration of the Sardinian soul. It is remarkable how so varied a people celebrate so much within such a small area. The diverse characters of the inhabitants match the marked contrasts between the coastal region and the interior.

What the descendants of settlers on the island of Sant'Antioco, who arrived from North Africa many centuries ago, have in common with those of long-established residents in Alghero, whose first language is Catalan, is that both communities cling to their own traditions, and not only in the food they eat – from couscous to lobster Catalane.

In the Easter ceremonies, the confraternitate, the brotherhoods, dressed in hoods and robes, file solemnly through town streets, giving an impression of deep piety and penitence, but the accompanying torch processions and bonfires date from pre-Christian times.

Macho festivals

Another Sardinian characteristic, the strong element of *machismo*, can be observed in the *matanza*, the catching of the tuna in early summer when shoals of the fish migrate east. The fishermen begin their elaborate preparations for the bloody massacre weeks beforehand; their mood is one of anticipation and intense excitement. And in the equestrian festival of San Costantino, which takes place in Sedilo in July, religiosity and male pride combine. Many a rider has paid with his life for taking part in the wild horseback entry into the pilgrimage church, but there has never been a shortage of volunteers.

FESTIVAL HIGHLIGHTS

Carnevale in Sardinia is marked with ghoulish parades and high jinks, many of which date back to pagan times. In Mamoiada and Ottana, in the Barbagia, there are masked parades while at Oristano *(Sa Sartiglia)* and Sant Lussugiu *(Sa Carrela è Nanti)* masked horsemen pound the old lanes.

Cavalcata Sarda (penultimate Sunday of May) in Sassari involves processions, colourful costumes and spectacular horse-racing.

Ardia (6 and 7 July) in Sedilo: dynamic bareback horseriders pursue a man representing San Constantino to a dry fountain whereupon much Vernaccia wine is consumed.

Candelieri, the Festival of Candles, in Sassari in mid-August: gigantic wooden candles are carried through the town in an ornate procession, which originated in the 13th century.

Corsa degli Scalzi: a bizarre barefoot race of white tunic-wearing young men carrying an effigy of Cabras's saint through the streets to the sanctuary of San Salvatore.

Madonna dello Schiavo (15 November) in Carloforte: a procession of a carved, wooden statue of the Madonna Nera, the Black Madonna – symbol of its Genoese inhabitants' miraculous journey to San Pietro from the island of Tabarka in the Bay of Tunis, and escape from enslavement.

Traditional Arts and Craftwork

Whether found in books, on the streets or in the home, the artistry of Sardinia represents cultural traditions passed down orally through the generations.

Authentic Sardinian crafts may have developed in conditions of poverty, isolation and oppression, but they also represent ingenuity, skill, pride and dignity.

On an island that has long been a world of its own, shepherds and farmers, miners and craftsmen had to develop their own creativity. Therefore from sheer necessity they learnt how to give expression to beautiful forms, depending on local raw materials.

Terracotta

One of the oldest Sardinian crafts is terracotta production, alive since prehistoric times. At the turn of 20th century practical *strexiaus* (craftsmen who made domestic ceramic items) started making artistic pieces, coloured by an application of the essence of fresh rockrose leaves.

Textiles

The island's rushes, asphodel, reeds, willow, myrtle, lentisk, straw and raffia have all been used to create baskets, hampers and mats. At Castelsardo in Via Marconi is the Museo dell'Intreccio Mediterraneo (Museum of Basket Weaving; see page 144).

The stiff, coarse wool of the island's sheep provides the raw material in the manufacture of carpets, wall hangings and furnishings. This craft also produces refined embroideries and lace. Motifs range from ornate geometrical patterns to designs from Byzantine art to the Baroque. Embroidered shawls with long fringes, adorned with colourful flower motifs and embellished with gems, are made in Oliena and often seen on festival days.

Jewellery

Together, gold and silver were the driving force behind the flourishing production of amulets, talismans and necklaces. Goldsmiths prospered in Sardinia in the 14th century, through the production of religious objects. Examples include buttons shaped like breasts, earrings, necklaces and brooches studded with gems, pearl and coral. Alghero is particularly famous for coral and jewels.

Woodcarving

Barbagia-style woodcarving gives us richly carved wedding chests – usually made of dark chestnut – with a variation of animal, bird, flower and abstract symbols.

Traditional decorations and lace in Nuoro's Ethnographic Museum.

Leatherwork

Leather handicrafts such as harnesses and horse saddles, belts, handbags, clothing, cushions and decorative objects are often embroidered with linen or silk thread folk motifs.

Metalwork

Sardinian knives – including the famous leppas with their sharp blade and shaft of ram or mouflon horn – are made in Pattada. Other ironwork featured around the island includes railings, sculptures, lamp and light fixtures and furniture. Sardinian wrought iron, with its magical designs, recall the exquisite arabesques of the Near East and Toledo in Spain, and primitive early history.

COSTUME AND JEWELLERY

The wearing of traditional costume and jewellery is still very much an integral part of the island's festivals and feast days.

At festival time in Sardinia the streets of the villages and towns become ablaze with men and women wearing brightly coloured traditional costumes. Sardinians are big festival-goers; in the past, high days and feast days were an opportunity to meet people from other villages and mark important occasions. In this closed island society costume and jewellery were not only indicators of where you came from but of social standing and wealth. Regional variations in costume are still apparent today, and are worn with pride by village members. In general, traditional dress for women consists of red waistcoats edged with gold filigree work, and worn over white blouses with lace cuffs and collars, decorated with an elaborate brooch. Full-length layered dresses of white, black and red are usual, and a black or white embroidered headscarf is often worn. The costumes are decorated with lots of accessories. Traditional costume for men is simpler but still very colourful, consisting of a red waistcoat, white shirt, red neckerchief and a black beret called a *berreta*. All this can be seen at Nuoro's ethnographic museum (see page 215).

The Mamuthones of Mamoida wear scary masks carved of wood in a festival thought to date back to pagan times.

Many of Sardinia's traditional costumes feature fine embroidery and petit-point, as this superb tunic and headdress from Desulo illustrate.

Traditionally, Sardinian women cover their head with an elaborately embroidered shawl, the result of years of work.

Festival jewellery includes su giunchigliu necklaces and filigree sos breves (silver cases) pinned to clothing containing images, prayers and magic spells.

TRADITIONAL JEWELLERY

Sardinian *prendas* (jewellery) is intrinsically linked to traditional costume. Made of gold, silver or fine filigree, it is handed down through the generations and reflects life, fertility and love. The quality and amount of jewellery is an important indication of social status. Worn on a dress or waistcoat, buttons have a small cylinder inlaid with a semi-precious stone at their centre. Necklaces come in two types: *su giunchigliu*, a long gold chain wrapped several times around the neck, or *su ghettau*, which has links adorned with large filigree balls. Precious stones are worn from a dark velvet choker *Maninfide* rings, featuring two clasped hands, are given by a fiancé to his intended. The most distinctive design for brooches is the *sinnai*, a large ruby or cameo set in a sunflower design. Typical feast-day earrings are bow-shaped with a pendant, or are butterfly-shaped and made of gold leaf. Earrings with figures of a bird and joined by two cones or pyramids are also worn, as are earrings in the shape of bunches of grapes.

Carved sheep's mask and traditional costume for the Ottana festival at Santa Teresa di Gallura.

Sardinia is arguably the most culturally distinct region of Italy, as shown by its folk dancing, costumes and musical traditions.

Couple dressed in traditional regional costume.

Making pizza at Hotel Mandra Edera in Abbassanta.

FOOD AND DRINK

Eating and drinking in Sardinia is a real treat. The food is simple, good value and gutsy, while the wines are some of the best produced anywhere.

Sardinian cooking comes from an agri-pastoral past, poor and simple. It is the cooking of shepherds and farmers who have never been rich but have made their simple dishes tastier by the use of aromatic herbs offered by the earth. An ancient inscription in the Grotta della Vipera in Cagliari mentions the use of saffron, the violet stigma of the crocus flower, in cooking. Other common aromatic herbs include myrtle, rosemary, wild thyme and mint.

Sardinian cooking may be peasant in origin but it has flavour, intelligence, versatility and an exotic nature. Some recipes are still prepared in the same way as they were thousands of years ago. The native cuisine of the island has also been influenced by other Mediterranean cultures such as the Arabs. For example, in the isle of San Pietro, which has links with Tabarka in Tunisia, a popular dish is *cas-cas*, the same as North African and Arab couscous. Another, *fregula*, looks like

Cutting salami in Paulolatino.

> The name for sardines is thought to have come from the young pilchards caught off the coast of Sardinia, and which were one of the first fish to be packed in oil.

couscous but is actually semolina pasta – it originated in ancient Rome and has a heavy Moorish influence.

In ancient times meat requirements were met by hunting or by keeping animals such as pigs, sheep, cows and goats or occasionally horses. White meat, especially poultry, was eaten only in small quantities: roast or boiled fowl was regarded as food only for invalids or pregnant women. Surprisingly for an island, fish fared no better (though the island did give the name to sardines, fished in copious numbers).

It is possible that the lack of appetite for seafood is explained by the fact that the Sardinians have never been a nation of seafarers. They have always regarded the sea as an enemy, ever bringing new waves of conquerors to their island. Even today the owners of the fishing fleets operating in Sardinian waters tend to come from Ponza, Naples, Genoa or Carloforte. The annual *matanza*, the tuna harvest, an event dating from Roman times, is these days mainly to supply the export market and is by and large backed by Japanese funds. Recent trends have led to a greater emphasis on fish in restaurants on the coast; around Cagliari, in particular, you will find excellent lobster, red and grey mullet, and in the Oristano-Cabras region, eel.

Breads

With regard to Sardinian bread, a variety of kneading techniques, handed down by women from generation to generation, and differing forms of leavening explain the remarkable range available on the island.

Bread is art in Sardinia, and the Baroque-like splendour of *coccoi*, the elaborately snipped and fashioned loaf of bread, is central

Fresh dough; good bread is one of the pleasures of Sardinian food.

Main dishes are usually a roast (*arrosto*) of suckling pig, lamb, kid, veal or wild boar, served with a delicious spicy sauce. Vegetable side dishes include lettuce, fennel, celery, radishes and artichokes.

to special occasions, such as Easter, Christmas, weddings and other *feste*. In Nuoro, *coccoi a puppia* are dolls made of bread that are given to children.

The variety of bread types across the island is staggering. The best-known is the *pane carasau* (sheet of music), a crisp, flat unleavened bread. As this type of bread keeps fresh for long periods, shepherds have traditionally taken a few *pane carasau* with them on their long wanderings. *Su pistoccu* (similar but thicker than *carasau*) and *su cifraxiu* (with a crisp crust and a soft interior) are sold in bakeries all over the island. Most restaurants serving typical Sardinian cooking list various types of breads among their specialities.

The traditional dish of *sa cordula*, found on most menus, is made of rolled lamb entrails stuck on a skewer and roasted on a spit.

Roast specialities

Arrosti, roast and grilled meat specialities, are a highlight of Sardinian gastronomy, particularly in the island's interior. Only the meat of young animals – lamb, kid, suckling pig and veal – is generally used.

There are two main methods of preparation. Firstly, there is carne a *carraxiu*. As in other Mediterranean countries (in particular Turkey), a hole is dug in the ground (stakes are laid in its base and driven round the inside to shore back the earth) and a deep trench is then dug round the hole, leaving about 15cm (6in) of soil as a "wall". The meat, usually the whole carcass, is placed inside the hole (which is liberally lined with herbs), and a fire is lit above. When this is sufficiently hot, the live ashes are raked into the trench. The heat bakes the meat evenly, with the herbs lending it a delicious aromatic flavour.

In the second method, the suckling pig, lamb, kid or veal is placed on wooden or metal spits. These are then positioned vertically or horizontally around the central fire and turned from time to time to ensure the meat cooks evenly.

In some districts the finishing touch is provided by a lump of bacon fat, which is wrapped in paper and then ignited. As it drips down onto the spit, the fat colours the meat golden brown and makes it crisp. In Sea and Sardinia D.H. Lawrence describes the roasting of a kid goat and the care that is taken in doing so, in great detail.

The most impressive *arrosti* are those served on special occasions: country festivals, saints' days or weddings. For the Sardinians, any cause for celebration naturally presents a social duty to provide good and plentiful food. You can sample an *arrosto*, usually described as a typical Sardinian speciality, in nearly every restaurant on the island.

Antipasto

The most popular antipasto (hors d'oeuvre), the *antipasto di terra*, is a selection of ham, smoked sausages, olives, chicken liver, *sa cordula* (lamb tripe, served rolled up and grilled or fried with peas), mushrooms and brawn. The island has a number of notable *salumi* such as *mustela sarda* (a mature peppered sausage, hung for 50 days)

burrida can be eaten as an appetiser or a main dish. It is made of dogfish, boiled in slices and then marinated for at least 24 hours in a sauce made of garlic, parsley, walnuts, vinegar, and the chopped dogfish livers. This grey sauce tastes considerably better than it looks.

Pasta and soup dishes

As elsewhere in Italy, in Sardinia a meal without pasta is unthinkable. Here it is almost always home-made; the most popular types are *malloreddus* (in the shape of ridged shells) and *maccarones* (shaped over a thin metal wire). These

You'll find spit-roasted pig at most Sardinian festivals.

and *sa suppressata*. Olives in brine are always present, succulent after a period of seasoning in salted water with wild fennel seeds. Black olives sautéed in oil and garlic, then preserved in chopped parsley and a little vinegar, are another island favourite.

A superb appetiser, *bottarga* is made from slated grey mullet roe which has been pressed and dried. *Bottarga* (often called Sardinian caviar) is served cut in thin slices and covered in olive oil. When grated with pasta it makes a delicious first course.

Other starters include *merca*, a dish of grey mullet simmered in salted water and wrapped in marsh grass, and *bocconi*, which consists of whelks simmered in salted water served hot. *Sa*

HONEY

Sardinia produces excellent honey. Flavoured by its native flowers, many different varieties of honey are available. Among them are eucalyptus, orange blossom and wild lavender. There is also a bitter honey made from pollen from the strawberry tree, which is prepared in December and is thought to prevent bronchial asthma. *Millefiori* or *miele della flora mediterranea* is made from a mixture of all the honey made throughout the year and is a good choice if you're looking for a pot of honey to take home with you. Honey can be bought in supermarkets, local shops or, best of all, at festivals and local fares from the people who make it.

are served in a fresh tomato sauce and herbs, sometimes with chunks of meat or pieces of smoked sausage and accompanied with a condiment of cheese melted in a bain-marie.

Two well-known stuffed pastas are *angiulotts* (ravioli-like parcels stuffed with ricotta or fresh cheese, spinach and saffron) and *culungiones* (large ravioli stuffed with potato purée, mint and a little cheese). Both are served with tomatoes or meat sauce.

Fregula is a granular pasta, similar to couscous. It is served with steamed clams, like pasta, or in broth as a thick soup. Thick broths of

really only served in Cagliari and a few other coastal places. Today there are a lot of tasty fish dishes to choose from, starting with the famous *ziminu* or *sa cassola*, a fish stew. Among the many different types of fish available in Sardinia, grey mullet, red mullet, *ghiozzi* (the local version of a *frittura de mare:* small fish tossed in semolina flour and then fried) and eels, both barbecued and fried, deserve a special mention. All of them may be cooked and eaten as a main course if they have been marinated in *scabecciu*, a sautéed sauce of oil, garlic and vinegar.

Cheese and ham being stored in Santu Lussurgiu, Oristano.

vegetables, meat and herbs are common; they are substantial, often meals in themselves. You could try *pecora in cappotto*, boiled mutton with potatoes, onions, celery and dried tomatoes prepared in Barbagia, or *suppa cuatta* (Italian *zuppa gallurese*), a dish with regional variations but generally made with large slices of bread and cheese arranged in a pan, sprinkled with grated *pecorino* and finely chopped garlic, then drowned in a hot meat broth. In Moni try *favata con lardo*, a soup of broad beans with sausage, lard and wild fennel.

Seafood dishes

Seafood cuisine is a recent addition to the menu; in fact, until recently *su pisci* was

Popular regional fish dishes include *l'aragosta alla catalana* (Catalan-style lobster), served with oil, vinegar and onions; *polpagliara*, small octopus simmered in a spicy sauce; *fregula cun cocciula* (baby clams), best eaten in Cagliari; and *orziadas*, sea anemones rolled in semolina and fried, also from Cagliari. In Oristano expect to see roasted mullet and eel soup on the menu; in Carloforte fish casserole and *musciamme* (dried tuna fish fillet); stuffed squid in Olbia; and roast cuttlefish in Dorgali.

Desserts and cheeses

A traditional lunch *alla sarda* – Sardinian-style – will conclude with cheese and dessert. The islanders have been manufacturing dairy products for more than 5,000 years, so it is not surprising that the range of fine cheeses made from sheep's, goat's or cow's milk is extensive. Gourmets will delight in the discovery of *caprino, fiore sardo, semicotto, caglio, casagedu, casu marzu, pepato and romano*.

All types of cheese are available, from soft curd to hard, with flavours ranging from slightly acid to mild and aromatic to piquant. Some are eaten simply with bread; others are grated generously over pasta.

Desserts are another Sardinian speciality; one particular favourite, *sebadas* (or *seadas*), consists of two circles of pastry, filled with a layer of curd cheese and fried in deep fat, then drizzled with honey. Invariably, a selection of fruit is offered at the end of a meal. This varies according to season. Popular, too, are dried fruits and nuts: almonds, hazelnuts and dried figs. A favourite confection at festival time consists of shelled almonds and orange peel dipped in honey.

The most commonly served *digestivo* has always been *aquavite*, an aromatic grappa with a high alcohol content. Another powerfully flavoured liqueur has also become popular among

Spaghetti alle vongole is mostly served on the coast.

TRADITIONAL BREADS AND SWEETS

Saludi e trigu! (Good health and wheat!) is a traditional New Year's greeting. There are countless variations of bread, from the shepherd's long-lasting *pane carasau* to the sublime *pirichitteddu*, baked in Cagliari on 3rd February in honour of Saint Biagio. The ethnographic museum in Nuoro (see page 215) keeps over 600 varieties of traditional breads, 100 of which are on display.

Sardinian sweets are closely related to religious festivals. Originally from Logudoro, *sebadas* pastries are covered with honey and filled with curd cheese flavoured with lemon rind. From the Barbagia come *sa voiardi* sponge fingers, which today are used to make tiramisu. *Biachittos*, small meringues with almond and lemon rind, and *amaretti* biscuits are popular everywhere. Campidano is famous for *pirichittus*, made from eggs, olive oil and flour, and *candelaus*, iced biscuits with almond paste and in the shape of flowers, animals, jugs, fruits and shoes. *Mustazzolous* biscuits are diamond-shaped and are eaten in honour of village patron saints. Finally, *sospiri* (sighs) are round sweets made of grated almonds, sugar, lemon and orange flower water. They are delicately wrapped in coloured tissue paper and eaten on special occasions.

Sardinians in recent years: *liquore di mirto*, distilled from myrtle. It is red in colour when it is manufactured from the berries, and clear if only the leaves of the plant are used. Be warned, it packs a punch.

Wines

The origins of Sardinian wine go back centuries. The old Nuragus vines (the name most probably comes from the nuraghe), together with the Vernaccia vines, are the oldest on the island. The Cannonau, Girò and Torbato vines date back to the time of the Catalans

Local wines can be excellent.

and the Aragonese, the Monica and Malvasia vines to the Byzantines, Vermentino vines to the Ligurians and Moscato and Nasco vines to the Romans.

There is a wide variety of local wines; most have a high alcohol content and are full-bodied, smooth and deeply coloured. The best-known bear the description Cannonau. Wines bottled in the cooperative cellars bear the DOC, a label guaranteeing quality; this certificate of authenticity is only awarded to wines from specific wine-growing areas. The varieties available range from heavy and lighter red wines, through rosés to whites. Most tend to be on the dry side rather than sweet or heavy; some are decidedly tangy. Cannonau wines are grown in

the eastern provinces and Dorgali. A lot of vineyards produce these wines; some have outlets where you can buy and taste wines.

> *The Sardinian version of Vernaccia, such as Vernaccia di Oristano, is different to the Italian varieties, being more sherry-like.*

Three wines from the district around Cagliari – Girò, Monica and Nasco – are red and sweet. The popular Moscato di Cagliari and Malvasia are available from the Cantina Sociale di Quartu Sant'Elena. Nuragus, from the nearby Monserrato winery run by the Cantina Sociale di Monserrato, is an excellent accompaniment to pasta, rice dishes, soup, white meat, fish and seafood. Meloni wines, produced by the Meloni Vini, come from vineyards throughout the island. At Selargius, the Santa Rosa estate specialises in dessert wines.

Vernaccia, perhaps the most famous Sardinian wine, is served as a dessert wine or as an aperitif and tastes rather like a dry sherry. It comes from the Cantina Sociale della Vernaccia, founded in 1953, and is grown in the fertile lower valley of the Tirso river.

Mandrolisai (red or rosé) wine from Sorgono is traditionally drunk during the feast of San Mauro and Santu Antine. The Cantina Sociale del Mandrolisai was formed in 1952 to improve the quality and distribution of the wine. Semidano, a white wine with a fruity and intense bouquet, is excellent with shellfish and also comes from this area. Another good wine to go with shellfish is Vermentino, which can also be drunk as an aperitif. It is a light wine and has an aroma of quince with a hint of bitter almond.

From the provinces of Oristano and Nuoro comes Malvasia, a sweet dessert wine. Look out for Malvasia di Bosa, one of the most outstanding DOC Sardinian wines, which featured in the documentary film *Mondovino*. The Malvasia white grape is thought to have come from the Greek port of Monemvasia, in the Peloponnese. Returning to red wines and moving to the Sulcis peninsula in the southwest, we find Carignano, a ruby red with an excellent consistency.

In restaurants the local wine (vino locale) is often served from jugs. It is usually very drinkable and cheaper than buying by the bottle.

Shepherds and Pecorino

The shepherd's way of life has come to symbolise Sardinia, but changes are inevitable if this aspect of island culture is to survive.

Sardinia's history has always been closely bound to that of its shepherds, whose lifestyle is as fascinating as it is full of privations. The native Sardinian sheep is small and hardy, able to withstand the

A group of enterprising businessmen from Rome established industrial cheese factories between 1385 and 1890, producing the *pecorino romano* (sheep's milk cheese), popular in Italy since Roman times.

Even as the first dairy production cooperatives were being formed, there were still extensive areas of land where farmers clung to the old order. The shepherd was upheld as a symbol of an entire culture which was in danger of disappearing as a result of the links being forged with other countries.

Pungent and tangy, *pecorino* is eaten with bread, grated over pasta and frequently used in cooking,

Pecorino romano, a sheep's milk cheese – pecora means sheep in Italian.

harsh conditions, and produces a high milk yield in spite of often poor pastures.

Sheep rearing developed under the Romans, in the Middle Ages and especially under Spanish rule and monastic orders like the Benedictines, as the island's inaccessible, barren land lent itself to sheep rearing rather than arable farming. Today the shepherd's lifestyle is under threat from modernity: continuing migration from the land, industrialisation of the island and the growing numbers of local inhabitants employed in the service industries. With this in mind, Unesco has been approached to protect the shepherd's unique way of life. It is also feared that a dangerous gap could arise between an impoverished interior and the wealthy tourist and industrialised regions of the island.

especially pesto. Today there are over 50 cheese-making factories in Sardinia, and *pecorino* is the island's main export product. Apart from *pecorino romano*, which amounts to just under half of overall production, they also make a sweet white variety of cheese known as *pecorino tipo toscanello* and *canestrato*, a delicious and strong-tasting sheep's milk cheese. The district around Gavoi is famous for its *pecorino fiore-sardo*, mostly exported to Puglia. In the Abruzzi, *pecorino fiore-sardo* is served with pears. Ricotta, an excellent curd cheese, is also made from *pecorino*. At one time ricotta and *pane carasau* formed the basis of the shepherd's diet; today it is mainly used in cooking, in the preparation of ravioli and *sebadas*, and served with a large spoonful of bitter-sweet Sardinian honey.

The bear-shaped Roccia L'Orso is a hit with tourists.

INTRODUCTION

A detailed guide to the entire island, with principal
sites clearly cross-referenced by number to the maps.

Church detail.

One can never go by appearances alone in Sardinia. By way of example, this book's first editor cited a vivid memory from his first visit to the island, way back in 1972, when he met some village youths in Orgosolo, who showed him their pistol and insisted on arranging "safe" accommodation for him. In the end, they all finished the evening eating spaghetti, drinking rough wine and playing cards – and it didn't seem to matter that everyone else in the bar carried shotguns.

Since those days, much has changed. Mass tourism may have turned the Costa Smeralda into a jet-set haunt, but of late ecotourism and city breaks are attracting new, urbane and more adventurous visitors to Sardinia. More traditional tourists are still attracted by the pristine beaches where white sand, rose-coloured cliffs and blue-green watery hues abound.

We begin with Cagliari, one of Europe's oldest cities and capital of the island. It has a little bit of everything: the cosmopolitan character of a port city, Spanish ambience in the Old Quarter, the luxuries of an Italian shopping mecca, and beaches and pink flamingo-flecked lagoons on its doorstep.

Spectacular sandy cove in the Golfo di Orosei.

We then travel up the east coast to Arbatax, a busy port and gateway to Sardinia's newest province, Ogliastra. Further on, past the spectacular Golfo di Orosei with its rocky coves and long sandy beaches, is Olbia, gateway to the Costa Smeralda, one of the most exclusive resorts in the Mediterranean. Then follows a tour of the dramatic countryside in the north – the Maddalena archipelago and seascapes of Gallura – before reaching Sassari. The most Italian Sardinian town has a cosmopolitan air and fine cultural attractions. Proceeding down the west coast, from Alghero to Oristano, we take in beguiling Spanish-influenced towns and then the fascinating southwest, with its colossal dunes and spectral mining landscapes. Finally we explore the Barbagia, which the Romans named after the "barbarians" they found there: this is the island's mountainous heart, where rugged Sardinian self-reliance lives on.

Such variety – wild landscapes and gorgeous beaches, the remains of an ancient culture, folk traditions and fascinating cities, make Sardinia almost a continent – *quasi un continente*, as the saying goes.

N

Sardinia

0   20 km
0   20 miles

T Y R R H E N I A N

S E A

S A R D I N I A N

S E A

Palermo

Trapani

Baunei

Santa Maria Navarrese

Arbatax

Lotzorai   Capo Bellavista

Bari Sardo

Villagrande Strisaili   Tortoli   125

1834

L. Alto del
Flumendosa   *Ogliastra*

P.ta Marmora
1829   Lanusei   Marina di Gairo

389   Desulo   Seui   Gairo   Loceri   Capo Sferracavallo

Tonara   Aritzo   Seulo   Jerzu

Sorgono   M.S.Vittoria
1212   Ussassai   Tertenia   P.s' Accettori
589

Gennargentu   Esterzili   Escalaplano   Capo S. Lorenzo

Fordongianus   Asuni   Orroli   Goni   Villaputzu   125

Busachi   Ruinas   Nuragus   Nurallao   San Vito
Muravera   Sarri Priamo

Allai   Nuraminis   Mandas   Sant' Andrea
Frius   Ballao   *Flumendosa*   Villasalto   Capo Ferrato

Ales   Usellus   Genna Spina   Orosno   Villamar   Guasila   Senorbi   Serri
Dolianova   Burcei   Parco dei
Sette Fratelli
M. S. Fratelli
1023   Casa di Marina

Arbore   Villaurbana   Barumini   Sardara   Sarluci   Serrenti   Settu
P. Serpeddì
1067   *Monte Genas*   Castiadas   Villasimius

Marrubiu   Simaxis   Su Nuraxi   Villatori   Assemini
Sestu
Sinnai   Quartu Sant' Elena
554   Geremeas   Capo Carbonara

Santa Giusta   Uras   Mogoro   Pabillonis   131   San Gavino
Monreale   San Sperate
Decimomannu   Uta   Selargius   Poetto   I. dei Cavoli

*Medio
Campidano*   Sanluri   Capoterra   Quartucciu   *Golfo di
Cagliari*

Terralba   San Nicolò
d'Arcidano   Gonnosfanadiga   M. Linas
1236   Villacidro   Serramanna   **Cagliari**

Gùspini   Arbus   Domusnovas   Siliqua   Stagno di
Cagliari

Pardu Atzei   Narcao   *Carbonia Iglesias*   Riserva Naturale
Foresta de
M. Arcosu   Sarroch   Nora

Flumimaggiore   Iglesias   San Giovanni
Suergiu   M. is Caravius
1116   Pula   I. Serpentara

Buggerru   Gonnesa   Giba   Gimestra   P. Maxia
1017   Domus
de Maria   Bithia

Portoscuso   Carbonia   Sant' Anna
Arresi   Sant' Antioco   Teulada   Capo Spartivento

**Isola di
S. Pietro**   **Isola di
S. Antioco**   Chia   *Costa del Sud*

Capo Altano
o Giordano   Porto Pino   Punta Mengà
I. la Vecca   Capo Teulada

I. Piana   I. il Toro

I. di Mal
di Ventre

**Parco Nazionale della
Penisola di Sinis**

I. Catalano   S. Giovanni
di Sinis   **Tharros**

Capo S. Marco

Golfo di Oristano   Santa Giusta

Putzu Idu   Riola Sardo

Cabras   **Oristano**

Badulu   Solanas

SARDINIA

Galleria Comunale d'Arte **8**

Università di Cagliari

Via La Vega

GIARDINI

San Michele, Colle di San Michele

Mercato San Benedetto, Parco della Musica

Piazza San Rocco

Via S. Rocco

Viale San Vincenzo

Via Tiziano

PUBBLICI

Via A. Manz

Viale Giardini Pubblici

Via S.S. Lorenzo e Pancrazio

Via Belvedere

Viale Buon Cammino

Viale Regina Elena

Via San Saturnino

Via S. Mauro

Via Del Giardini

Via Ozieri

Via Ottone Bacaredo

Via V. Mons

Via Macomer

Pinacoteca Nazionale

Cittadella dei Musei **1**

Museo Archeologico Nazionale

Museo d'Arte Siamese

Via San Giovanni

Via Ozieri

Via Tempio

Fra' Nicola da Gesturi

Anfiteatro Romano **19**

Facoltà di Scienze

Piazza Arsenale

Collezione delle Cere Anatomiche di Clemente Susini

Via Bosa

Via Anfiteatro

Via Laconi da

Porta Cristina

Torre di San Pancrazio

San Domenico

Piazza San Domenico

Facoltà di Economia, Commercio e Giurisprudenza

Via Porcell

Piazza Indipendenza

Viale Regina Elena

Via San Giovanni

Via San Antonio

Via San Giacomo

ORTO BOTANICO **18**

Ospedale San Giovanni

Cliniche Universitarie

La Purissima

Vico P. Martini

Via Martini

Via Nicolò

STAMPACE

Via S. Giorgio

Via Colle d'Appello

Santa Croce

Palazzo Regio **2**

Piazza Palazzo

CASTELLO

Cattedrale di Cagliari **3**

Piazza San Domenico

Via Piccioni

San Giaco **14**

Via Tigellio

Sant'Efisio **13**

Via C.F. Fara

Via Santa Croce

Via Stretta

Via Genovesi

Museo del Duomo **4**

Palazzo di Città

Piazza Carlo Alberto

Via del Duomo

Via Lamarmora

Piazza San Giacomo

Piazza Marghinotti

Villa di Tigellio

Via V.A. Carbonazzi

Ignazio da Laconi

Cripta di Santa Restituta **12**

Via Sicilio Pintor

Via Margherita

Bastione Santa Croce

Bastione Santa Croce Nuovo

Il Ghetto

Via Canelles

Via Fossario

San Michele

Via Azuni

Mercato Santa Chiara ★

Torre dell' Elefante **5**

San Giuseppe

Palazzo Boyl

Sant'Anna

Piazza Yenne

Università **6**

Collezione Sarda Luigi Piloni

Porta dei Due Leoni

Via Università

Terrazza Umberto I

Bastione di San Remy **7**

Piazza Costituzione

Via Sulis

Corso Vittorio Emanuele II

Via Porto Scalas

Via G. Spano

Piazza Martiri

Via Manno

Infopoint

Fabbrica della Creatività

Via Carloforte

Via Caprera

Via Goffredo Mameli

Via Goffredo Mameli

Via Angioi

Via Carlo Felice

Santo Sepolcro **11**

Santa Rosalia

V. Principe Amedeo

Via Torino

Pia Reg Marghe

Colle di Tuvixeddu, Necropolis of Tuvixeddu

La Carmine

Via Maddalena

Via Malta

Via G. Maria

Via Sassari

Piazza Sto Sepolcro

Via Napoli

Piazza Dettori

LA MARINA

Via Baille

Via Collegio

Via Lepanto

Via Arquer

Vidio

Viale Trieste

Via V. Tavolara

Poste e Telecomunicazioni

Palazzo del Consiglio Regionale

Via Crispi

Museo del Tesoro e Area Archeologica di Sant'Eulalia **10**

Piazza Sant' Eulalia

Via Mercato Vecchio

Via Barcelona

Via Sardegna

Via Concezione

Via Cavour

Piazza del Carmine

Palazzo Municipale **9**

S.E.A.R.C.H.

Piazza Matteotti

Via Roma

Via Sardegna

Via Roma

Regina

Via Roma

Stazione FS

Via Sassari

Via S. Agostino

Stazione Arst

Calata Azuni

Infopoint

Stazione Marittima

Calata Via Roma

Porto Interno

Cala Darse

Darse

Cagliari

High defensive walls of the Bastione di San Remy.

CAGLIARI

This fortress town hewn out of limestone hills is Sardinia's
thriving capital of culture and commerce, honouring its historic
charms while cautiously moulding a stimulating city of the future.

Cagliari is the island's capital and largest town, with a population of almost 150,000 and a refreshingly down-to-earth charm. The wealth of precious objects and architecture to be found here tells of the city's complex history, which on more than one occasion has determined the fate of the entire island.

The name Cagliari is derived from the 12th-century Spanish *callaris*, meaning "a rocky place", and looking across the limestone hills and fortifications of Castello, the name certainly fits.

The charm of the capital

Like its geography, the city and its inhabitants remain solid yet adaptable. From the buzzing Marina backstreet restaurants and Via Roma porticoes to the serene heights of Castello's historic fortifications and panoramic terraces, there is a sense of unhurried bonhomie and quiet confidence. Sardinia's capital has metropolitan verve – with traffic, port activity, tourism, shopping and smoking industrial satellites – but instead of the sense of chaos and posturing of mainland Italian cities, Cagliari has an understated allure and grace. You can explore its *quartieri* easily on foot – wandering through medieval backstreets, past Renaissance and 19th-century palazzi and the Cittadella museums, then,

after a seafood lunch in a rustic trattoria, you can sprawl out on Poetto's white sands in the late afternoon.

In recent years, new creative spaces showcasing artistic talents have been added to Cagliari's historic attractions. After flirting with the idea of iconic museum architecture to spur an economic revival, the council is now focusing on enhancing the Marina and waterfront, encouraging imaginative conversions of old industrial buildings. In 2014, Cagliari lost its bid for European Capital of Culture 2019

Main Attractions

Cittadella dei Musei
Cattedrale
Torre dell'Elefante
Università
Bastione di San Remy
Galleria Comunale d'Arte
Centro Comunale d'Arte e
  Cultura EXMÀ
Nostra Signora di Bonaria
Orto Botánico
Anfiteatro Romano

*Inside the T Hotel, one of Cagliari's
trendiest hotels.*

View of Cagliari.

to mainland Matera. Bad luck struck again in 2015 when the opening races of the America's Cup scheduled here had to relocate to Portsmouth, England, at the eleventh hour.

Phoenicians, Carthaginians and Romans

Archaeological finds from Sant'Elia, Santa Gilla, San Bartolomeo and Calamosca prove that the first inhabitants settled on this part of the island at the end of the 3rd millennium BC. Expansion came with the Phoenicians who, plying their trading routes between their native shores (the present-day Lebanon) and the Iberian peninsula, moored their ships at the Golfo degli Angeli, and colonised the area, building a series of trading ports. Carthaginians, descendants of the seafaring Phoenicians, continued the conquest by crisscrossing Sardinia with an important network of roads radiating out from Cagliari. The town developed into one of the most important trading centres on the East–West Mediterranean axis.

It is estimated that around 20,000 people lived in Cagliari in Roman times. Remains of the Roman city include the **Villa di Tigellio**, a complex of three Roman houses dating from the 1st century AD, the **Anfiteatro Romano** (Roman Amphitheatre), built directly in the rock of a natural valley, and the recently discovered archaeological area of Sant' Eulalia in the Marina quarter..

Cagliari in the Middle Ages

During the Byzantine era and the occupation by the Vandals the town continued to grow in importance, and the spread of Christianity rapidly elevated Cagliari to a sort of spiritual and moral capital. The year AD 704 marked the beginning of Saracen incursions along the southwest coast of Sardinia. Fear of the sea and the invaders it carried to the island wrought fundamental changes, and for almost three centuries Cagliari was to remain cut off from world history. This isolation may have been why Sardinia's first *giudicato*, a defensive alliance with its own jurisdiction, was formed around Cagliari. The town established contact with the French towns along the Mediterranean coast and began trading with the city states of Genoa and Pisa, which were subsequently to dominate the history of Cagliari and even Sardinia itself, first as partners and then as conquerors. Under Pisan rule, the town enjoyed a considerable demographic, artistic and economic revival.

The Spanish, the House of Savoy and Italy

In 1326, following the decline of Pisa, Cagliari fell into the hands of the royal house of Aragon. Their first action was to expel all native Sardinians from the castle. In 1418 it became the official residence of the Viceroy of Sardinia, who replaced the Governor General. In 1421, in the presence of the King of Aragon, Alfonso V "The Magnanimous", the Viceroy of Sardinia, Bernardo de Centelles, inaugurated the island's first parliament. Under Aragonese rule the city's administrative system built up by Pisa was dismantled and replaced by a new arrangement resembling that of Barcelona.

Under Aragonese and Spanish rule, Cagliari's position as an important port and trading town was reinforced, and the university was founded. However, a number of unwelcome measures aggravated the local population and the Spanish were driven out, aided by a British fleet. Following the Peace of Utrecht, Duke Victor Amadeus II of Savoy became the King of Sardinia (1718). Then, in 1720, Sardinia, along with Naples, Milan and the Spanish Netherlands, was formally handed over to the Austrian Empire by the Spanish; and the island was passed on to Luigi Departes, the emissary from Savoy.

As part of the Kingdom of Savoy-Sardinia, Cagliari suddenly joined the international political arena. In the wake of the turmoil which Napoleon spread across the whole of Europe, Cagliari was to become the refuge of Charles Emmanuel IV and then Victor Emmanuel I of Savoy. In the 19th century a succession of famines and epidemics plagued the inhabitants, exacerbated by the indescribable sanitary conditions in which the population lived. The ancient regime was toppled, replaced by a new governor, namely Italy. Railways, industrialisation and new ideas brought "Fortress Cagliari" into the modern world.

Castello quarter

A good place to start a tour is from the Castello quarter, the large ancient stronghold of the town, over which the two medieval towers of Torre di San Pancrazio and Torre dell'Elefante rise. The highlight here is the city's museum complex, the **Cittadella dei Musei ❶**, situated on Piazza Arsenale in the heart of the Old Town. Until 1966–7, when it was allocated to its present role as a documentary and cultural witness of local history, the building itself experienced a very turbulent past. The present structure rises above the remains of the ancient Piedmontese fortress and arsenal. Standing on the highest point of Cagliari, it affords a spectacular view over the town and the bay. The two architects of the Cittadella, Gazzola and Cecchini, were successful in adapting historic

The EXMA building (the town's former abattoir) is decorated with cows' heads.

Laundry drying from balconies adds colour to the streets.

elements to new uses, incorporating the Renaissance portal and splendid statue of Santa Barbara into their concrete modernist vision of curvy walkways and straight lines.

City museums

The Cittadella complex houses four museums. The **Pinacoteca Nazionale** (National Art Gallery; tel: 070-662 496; www.pinacoteca.cagliari.beniculturali.it; Tue–Sun 9am–8pm) contains an important collection of *retabli* polyptychs. Polyptychs were introduced by the Aragonese during their conquest in the 14th century. The huge paintings were used as altarpieces, usually divided into three sections and placed behind a main altar, or they acted as the main focus of a side chapel. Intended to be instructive visual depictions of religious themes and the lives of saints, the central panel of a polyptych often features the most important events in a saint's life. Most of the *retabli* in the collection come from the church of San Francesco in Cagliari and are attributed to painters known only by the title of Master and

the village in which their work was first recognised. The *retablo della Porziuncola* by the Master of Castelsardo, painted in 1492, is probably one of the best examples of this particular period and style of painting.

Also contained in the Cittadella's complex is the **Museo d'Arte Siamese** (Siamese Art Museum; tel: 070-651 888; www.museicivicicagliari.it; Tue–Sun mid-June–mid-Sept 10am–8pm, mid-Sept–mid-June 10am–6pm). The collection was bequeathed to the town by Stefano Cardu, a Sardinian at the court of the King of Siam in the 19th century. The collection contains Chinese and Siamese objets d'art dating back to the 11th century.

One of the most unusual museums in the complex is the **Collezione delle Cere Anatomiche di Clemente Susini** (tel: 070-675 7624; http://pacs.unica.it/cere; Tue–Sun 9am–1pm, 4–7pm), which displays 23 disquietingly realistic anatomical wax models based on originals made by Clemente Susini in 1803. This is not recommended for the squeamish.

Inside the Museo Archeologico Nazionale

Contained within the complex is the city's best museum: the **Museo Archeologico Nazionale** (tel: 070-684 000; www.archeocaor.beniculturali.it; Tue–Sun 9am–8pm). The exhibition rooms contain displays of prehistoric and early finds as well as a large number of objects illustrating the long history of the island. The first appearance of human beings in Sardinia dates to the early Palaeolithic Age (350,000 years ago), but the earliest material displayed in the museum dates back to the Neolithic period (6000–2700 BC) including pottery, obsidian tools and small fat female statuettes, which formed part of the Great Mother Goddess cult, often found in *domus de janas*. Of particular interest are the *bronzetti* (recent and late Bronze Age bronze statues) representing people in religious contemplation, along with those depicting archers, *navicelle*

Roman marble torso in the National Archaeological Museum.

nuragiche (Nuraghic small boats) and votive gifts from nuraghe and Nuraghic villages, grave temples and sacred springs. The majority of human figures represented are males, but among the female representations there are some extremely expressive female figures, the so-called "mothers". Seated on round stools, the figures embrace their sons on their laps. One female figure holds a naked adult in her lap instead of a male infant. This figure is interpreted as being a Nuraghic Madonna with her dead son – God.

The Phoenicians' time on the island is marked by a collection of valuable objects discovered in sites scattered along the coast: imported Etruscan Bucchero vases found near Cagliari, Phoenician ceramic pots with mushroom-shaped rims and Greek cups and plates. Of great value is the fabulous Carthaginian glass paste necklace found in Olbia, which has large beads representing colourful human faces and animals. The juniper-wood statuette of a *kore* (a girl wearing festive dress) was discovered in the former Punic settlement of Olbia, as was a particularly well-preserved example of the apotropaic terracotta masks which were manufactured extensively by the Phoenicians to ward off malevolent spirits.

The Roman period in Sardinia is represented by glass vases and bottles, used to import wine from central Italy. Sigillata Italica or Arretin ware, a new type of tableware, was adopted during this time by those who could afford it. Lead ingots with the seal of the Emperor Hadrian produced in the south of the island and exported to Rome have also been found.

The last section of the museum's ground floor contains a collection of early Christian and medieval artefacts which includes metal objects such as jugs, lamps, incense burners, silver and bronze fibulae, and a number of Afro-Mediterranean clay oil lamps with varied decorations and designs. It provides a rare opportunity to appreciate the culture of the Byzantines and Vandals, the island's early invaders.

Palatial splendour

From Piazza Arsenale outside the Cittadella and passing under the Palazzo

Nuraghic sculpture in Cagliari's archaeological museum.

Interior of the Palazzo Regio.

delle Seziate, you arrive in Piazza Indipendenza. On the right is the building which housed Sardinia's mint during the 14th century and later an archaeological museum.

The **Piazza Palazzo**, created after the removal of bomb-damaged World War II buildings, has always been the centre of civil authority on the island. The **Palazzo Regio** ❷ (Royal Palace or Palazzo Viceregio; Mon–Fri 9am–8pm, Sat–Sun 9am–6.30pm) is the seat of the prefecture. An older building, home to the Viceroy sent to rule the island by the King of Aragon, stood here from the 14th to the 18th centuries. The present building was constructed in the 18th century on the orders of the Kings of Sardinia. Inside, it is worth taking a look at the fine staircase leading up to the *bel-étage* designed by the military engineer De Guibert, as well as at Bruschi's allegorical and realistic frescoes in the Provincial Assembly Chamber.

Cagliari's cathedral

The **Cattedrale di Cagliari** ❸ (www.duomodicagliari.it; Mon–Fri 8am–12pm

and 4–8pm, Sat–Sun and holidays 8am–1pm and 4.30–8.30pm) was built in the 13th century, but only the belfry and the supporting beams of the main doorway remain from the original building. The cathedral has been remodelled on a number of occasions, finally receiving its Romanesque facade in 1930 in the style of Pisa and Lucca.

The Catalan Gothic-style chapel in the right transept is evidence that the building plans were changed when the invading forces of Aragon conquered the town in 1326. Inside the cathedral are two works of art of particular interest. The first is the carved reliefs of the two stone pulpits by Guglielmo da Pisa which flank the main doors. The engravings were originally commissioned in 1160 for Pisa's cathedral and later donated to Cagliari. During modernisation of the church in 1600 the original pulpit, formed by eight panels, was split into the two we see today. The engravings show 16 scenes from the life of Christ, including the *Last Supper and the Sermon on the Mount.*

In the Gothic-Catalan chapel on the right transept is a copy of a 15th-century triptych, the *Trittico di Clemente VII*, attributed to the Flemish Rogier van der Weyden (1399–1464), the official painter of Brussels. The painting originally belonged to Pope Clement VII, but during the sack of Rome in 1527 it was stolen and ended up in Cagliari, where the original can still be seen in the **Museo del Duomo** at Via Fossario 5 (Treasury; www.museoduomodicagliari. it; Tue–Fri 4.30–7.30pm, Sat–Sun 10am–1pm and 4.30–7.30pm). Also worth seeking out here amid the silver, wooden and wax sculptures is a six-panelled polyptych, the *Retablo della Crocefissione* by Michele Cavaro (1517–84).

Under the cathedral is the crypt, carved out of the rock that forms the foundation of the cathedral; it's decorated with depictions of saints by local artists and contains the tombs of many notable people, including the wife of Louis XVIII of France. The crypt is an atmospheric space – you can often duck down here to find yourself with just an eerie silence and the cool, aged stone as company.

The **Palazzo di Città** ❹ (tel: 070-677 6482; www.museicivicicagliari.it; Tue–Sun 10am–6pm, mid-June –mid-Sept until 9pm) is the old town hall; today it has an 18th-century facade, but the original building existed during Pisan rule. For centuries it was the seat of one of the branches of Sardinia's Parliament. Some of its handsome, newly restored spaces host permanent collections of wooden sacred sculptures, ceramics and jewellery as well as temporary exhibitions and cultural events.

The whole of this quarter is crossed by the long Via Lamarmora, where the street-level rooms of nobiliary buildings, once used as stables and store rooms, have been transformed into quaint antique shops and artisans' workshops.

University quarter

The quarter is delimited to the west by the imposing **Bastione Santa Croce**. The view of the gulf, of Santa Gilla lagoon and of the Stampace quarter is breathtaking. The **Basilica di Santa Croce** (www.santacrocecagliari. it; free) was built in 1661 over a synagogue abandoned after the edict of Ferdinand the Catholic in 1492,

Colourful ceramics make great souvenirs.

A wedding party outside the cathedral.

Playing inside the cathedral.

Mosaic in the Cattedrale Santa Maria del Castello.

which expelled all Jews and Muslims from his land, which at the time included Sardinia.

The **Torre dell'Elefante** ➎ (www. beniculturalicagliari.it; daily 9am–5pm), at the end of the Via Santa Croce, was built in 1307 by Giovanni Capula, a local architect, who also built the **Torre di San Pancrazio** (same hours) – the northern gate of the Castello district. The Torre dell'Elefante owes its name to the little elephant carving placed upon a plinth on its facade, under which the head of Marchese di Cea was displayed for 17 years after the tower was built. The spiked gates of the tower loom sinisterly over passers-by, which combined with a strong wind can evoke echoes of the grisly deeds that took place here.

The **Università** ➏ just to the south was established in 1606; today the rectorship, together with the library, is housed in the former Tridentine Seminary building, which dates to 1700. The noteworthy **Collezione Sarda Luigi Piloni** (tel: 070-675 2420; Mon–Fri 10am–1pm, Jul–Aug also Tue and

Thur 4.45–7.45pm; free) is also kept in the same building. The collection contains 206 geographical maps of Sardinia dating from the 16th century, 54 paintings covering the same period by painters local to or related to the island, prints and drawings of 19th-century Sardinian costumes and a valuable collection of local carpets, packsaddles and chest covers.

The **Museo di Geologia e Paleontologia D. Lovisato** (Geology and Palaeontology Museum) and the Mineralogy Museum, **Museo di Mineralogia** (both museums in the Earth Sciences Department, Cagliari University, Via Trentino 51; Mon and Fri; tel: 070-675 7753 or musei.dister@unica. it for an appointment) are devoted to the geological history of Sardinia. The displays include fossils and rocks gathered in the first half of the 19th century and a splendid collection of minerals from Sardinia's mines.

Bastione di San Remy

At the end of Via Università, on Piazza Costituzione, is the **Bastione di San Remy** ➐, which was used to defend the castle to the south. The bastions were built upon old city ramparts in the early 18th century by the Baron di San Remy. He became the first Piedmontese Viceroy of Sardinia and made his name by enlarging the island's fortifications.

The Bastione can be reached via a magnificent staircase in yellow and white limestone built in 1902, which rises in grand stages and is framed by an imposing roofed structure with giant arches. Halfway up is the *passeggiata coperta*, a long covered arcade with bold orange walls and geometric-designed marble flooring. Its cavernous interiors are perfect for lingering, people-watching and perusing the latest exhibition.

Spectacular views of the city, surrounding landscape and sea open up from the expansive terrace of the Bastione, which is dotted with trees, benches and a few café-bars – a favourite evening hotspot and a place to see and be seen. Glass lifts are also available to the summit from a few corners and metal walkways.

Overlooking the terrace, you can't miss the peachy-hued, neo-classical **Palazzo Boyl** (1840), built over what remained of the Torre dell'Aquila (Eagle's Tower), one of the ancient Pisan towers that stood at the entrance of the city.

The Galleria Comunale d'Arte

Back at the foot of the Piazza Arsenale on the northern edge of Castello, walk down Viale San Vincenzo and you will come to the pleasant **Giardini Púbblici** (daily). In the middle of the gardens is the **Galleria Comunale d'Arte ❽** (tel: 070-677 7598; www. museicivicicagliari.it; Wed–Mon 10am–6pm, mid-June–mid-Sept until 9pm). The gallery has a collection of modern works by Sardinian artists and stages exhibitions of contemporary artists. Among the most notable works in the museum's collection are paintings by Tarquinio Sini from the 1920s and

Giuseppe Biasi. Early 20th-century work by Francesco Ciusa, who was honoured at the 1907 Venice Biennale, is also on show here – particularly impressive is his piece *La Madre dell'Ucciso*.

La Marina quarter

The narrow Marina quarter to the south, originally surrounded by walls, has always been tied to the ups and downs of the port's commercial activities. Its alleys are lined with a succession of welcoming little *ristoranti*. The quarter is more or less a rectangle closed on one side by Largo Carlo Felice and the elegant building of La Rinascente store, on the other by Piazza Amendola with its enormous ficus trees, palms and jacarandas. To the north the quarter ends with the pedestrian street Via Manno, under the Bastione di San Remy.

On Via Roma, parallel to the port, is the imposing, Gothic-meets-Art Nouveau **Palazzo Municipale ❾** (or Palazzo Civico; tel: 070-6771; Mon–Fri 9am–1pm; by appointment only), the town hall, which was built in the

Strolling along Via Roma.

TIP

Il Bastione di San Remy attracts collectors and the curious to its bric-a-brac and antiquarian market (Jun–Sept Wed–Sun 6.30pm–midnight, Oct–May Sun morning only).

20th century. Nearby is the **Palazzo del Consiglio Regionale** (regional government offices) in Via Sassari, built in the 1980s. This frequently criticised concrete-and-steel building contains a fine series of sculptures by the Sardinian artist Costantino Nivola (1911–88).

Via Roma enjoys a sunny position overlooking the sea. By day a multitude of little cafés under the porticoes are crowded and lively. The main harbour nearby provides a link with the Italian mainland and other Mediterranean ports, including Tunis. The **Via Manno**, the **Largo Carlo Felice** and some sections of the **Via Roma** have become popular shopping streets.

Roman remains

Today the main historic and cultural reference point in La Marina is the 14th-century parish **church of Sant'Eulalia** in Piazza Sant' Eulalia. Under the church, recent archaeological excavations have discovered parts of the old Roman town, which can now be seen as part of the

Colourful ceramics for sale.

Museo del Tesoro e Area Archeologica di Sant'Eulalia (MUTSEU, Vico del Collegio; tel: 070-663 724; Tue–Sun 10am–1pm, 5–8pm). Apart from containing part of the Roman town, the museum contains wooden sculptures, silver objects, vestments and paintings.

The **church of Santo Sepolcro** (Piazza Santo Sepolcro, off Via Dettori; daily 9.30am–12pm and 4.30–7pm) belonged to the Templars from 1248 to 1311. It was then entrusted to the main confraternity of the Cross, which took care of the burial of the poor and those who were condemned to death. In 1538 lumps of earth brought from the Holy Sepulchre in Jerusalem were scattered here.

Nearby Via Manno, Viale Regina Margherita and Piazza Martiri were the haunts of writers and travellers such as D.H. Lawrence and Grazia Deledda.

Stampace

Stampace is one of the four historical quarters of Cagliari, easily reached on foot from Piazza Yenne, under and west of the castle. In the past it was inhabited by artisans and artists, who congregated around Via Azuni and what is today the Corso Vittorio Emanuele II.

Stampace has many churches, including the Jesuit complex of the **church of San Michele** (Mon–Fri 8–11am and 7–8.30pm, Sat–Sun 9am–12pm and 7–9pm), built at the end of the 17th century in a Spanish Baroque style. Right at the centre of Stampace, in Via Santa Restituta, is the **Cripta di Santa Restituta** ⑫ (tel: 070-677 0168; www.beniculturalicagliari.it; Tue–Sun 10am–1pm). It is a large room with traces of Punic and Roman presence later transformed into a Palaeo-Christian church. The crypt is tied to the worship of Saint Restituta, whose statue, dating from the 5th century, was found during excavations.

Popular festival

The nearby **church of Sant'Efisio** ⑬ (Tue–Sun 9am–12.30pm, 4–8pm) was built in 1700 and is the headquarters of the Gonfalone brotherhood which organises the colourful **Festa di Sant'Efisio**, a folk festival

at the beginning of May each year. The festival is the biggest in Sardinia, and the whole town is involved in its preparations. Saint Efisio is credited with saving Cagliari from the Black Death, and is revered throughout the island. During the festivities the saint's statue is carried to a tiny church in Pula which stands on the spot where he was martyred. Garlanded oxen draw the statue through the town on a richly decorated cart, escorted by elegantly costumed riders and followed by a vast crowd. The sound of *launeddas*, Sardinian flutes, accompanies the party.

Villanova

The **Villanova quarter** is made up of small houses originally inhabited by farmers who cultivated the fields on which the modern town has developed. Today the houses are part of a labyrinth of narrow and long alleys which give Villanova a lively and colourful atmosphere. The 15th-century **church of San Giacomo** ⑭ (winter Mon–Sat 7–11am and 5.30–7.30pm, Sun 7am–12.30pm and 5.30–7.30pm,

Catching up with the news on Via Roma.

View over Cagliari to the surrounding lagoons and hills beyond.

TIP

East of the city centre on the Sella del Diavolo promontory is a beautiful rocky beach with a swanky bar, pool and solarium platform, perfect for a relaxed bathing and sunset *aperitivi* (La Paillote, Località Cala Fighera, Viale Cala Mosca; tel: 070-371 584; www. lapaillote.it). A rough track nearby leads to the secluded Cala Fighera, popular with nudist bathers.

Cacti growing in the Orto Botánico.

summer Mon–Sat 7–11am and 6–8pm, Sun 7am–12.30pm and 6–8pm), on the piazza of the same name, is an important centre for the traditional and folkloristic liturgical rites that take place during the celebrations of Holy Week.

Churches and art centres

Outside the four historical quarters there are some very important churches in Cagliari: one is the **Basilica di San Saturnino** (tel: 070-659 869; Tue–Sat 10am–1pm and 3.30–7.30pm, though often closed) on the Piazza San Cosimo, just off the Via Dante. Built on the site of an early Roman necropolis, this Romanesque basilica is the oldest church on the island. Saint Saturno, the patron saint of Sardinia, was beheaded in AD 303 during a time of Christian persecution; his body was buried in a crypt over which the Basilica di San Saturnino was built.

At the corner of the same square is the **church of San Lucifero** ⑯ (tel: 070-656 996; visits only by appointment). The side door of the church

bears the coat of arms of Aragonese Cagliari, placed next to two dogs, symbols of the Dominicans. Excavations have revealed a Palaeo-Christian complex formed by three chapels dating from the 5th–7th centuries under the church. On Via San Lucifero is the **EXMÀ building** (see page 108).

In Piazza Bonaria is the **Basilica di Nostra Signora di Bonaria** ⑰ (tel: 070-301 747; www.bonaria.eu; 6.30– noon and 4.30–7pm), built in 1704. The basilica dominates the skyline as you approach Cagliari from the sea and is believed to give protection to sailors. A flight of steps leads up to an impressive neoclassical facade. Next to it is the less impressive but older **church of Bonaria**, built in 1326, which contains a 14th-century wooden Madonna – the centre of devotion on its main altar. This was the first church to be built in Sardinia in an Aragonese-Gothic style immediately after the arrival of Alfonso of Aragon to commemorate the conquest of Cagliari.

In the cloister of the convent is the entrance to the interesting **Museo del Santuario di Nostra Signora di Bonaria** (tel: 070-301 747; www. bonaria.eu; 6.30–noon, 4.30–7pm), where religious objects and ex-votos are kept, many of them in the shape of boats and ships and dating from the 18th century. The museum also contains finds from local excavations and the mummified bodies of a family who died from the plague in the 17th century.

Green spaces and a Roman amphitheatre

Cagliari has one of Italy's most famous botanical gardens, the **Orto Botánico** ⑱ (Viale Sant'Ignazio da Láconi; tel: 070-675 3522; summer Mon–Fri 9am–1pm and 3.30–7.30pm, winter Mon–Fri 9am–1pm; guided visits by appointment). Founded in 1858 by the town's university, it is divided into three climatic environments: Mediterranean, Tropical and

Rocky-Arid. As well as the splendid variety of plants from all over the world, there is a Punic water tank, a Punic-Roman quarry and the remains of a Roman aqueduct.

To the north of the botanical gardens is the **Anfiteatro Romano** ⑲ (Roman Amphitheatre; tel: 070-652 956; www.anfiteatroromano.it; May–mid-Oct Fri–Sun 9am–6pm, mid-Oct–Apr Sat–Sun 10am–6pm). Dating from the 1st century AD, the theatre was carved out of the rock on the hill and had a capacity of around 10,000. Today's spectators come not for bloody gladiatorial battles but for jazz and other music events. Another major complex of Roman remains is located to the south of the botanical gardens. The **Villa di Tigellio** (tel: 070-4092 306; summer 9am–1pm, 4–8pm, winter 9am–5pm) is in fact not a single building, but a residential neighbourhood.

Hills and beaches

The hill of **Monte Urpino** rises for over 100 metres (330ft) between the modern quarters of eastern Cagliari and the Molentargius coastal marshes. Covered by pine trees, it is, together with the **Colle di San Michele** and **Colle di Tuvixeddu**, one of the few parks in town. Colle di Tuvixeddu is home to the Phoenician-Punic necropolis opened to the public in 2014 after decades of excavation works. Dating back to 500BC–200BC, the **necropolis of Tuvixeddu** is one of the largest in the Mediterranean (Sat–Sun, summer 9am–6pm, winter 10am–4pm; park free, open from dawn till dusk). In the Parco di San Michele is the 10th-century San Michele castle bearing the same name, usually used for exhibitions but closed for restoration since 2015. A road leads to the top of the hill, where there is a stunning view over the town and the lagoons that surround it. If your itinerary can fit in a day at the beach then head for **Poetto,** one of the longest beaches in Italy, with views across to the foothills of the Sella del Diavolo. The Marina Piccola, at the southern end of the beach lined with restaurants and bars, has a lively atmosphere.

A stylish lookout for the lifesavers, Cagliari beach.

The steps of the Basilica di Nostra Signora di Bonaria.

CAGLIARI FOOTBALL

Cagliari Calcio football team play their home games at the Stadio Comunale Sant'Elia, which hosted three games at the 1990 World Cup. Following renovation in 2014, the stadium now has a capacity of 16,000, although Cagliari Calcio would have liked the venue to accommodate 30,000 spectators but the council put a stop to the project.

The Rossoblu were founded in 1920 by a surgeon, and their finest hour to date came in the 1969–70 season, when they were inspired by Italian football legend Gigi Riva to Lo Scudetto, the Italian Serie A championship. Recent years have seen lots of yo-yoing up and down the divisions. Tickets are available at Cagliari Point, Viale La Playa 15 (tel: 070-604 201; www.cagliaricalcio.net).

Inviting Lido di Orrì beach, near Tortolí.

CAGLIARI TO ARBATAX

This stretch of coast covers a wide range of terrain, from
the Sette Frattelli peaks to the seaside resort of Villasimius
and on to the wild mountains and beaches of Ogliastra.

The road from Cagliari to Olbia,
the Eastern Trunk Road or SS
125, is known as the **Strada
Statale Orientale Sarda**. It is one of
the main traffic arteries in Sardinia,
and has received much investment in
recent years – with impressive tunnels
and raised sections speeding the journey into this mountainous region.

Setting off from **Cagliari ❶** (see
page 99) via the Viale del Poetto,
you will come to **Quartu Sant'Elena
❷**, where the **Casa Museo Sa Dom'e
Farra** (Via Eligiu Porcu 143; closed for
renovation, call tel: 070-812 340 for
information), an original Campidanese farmhouse displaying traditional
agricultural implements and domestic
tools, is well worth stopping off for.

Mountains and maquis

A few kilometres inland, the SS 125
runs past the **Monte dei Sette Fratelli ❸** (Seven Brothers), a small
range of mountains with peaks up to
1,000 metres (3,280ft) high. The Sette
Fratelli regional park is characterised
by a forest-maquis formed by holm
oaks, cork trees and arbutus (strawberry trees). There is also a protected
area for the rare *cervo sardo*, the short
Sardinian stag. Following the gorge of
the Rio Cannas, the SS 125 arrives at
San Priamo and connects itself with
the coastal road a few kilometres
before Muravera.

Boats in the bay of Punta Valentis, Villasimius.

Villasimius and Isola dei Cavoli

Sardinia's main seaside resort on the
southeast coast is **Villasimius ❹**. It
has enjoyed a remarkable boom in
recent years and is now dotted with
holiday complexes, apartment blocks,
hotels and villas catering to large
numbers during the summer months.
Unfortunately some tourist developments have blighted the countryside
in the area.

Villasimius's star-shaped 17th-cen-
tury **Fortezza Vecchia** (Old Fortress)

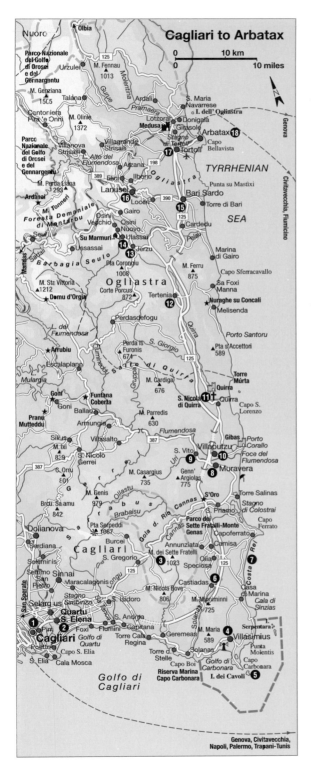

Cagliari to Arbatax

0   10 km
0   10 miles

rises up above the harbour. Built for military purposes and coastal protection, it now relates the history of piracy from Byzantine times to more recent Arabic seafaring invaders. Each July Villasimius's *Sagra della Madonna del Naufrago* (Festival of Our Lady of the Shipwrecks) sees a procession of fishing boats and the scattering of flowers around the Isola dei Cavoli, to mark lives lost at sea.

Villasimius lies on the northern edge of a promontory which extends to **Capo Carbonara**; from the road there are breathtaking views of the sea and a scattering of tiny islands, the largest of which are the **Isola Serpentara** and the **Isola dei Cavoli** ❺. Cavoli is dominated by an imposing lighthouse which houses a sea research centre. You can visit by boat as part of an excursion package (see page 241). Scuba-divers will enjoy the sea around the headland, being rich in vegetation and marine life.

The Costa Rei and the Sarrabus region

A few kilometres inland is the hamlet of **Castiadas** ❻, surrounded by a vast agricultural area created by a penal colony that was established in 1875. At the time, open-air convict colonies were common in Europe and were founded on the assumption that hard work would aid rehabilitation. The convicts constructed all the buildings in the colony, including a hospital. The result is the small, partially restored hamlet we see today.

Back on the coast are the seemingly endless beaches of the **Costa Rei** ❼, dotted with tourist villages, which reach right up to the foothills of **Capo Ferrato**, the lagoons of **Feraxi** and **Colostrai**, and the salt works of the **Peschiera**; the coastal marshes here attract many different species of birds, including flamingos, white egrets and herons. The flat coastal strip gradually gives way to the mountainous foothills of the Sarrabus region, through which, flanked by fields and citrus plantations, meander the **Flumendosa** and the **Picocca** rivers. Although no larger than 180 sq km (70 sq miles), the area includes a range of stunning landscapes, encompassing plains and ranges of mountains as well as lakes and superb stretches of coast.

Muravera

At the mouth of the Flumendosa river is **Muravera** ❽, a town swelled by summer visitors and surrounded by fragrant orange groves.

Muravera was inhabited at the time of the Nuraghic civilisation; later on, under the Romans, the town must have acquired a certain importance in view of its situation on the Roman road to Olbia. The community is divided into the three districts of Castiadas, San Pietro and Costa Rei. In the vicinity, near Costa Rei, there are 22 Neolithic menhirs; six of them are still in their initial vertical positions. Comparisons with similar ancient structures on other sites in Northern Europe seem to indicate that their purpose was to mark the passage of the seasons. A further 42 menhirs can be seen on the site of the **Nuraghe Scalas**. Of artistic interest is Muravera's 16th-century church of **San Nicola di Bari** (daily), which was built in Catalan Gothic style.

The little town itself has retained numerous folkloric customs, and every year various festivals take place. The **Sagra degli Agrumi** (Citrus Fair), which usually takes place on a Sunday in April, features processions of folk groups wearing traditional embroidered costumes and playing traditional instruments such as the prehistoric *launedda*, a flute-type instrument traditionally used by shepherds.

Villages along the Flumendosa river

The village of **San Vito** ❾, northwest of Muravera, has around 4,000 inhabitants and a parish extending over an area of 230 sq km (90 sq miles) of mainly mountainous countryside. To the south are woods and oak groves; in the middle rise the peaks of the Monte dei Sette Fratelli; in the north lie the mountains of the Sarrabus. The entire area is a refuge for wildlife:

TIP

Those after adrenalin rushes should contact amiable outdoor guide Mariano at Ogliastra Adventure for treks, climbs, canyoning, quad biking and parachuting (www.ogliastraadventure.it).

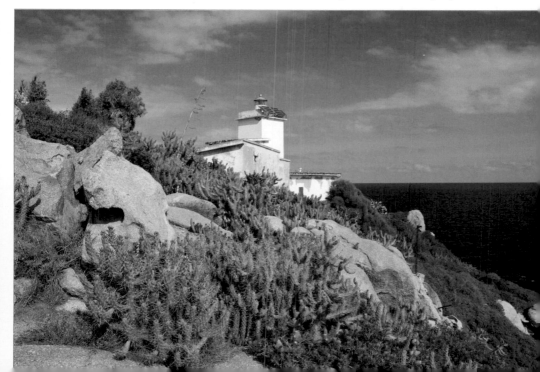

The lighthouse (il faro) of Capo Ferrato.

Deer inhabit the woods and oak groves of the southeast.

Porto Corallo, Villaputzu.

the Sardinian partridge, ring and turtle doves, wild boar and rabbits, the hobby and the Sardinian deer all inhabit the area in large numbers.

Mining – for silver and other minerals – was once a major industry in the area, especially on Monte Narba, and as a result the village of San Vito enjoyed a fourfold increase in its population at the turn of the 17th–18th century. Large numbers of convicts were used as forced labour in the mines. Since the completion of the **Flumendosa Barrage**, the river valley – previously subject to frequent flooding – has been exploited more intensively for agriculture.

Worth seeing in San Vito is the **parish church**; it has a fine facade, twin belfries and an interesting crucifix in one of the side chapels. The district has a rich craft tradition and produces some excellent handicrafts, such as colourful embroidery and basketwork, as well as *launeddas*. The local cuisine is also justly famous. It includes Sardinian specialities such as roast kid, *culingionis de patata* (a type of ravioli filled with cheese) and *pardulas cun meli* (pastry

cases filled with a delicious mixture of honey, egg and curd cheese).

In a field near San Vito an ancient grave containing 14 skeletons and a rich store of funeral gifts has been unearthed. The collection of gold and silver earrings, bangles, fibulae and pottery dating from the 5th and 4th centuries BC can be seen in the archaeological museum in Cagliari.

Silver mining

Villaputzu ⑩, a small town of 5,000 inhabitants, lies just east of San Vito along the SS 125; it sits on a small plain formed by the detritus deposited by the Flumendosa river. Views extend across to the Mediterranean *màcchia* on the hills of the Sarrabus, a tangle of wild strawberries, mastic trees, phyllirea, juniper bushes and low-lying holm oaks. A closer look reveals the remains of two silver mines, **S'Acqua Arrubia** and **Gibbas**, which lie in the middle of the small coastal marshes of **Porto Corallo**. Both were in operation until the beginning of the 20th century.

At the end of the 14th century Villaputzu was the scene of the fierce quarrels between the Sardinian rulers of Arborea and the Aragonese. During the 16th century the **Fortezza Gibas** and the **Porto Corallo** were constructed to protect the town from the increasingly persistent attacks of the Turks operating off the North African coast.

Churches, castles and rockets

Around 20km (12 miles) north of Villaputzu just off the SS 125 stands the pretty little Romanesque church of **San Nicola di Quirra ⑪**. It was built entirely with bricks, very rare in Sardinia, by the Pisani in the 12th century and is surrounded by *cumbessias* (shelters for pilgrims). On a broad plateau demarcated by precipitous cliffs perches a grim fortress, the **Castello di Quirra**. The view is breathtaking. Folk festivals are still important in the area, and during the *Sagra di Sant'Antonio del Fuoco* a giant bonfire is lit on the village square in accordance with an ancient pagan rite.

The SS125 climbs up to the **Salto di Quirra**, a very large, high plateau with scenery of great natural beauty. The plateau can be reached more easily by following the panoramic road that goes up to **Perdasdefogu** and leads to **Monte Cardiga**. The presence of military vehicles and futuristic radar stations around Perdasdefogu hints at the presence of the Italian Air Force: you may even see or hear rockets blasting off while passing the area's spectacular *tacchi* – the high limestone plateaux often separated by deep canyons, reminiscent of Spaghetti Western film landscapes.

Gateway to Ogliastra

The province of Ogliastra has been dubbed an *isola nell' isola* – "an island within an island" – as its mountains and rugged coastline cut it off from the rest of the world. This characteristic has meant that, like the dramatic *tacchi*-studded landscape, its culture and traditions are largely untouched.

The gateway to the provinces of Ogliastra and Nuoro is **Tertenia** ⑫,

which lies in the middle of a largely uninhabited region divided into three main districts: Sapala, Quirra and Villamonti. There are many springs in the vicinity, as well as a mountain torrent, the Sibiri or Rio Sibi, and a number of mountain peaks such as the San Giovanni. Between the two regions of the Sarrabus and the Ogliastra, at the southern end of the Jerzu district, you may be lucky enough to come across a *petra fitta*, a monolith usually in the form of a phallus, or a flat, altar-like *petra de s'altari*.

Ancient monuments

There are a number of well-preserved nuraghi in the region around Tertenia; some of the best examples are the **nuraghe su Concali** and the **nuraghe Longu**, along the coast of the Marina di Tertenia south of the coastal tower of Sarralá.

Travellers interested in churches will enjoy visiting those of the Beata Vergine Assunta, Santa Lucia, San Pietro, Santa Sofia or Santa Teresa. Ideally, time your visit to coincide with one of their festivals, such as *Vergine*

The European bee-eater (merops apiaster) can be seen in many parts of the island in the summer before it heads south to Africa for the winter.

The road towards Tertenia.

TORRE MURTA DIGS

Near **Torre Murta** can be found the intriguing remains of an ancient settlement dating from the 3rd millennium BC, including a *domus de janas*. In 1966, an archaeologist discovered the ruins of a Phoenician settlement. It is likely that the site of the Acropolis of Sarcopos, a Phoenician-Carthaginian temple-fortress, must also have stood near here. The Latin *Itinerarium* of Antoninus, written at the beginning of the 3rd century AD, refers to the town of Sarcopos as being situated near Porticenses (Tertenia) and Ferraria (San Gregorio). North African pottery finds in the area date from the 6th and 7th centuries AD; local clay artefacts indicate that the area was inhabited during Vandal and Byzantine times.

Assunta (Assumption) in August or the festival in honour of St Sebastian (January). The festivities attract visitors from the surrounding villages as well as foreign tourists.

Winemaking cooperative

Further to the west, a few miles from the SS 125 between Tertenia and Bari Sardo, on a long ridge surrounded by hilly country, lies the slightly larger town of **Jerzu** ⑬. A noble Cannonau vintage is produced in its vineyards; in former times the farmers themselves would make the wine, but nowadays this is undertaken almost exclusively by the cooperative wine cellars. The neighbouring countryside is mostly mountainous. The cone-shaped **Punta Corongiu** affords a spectacular view of the Tyrrhenian Sea; on clear days one can even see the summits of Villacidro on the other side of the island, towering above the smaller mountain peaks and wooded slopes.

Jerzu's most important festival of the year is the **Sant'Antonio di Padova** held on 13 June in honour of St Anthony of Padua, to whom one of

the town's churches is dedicated. Other buildings of note which are worth a quick visit include the churches of St Sebastian and St Erasmus.

Ulassai and Bari Sardo

The picturesque town of **Ulassai** ⑭ is situated in a canyon which formed itself between two *tacchi*. Of great interest for its beautiful concretions is the **Grotta Su Marmuri** (Apr–Oct, 60-minute guided tours, hours vary; tel: 0782-79859 for details), part of the limestone massif at the back of the village. The grotto has a large entrance and long caves where the constant 12°C (53°F) temperature requires the use of a pullover even in summer. Contemporary artworks by Maria Lai (1919–2013) that explore myths and mountain life can be seen scattered around Ulassai's landscape, as well as in an old railway station building, the **Museo Stazione dell'Arte** (tel: 0782-787 055; www. stazionedellarte.it; daily 9am–7pm, May–Sept until 8.30pm). Continuing towards Gairo in the Rio Pardu Valley you come across the ghost village

Hiking in the Jerzu hills.

of **Osini Vecchio**, abandoned in 1951 after landslide damage.

Further north on the SS 125 is **Bari Sardo** ⓯. The origin of the name lies in its *abbari* (marshy ground). Historically the town enjoyed considerable importance; in former times it was famous for flax and the manufacture of linen. Today the town derives most of its income from cattle breeding and agriculture, the best products being its red and white wine, and various types of fruit: lemons, oranges, pears, plums and apricots. In the mountains there are still many species of wild animals: rabbits, ring and turtle doves, partridges and wild boar. The stretch of coast near **Marina di Cea** has become popular with tourists.

Lanusei and oak forest

The little town of **Lanusei** ⓰ lies away from the coast, perched on the eastern foothills of the Barbagia surrounded by mountains. Now a bishopric and the seat of the local courts, Lanusei is the proud setting of the first Salesian-Sardinian foundation (a Catholic order known for its charitable works established by the followers of St John Bosco), and there are a number of interesting aristocratic buildings. The town also has numerous schools and colleges, lending it a youthful vibe. A handicraft fair is held in summer on the main square. In the **Duomo** (Cathedral of St Mary Magdalene: daily) are some interesting paintings and canvases of Delitala, an important 20th-century Sardinian painter.

The **church of Santos Cosma e Damiano** (dedicated to two brothers, the patron saints of doctors, who were canonised following their martyrdom in the 4th century) is in the neighbourhood, on the way to Bosco Selene. This is the town's surrounding holm oak forest, which, at 1,000 metres (3,280ft) above sea level, has some commanding views of the valley below as it descends to the sea, and numerous walking trails. The **Bosco Selene Archaeological Park** (tel: 0782-41051; Tue–Sun 10am–1pm and 3–5pm) consists of two *tombe di giganti* and part of a large Nuraghic village.

Jerzu is built on several levels up the hillside, and vineyards cling to the steep slopes around the town.

VILLAGRANDE STRISCAILI

Further north, towards the wild, untouched Gennargentu mountain range and Sardinia's highest peak. Punta La Marmora (1,834 metres/6,000ft), there are fabulous opportunities for outdoor pursuits, relaxation and discovering the generous hospitality of some of the healthiest people on earth.

Due to a unique blend of simple diet, unpolluted water and air, a shepherd's life of hard graft and some favourable genes thrown in, the people of Ogliastra have a better chance than most to live to the grand old age of 100. Indeed, the province boasts one of the highest concentrations of centenarians in the world: at Villagrande Striscaili the highest level of male longevity in the world was recorded for those born between 1880 and 1901.

Deep in the ancient Bosco di Santa Barbara, a vast woodland in Villagrande Striscaili, a new colourful hotel has emerged where you can discover Ogliastra's secrets of longevity and revel in its simple pleasures. Traditional beautifully presented Ogliastra cuisine is served, and a spit for wild boar roasts caters for groups who dine on granite tables under ancient trees. Concerts, outdoor theatre, art shows and various craft events add vibrant cultural life. There are also a variety of family packages available (www.hotelorlandoresort.com).

TIP

At Arbatax port you can hire a *gommoni* speedboat and tour guide Marco Nonnis to explore the spectacular coastline of limestone cliffs, grottoes and pristine beaches of the Golfo di Orosei. Tel: 338-422 8788. www. velamarearbatax. t.

Tortolí

Tortolí ⑰ lies further to the north in a small, fertile plain surrounded by agriculture. In former times the marshes and lakes surrounding Tortolí increased the risk of malaria infection and gave the town a reputation for being an unhealthy place to live. Times have changed – tourism, the port, the industry of nearby Arbatax, a new airport and the fertile surrounding countryside have all helped make Tortolí one of the liveliest towns in the Ogliastra region – as witnessed by its numerous schools, restaurants, shops and hotels.

To the south of Tortolí flows the river of the same name, its banks a haven for various species of water bird, including cranes and flamingos, whose more usual homes are Andalusia, the Camargue and the lagoons of Cagliari.

Arbatax and a steam train

A few miles further on is **Arbatax** ⑱, a well-known seaside resort buzzing gently with commercial, ferry and leisure vessel traffic, with connections to the Italian mainland as well as other ports on the island. Industrial drilling

platforms are produced in the port of Arbatax, and this industry, along with tourism, has brought the district regular employment and prosperity. There are a dozen or so sandy beaches around Arbatax, ranging from long, curvy, family-orientated **Spiaggia di San Gemiliano**, to intimate **Porto Frailis**, backed by rocks and the luxury hotel of La Bitta.

The small **Trenino Verde** (Green Train; tel: 070-265 7612; www.treninoverde.com), formed by a 1930s steam locomotive and two vintage carriages, leaves Arbatax and follows the winding narrow-gauge railway track built in 1894 until it reaches Mandas, where you can jump on a regular train to Cagliari. The railway was built so that the heart of the wild southern parts of the island could be accessed and the rich mineral deposits and forests of the region could be exploited commercially. As the Trenino Verde slowly climbs through the mountains, heading through some of the wildest landscapes on the island, it sometimes stops to avoid wild animals on the track, reminiscent of D.H. Lawrence's train journey described in his book *Sea and Sardinia*, written in 1921.

Ancient shoreline defence.

GOLFO DI OROSEI TO OLBIA

Covering one of Europe's wildest and most spectacular coastlines, the Golfo di Orosei, this tour heads deep into the limestone mountains where ancient traditions flourish, then via beguiling bays to tourist boom town Olbia.

Boat tours from Cala Gonone can take you to the Grotte di Cala Luna.

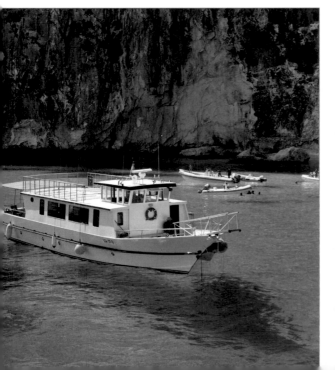

All along this stretch, as far as busy Olbia, there are beautiful bays and ancient villages where intriguing traditions and festivals flourish. From Arbatax and Cala Gonone you can charter boats for memorable day-trip adventures along the incomparable Golfo di Orosei, Sardinia's wild, untouched coastline. As well as challenging walks in the limestone mountains – some paths lead down to isolated coves – there's abundant wildlife, including nimble-hoofed mouflon (wild sheep), and awe-inspiring natural features. From Oliena north to Orosei and Posada the rolling hills of the Baronia produce excellent wine, olives and almonds.

A charming little village by the sea, **Santa Maria Navarrese ❶** forms part of the community of Baunei. It developed around the church of the same name which has an olive tree in its courtyard said to be over 1,000 years old. According to legend, the church was founded by one of the daughters of the King of Navarre in gratitude for being saved from a shipwreck. The church stands on the site where she reached land. The town lies on the southern coast of Montesanto and contains hotels, restaurants and holiday villas.

Its environs are wild and untouched and stretch in the east as far as the cliffs overlooking the Tyrrhenian Sea. Goat and pig herds still wander among the holm oaks, arbutus and the shrubs of the Mediterranean *màcchia* (scrub), to feed on the profusion of berries and acorns.

The town of **Baunei ❷** is known for its hard-working population. Today, few local residents pursue the area's traditional occupations of woodcutting or weaving; most are employed in jobs associated with tourism, the manufacture of sweets or wine production.

Dramatic coastline of coves and canyons

The vast landscape surrounding Baunei is exceptional – rugged limestone mountains, untouched by development, fall dramatically into azure waters. It is here that you begin to understand how the geology of Ogliastra defines this province's character and how isolation has preserved its traditions. It is enclosed by mighty natural barriers: the Supramonte mountains and the Codula di Luna river to the north, the Gennargentu mountains to the west, and the hills of the Salto di Quirra to the south. The coastline looks like a huge mountainous amphitheatre looking out towards the Tyrrhenian Sea.

The coast is characterised by high cliffs, false inlets carved into the malleable limestone and pristine beaches with crystalline water. The **Altopiano del Golgo** (1,000 metres/ 3,280ft) is a large depression in the limestone rock covered by a flow of basaltic lava, where the enormous **Golgo Ravine** (295 metres/967ft) opens up. Not far away is the simple church of San Pietro di Golgo, built in the 18th century, and surrounded by rustic *cumbessias* (pilgrim's houses).

From the plateau it is possible to walk down the **Codula de Sisine**, a 4km (2.5-mile) narrow limestone canyon of great natural beauty formed by the Supramonte di Baunei that ends at Sisine beach surrounded by majestic cliffs. The **Cala Goloritzè** is dominated by l'Aguglia, an enormous pinnacle reaching 100 metres (328ft) high, popular with free-climbers.

From Baunei the main road, the SS 125, continues northwards. On one side is the **Gola su Gorroppu**, a spectacular canyon 500 metres (1,640ft) deep and 4km (2.5 miles) long in its most spectacular part. On the other side is the **Genna Silana Pass** (1,017 metres/3,336ft at its highest point). You can follow the Gola su Gorroppu on foot, but in the final section it is necessary to use ropes to get over some vertical cliffs and ponds, so a local guide is essential.

The path that leads down the large canyon of Cala Luna, the Codula di Luna, is about 8km (5 miles) long and starts from the Supramonte di Urzulei. It takes about three hours to

Pristine beach near Baunei.

GOLFO DI OROSEI BOAT TRIP

The 36km (22.5 miles) of rugged coast between the Porto di Arbatax and Porto Cala Gonlone is a must-see. Boats can be chartered from both ports, preferably with a guide, as local knowledge and skill is needed to negotiate hidden sea caves and rocky shoreline. Pack a lunch, drinks, swimming costumes and sun protection for an unforgettable day out.

Beyond the otherworldly brick-red granite turrets of the Rocce Rosse of Capo Bellavista, and L'Isolotto dell'Ogliastra, the limestone wonders begin to unfold. Gulls, shearwaters, shags and other seabirds encircle the towering cliffs, and wild mouflons and goats move amid blotches of *màcchia* scrub. Around each jagged corner the limpid waters of various hues of blue and green ripple over white pebbles. Small craft and gleaming super yachts drop anchor, and tanned bodies wade to the shore carrying supplies. Towards Cala Gonone charter boats ferry day-trippers to Cala Sisine and Cala di Luna. Away from the numbers, in the intimate coves of Porto Pedrosu, Cala Goloritzè and Cala degli Innamorati, you may see a diver plunging the shallower depths to spear fish and collect *ricci* (sea urchins).

Boat companies include Cala Luna (tel: 0784-93133; www. escursionecalaluna.it) and David e Golia (tel: 338-958 3436; www. davidegolia.it).

Golfo di Orosei to Olbia

```
0        10 km
0             10 miles
```

walk the easy-to-follow path, which passes through *màcchia* scrub and the entrances to many caves. The village of **Urzulei** ❸ is on the left-hand side, clinging to a wooded hillside and sheltered from northerly and south-westerly winds. It lies at the foot of **Punta is Gruttas**, in the midst of varied terrain where the shepherds allow their flocks to roam wild. Continuing towards Dorgali, beyond Urzulei the road is full of tortuous bends, more than compensated for by the awe-inspiring views.

Gonone and Luna beaches

Barely 2km (1 mile) before Dorgali, there is a road tunnel through the Monte Bardia. The views as you exit the tunnel are magnificent: a gentle limestone hill falls away towards the sea. Juniper, rosemary and other aromatic Mediterranean plants blossom under ancient holm oaks. Spreading out in the distance, **Cala Gonone** ❹ is a former fishing village with views extending across glistening emerald waters – nowadays it is a sizeable town with hotels, villas, flats, apartment houses and campsites.

Cala Gonone is the starting point for boat trips along the 40km (25 miles) of wild cliffs, bays and beaches. Grottoes with little sandy beaches are visible at sea level, but many of the most magical sea caves are kept secret by local guides.

The most famous grotto of all is the huge **Grotta del Bue Marino**, renowned for its spectacular caves which are thought to extend for about 8km (5 miles), although only 1km (0.5 mile) of the caves is open to the public. The grotto was also home to Sardinian monk seals until the 1950s, and along this stretch nests the elusive Eleonora falcon.

The most popular beach in the area is **Cala Luna**, described as one of the most beautiful beaches in the Mediterranean because of the flowering pink oleanders that reflect themselves in the tiny fresh-water lagoon behind the beach. The beach is surrounded by six grottoes and high rocks. A daily boat service allows you to reach parts of the coast which are otherwise only accessible by long and tiring walks.

Dorgali and Nuraghic villages

Dorgali ❺ extends along the foot of the Monte Bardia, which protects the town's inhabitants from the sea breezes. Cattle farming and agriculture have been practised here since earliest times; the vineyards of the nearby community of Oliena to the west are famous for their noble Cannonau vintages. Dorgali itself thrives on a flourishing handicrafts industry: cork, wood, wool, gold and silver items are all produced by a variety of medium-sized firms, most of them are also involved in local tourism.

The principal sights in and around the town include the impressive Nuraghic village of **Serra Orrios** (daily 9am–1pm and 3–7pm), 11km (7 miles) northwest of Dorgali near the SS 125. This is one of the best-preserved Nuraghic villages in

Sardinia, dating from the 10–12th centuries BC. The 70 round huts in the village are grouped in six clusters, each with a central well. A small temple area has also been discovered. About 15km (9 miles) northwest of Dorgali is the Marreri Valley, near the village of La Traversa. On the road that connects Dorgali with the SS 131 you will see signposts to the giants' tomb of **Sa Ena'e Thomes**. The tomb has a high stela carved in granite.

Heading north from Dorgali, about 4km (2.5 miles) on the right-hand side of the SS 125 you will see a sign for the **Grotta di Ispinigoli** (tel: 0784-927 200). The cave contains a 38-metre (125ft) stalagmite – the highest in Europe. Some interesting archaeological finds dating from the time of the Phoenicians have been discovered here.

Four km (2.5 miles) from Dorgali, on the road that connects the SS 125 with Cala Gonone and not far from the tunnel, is the turn-off for the **nuraghe Mannu** (Area Archeologica del Mannu; tel: 0784-927 200;

If you are visiting the Su Gologone spring, bring some food with you and enjoy lunch at one of the picnic tables in the eucalyptus wood surrounding the spring.

Inside the Grotta di Ispinigoli.

FROM SMALL ACORNS

Uhe residents of Uzulei and Baunei still bake *pan'ispeli* – acorn bread, at one time prepared all over the island – which was even mentioned as a Sardinian staple by Pliny the Elder in the 1st century AD. The local recipe for the dough goes something like this: soak some clay and wood-ash particles in water, then decant and pour the water into a large pot. Place the pot on the stove and add some shelled acorns (the ash particles act as a leach and remove the bitter taste from the acorns, while the clay softens them). A smooth paste will gradually form. Stir continuously, and cook until it is dark red, almost brown in colour. Allow the mixture to cool and solidify. Place the dough in the sun to dry. The acorn bread has a slightly nutty taste.

The giants' tomb of Sa Ena'e Thomes, one of the best preserved on the island, dates from around 1800 BC.

The mighty Supramonte mountains.

Apr–Sept daily 9am–12pm and from 3–4pm until 6–8pm), an excavated site and in a panoramic position over Cala Gonone. Archaeological finds dating from Palaeolithic times have also been discovered in the **Grotta Corbeddu** in the Lanaittu Valley, which during the 19th century was used as a shelter for the bandit of the same name.

The Valle Lanaittu to Oliena

The gateway to the Supramonte, the Valle Lanaittu, is covered by holm oaks and juniper bushes, which provide shelter for the mouflon that roam the hills. At the top of **Monte Tiscali** ❻ (515 metres/1,690ft) a wide crater opens up and inside is the Nuraghic village of **Tiscali** (tel: 0784-927 200; daily 9am–5pm, May–Sept until 7pm). The name has become synonymous with the European internet provider of the same name, founded by Renato Soru, the left-leaning governor of Sardinia (2004–9). Discovered in the 19th century, Tiscali consists of

a number of round dwellings with limestone walls. It is thought that the village was inhabited up to the time of the Roman invasion and its high walls and surrounding terrain acted as natural defences. To get to Tiscali, take the turn-off on the right near Su Gologone and leave your car about 2km (1 mile) after Grotta sa Oche following the main dirt road. Follow the red-and-white marks on the rocks to the chasm of Tiscali; the walk to the crater village takes a little over 1.5 hours.

Returning to the SS 125 towards Olbia, a few kilometres past Dorgali you can turn off towards pretty **Oliena** ❼. The little town lies in a lovely setting at the foot of Punta Corrasi, separated from Dorgali by the Valle Lanaittu. The most noteworthy sight in Oliena is **Su Gologone**, a spring situated near the hotel and restaurant of the same name. Gushing in a torrent from the limestone cliff, it is the most important spring in Sardinia, flowing at 400 litres (106 gallons) of water per second before joining the Cedrino river.

The beauty of the surrounding countryside, coupled with the hospitable nature of the inhabitants of Oliena, is famous in Sardinia. In and around the town are numerous late Romanesque and Pisan-style churches, all completed before the 14th century. The town centre is dominated by the **Chiesa di Santa Maria** (daily); at Easter this is the scene of one of the most popular religious ceremonies in Sardinia. **S'Incontru** (The Encounter) marks the meeting between the Virgin Mary and the resurrected Christ. The brightly coloured costumes, shawls and filigree jewellery for which the town is famous are all on display during the festival. The ancient churches of **Santa Croce** and **San Lussorio** are worth a visit; from 21 August the latter forms the setting for a popular festival combining both sacred and secular elements.

The Jesuits played a key role in the town's history. They were responsible for establishing the **parish church of St Ignatius Loyola** (daily), named after their founder. In the church offices is a varied collection of paintings and old manuscripts.

During the 16th and 17th centuries, the Jesuits painstakingly undertook the development of 16,000 hectares (39,500 acres) of mountainous countryside: some of this was later sold off to local farmers, but 4,000 hectares (9,900 acres) are still in the possession of the society today. Thanks to their skills and their diligence, Oliena is now a thriving agricultural community, although it's best-known as a producer of olives and wine, notably Cannonau.

From Oliena to Orosei

The SS 129 to Orosei is bordered by hills covered with olive and almond trees. Lowland stretches occur from time to time, mostly given over to viticulture except when the local livestock farmers use them as grazing for their animals, principally sheep. Now and again the way leads through rough countryside, where the parched clay soil supports oleander, *màcchia* scrubland vegetation, arbutus and the thorny Sardinian gorse, the flowers of which blossom

Olive, oak and juniper trees grow in abundance around Oliena.

Standing at the entrance of the Nuraghic village of Tiscali.

The church of Rosario, one of three churches in the centre of Orosei.

Orosei.

in spring and early summer, covering the landscape in a magnificent carpet of yellow.

The valley of the **Cedrino river** is marked by a mighty dam constructed to prevent the regular destruction caused by flooding when the river bursts its banks. On one occasion, however, the dam was unable to contain the deluge; the waters devastated the valley and the ancient villages of **Galtellì**, **Loculi**, **Irgoli** and **Onifai**. Of the four settlements, Galtellì lies on the right bank; Loculi, Irgoli and Onifai are on the left. Galtellì was the most important town in the region until the Middle Ages, and was the bishopric until 1496. However, the ravages of malaria and frequent pirate raids meant that for a long time its population lived in poverty.

The houses and churches of the four villages, especially those of Irgoli and Galtellì, bear silent witness to a peasant culture and its religion, displaying fine examples of a formal but modest Mediterranean architectural style: tiled roofs, courtyards, archways, and belfries which – large or small – seem to cling to the ground rather than soar heavenwards. A good example of a 17th-century house is **Casa Marras** in Galtellì, which has been transformed into an **ethnographical museum** (tel: 0784-90005; May–Sept 10am–1pm, 4–8pm).

The historic capital of Orosei

Located on the final section of the SS 129 is the small town of **Orosei ❽**, with an elegant, bustling centre and whitewashed stone buildings overlooking colourful courtyards. The former capital of the Baronia region, the town had its golden age under Pisan rule, when it developed into an important harbour on the Cedrino river. Malaria and the silting up of the river caused its decline.

Three churches stand on the central Piazza del Popolo; the **Chiesa del Rosario** has a Baroque facade, while the parish church of **San Giacomo Maggiore**, at the top of a large flight of steps, is surmounted by an unusual group of small domes.

Not far from here are the *"palatzos Betzos"*, ancient homes belonging to noble families. Among them is the **Museo Don Nanni Guiso** (tel: 0784-997 084; May, June, mid- to end Sep Tue, Fri, Sat, Sun 9.30am–midday and 5–7pm; July to mid-Sep Tue–Sun daily, Mon 9.30am–12.30pm and 5–10pm), an eclectic museum displaying surprising miniature theatres from the 18th century, antique books on Sardinia, old costumes and drawings of important Italian artists.

The **church of Sant'Antonio Abate** is enclosed in a large courtyard with a Pisan tower, and contains 15th-century frescoes. Every year on 16 January a big bonfire is lit at the centre of the courtyard in honour of the patron saint. Further celebrations are held in the **parish church of San Giacomo** in honour of Nostra Signora del Mare (Our Lady of the Sea) in the second week in May. Orosei is clearly prospering, not only from tourism – its long sandy beaches (including Cala Liberotto and Cala Ginepro) are a big draw – but also from agriculture and a steady income from its marble quarries.

About 30km (19 miles) inland from Orosei near the Monte Albo woods, in the region of Barbagia, is the village of **Lula 9**, where the important sanctuary of San Francesco di Lula stands. According to tradition it was founded by bandits in 1600, who believed that Saint Francis was their protector.

Near the sanctuary is a church and a number of *cumbessias* (pilgrims' houses). It's an evocative spot, and becomes very lively in the first week of May when thousands participate in a pilgrimage to the shrine, and food and wine is aplenty.

Siniscola and limestone cliffs

North of Orosei the SS 125 follows the coast. The invitingly clear sea here is as unpolluted as it looks. After driving for a short while through pine groves and characteristic Mediterranean vegetation, you will reach the twin villages of Capo Comino and Santa Lucia, before arriving in **Siniscola 10**, and its coastal suburb, La Caletta, with its own harbour and a pretty beach.

During the latter part of the 20th century, tourism and a number of small industries – including a lime kiln and a cement works – have resulted in a more rapid population growth rate in Siniscola than in any of the other towns or villages within the province of Nuoro, apart from the regional capital, Nuoro itself. Today Siniscola has some 11,000 inhabitants.

In earlier times Siniscola was the seat of the barons of Monte Albo, under whose jurisdiction also lay the towns of Lodè and Torpè in the interior and Posada and San Teodoro on the coast. The defensive towers, Santa Lucia and Caletta, and the fortified wall around the town, were built following persistent raids by Turks in the 16th century. On the main street, Via Sassari, stands the 18th-century church of San Giovanni Battista, decorated with a fresco cycle showing the life of St John the Baptist.

Marble quarry in Orosei.

The name of Posada's Castello della Fava translates as "bean castle". It gained its name during the time of the Moorish invasion.

Lighthouse on the coast of Olbia.

Not far from Siniscola lie the mountains **Remule** and **Monte Albo**. What these mountains lack in height they more than make up for by their awe-inspiring, strangely shaped limestone cliffs. At dawn they greet the day with a shimmering pale pink hue; by midday they are a dazzling white; and as dusk falls they are suffused in a blaze of crimson.

Posada's tourist boom

Further north, perched on top of a limestone hill, is the town of **Posada** ⓫, dominated by the 12th-century ruins of Castello della Fava. Stairs lead to the top of the castle's tower, from where there is a panoramic view of the surrounding countryside, much of it planted with fruit trees, the sea and the Posada river. The town itself is worth exploring; follow the winding alleyways and steep stairways until you come across delightful small squares, all reminders of Posada's medieval roots.

Posada and San Teodoro further up the coast, together with Budoni between the two, have experienced rapid economic growth in recent decades, mainly thanks to the tourist boom. There are numerous hotels, apartments and rooms in private houses to accommodate the hordes of visitors who come every summer to the beaches between Siniscola and Olbia.

The road to Olbia

The coast between Posada and Olbia has some of the finest beaches on the east coast. The remaining stretch of the SS 125 as far as Olbia is some 35km (22 miles) long and leads through one of the most enchanting regions in the whole of Sardinia, past the Cala Coda Cavallo, the Spiaggia di Salinedda beach, and a succession of bays – Cala Ruia, Cala Suaraccia and Cala Purgatorio to the foothills of Monte Petrosu and the picturesque beaches of Porto Taverna, Porto San Paolo and Porto Istana.

Olbia ⓬ has a modern airport and a flourishing port, and is the main arrival point for people staying on the Costa Smeralda – except for those arriving by yacht. Thanks mainly to the growth in the tourist industry, Olbia has expanded rapidly in the past two decades. Its first population boom occurred in the 1920s, when a group of foreign industrialists developed local cheese production and mussel farming.

Despite its Greek name (*olbius* means happy), the town was not founded by the Greeks. There is no doubt that the Carthaginians once lived here; when the Romans conquered Sardinia (238 BC), Olbia ceased to rely purely on its economic value, and acquired military power as well as strategic importance. In those days the town was connected to the rest of the island by three roads; they served as highways for the legions as well as for the transport of goods.

Later, during the Christian era, these roads were a great aid to the Christian missionaries in their progress to convert the islanders. But the town's golden age occurred under the Romans. In 1904 a hoard of money was found in the necropolis; the 871 gold coins bear the portraits of 117 different Roman families and include 312 different currencies. The break-up of the Western Roman empire during the 5th century BC marked the beginning of a long period of decline in the fortunes of Olbia. The town repeatedly fell prey to Arab raids from the 8th century onwards, and many of its inhabitants fled to the interior.

It was not until the turn of the millennium that it began to flourish again, initially as the first capital of the *giudicato* of Gallura, and later under Pisa, when it acquired the status of a free city. During this time the town was rechristened Terranova, a name which it bore until 1939.

Olbia is now a modern city and usually passed through on the way to somewhere else. In 2013, the town was severely hit by floods caused by Cyclone Cleopatra. Worth a visit, however, is the Romanesque **Basilica of San Semplicio** (daily 6.30am–12.30pm, 4–7pm), built between the second half of the 11th century and the beginning of the 12th century. It contains frescoes of the same period that represent two bishops (San Semplicio and San Vittore) and a fragment of a fresco depicting only the heads of a group of people.

Isola di Tavolara, a marine reserve.

BEACHES, BAYS AND ROCKY ISLANDS

Beautiful beaches and isolated coves are to be found along this stretch of the east coast. Some of the best beaches are **Su Tiriarzu** at Posada, **Budoni**, the sandy beach of **l'Isuledda** on the peninsula of the same name, and the beach of **La Cinta**, a narrow strip of sand 3km (2 miles) long that separates the coastal marsh of San Teodoro from the sea, not far from the mighty foothills of Punt'Aldia.

Lurking offshore, amid the primordial granite coastal landscape, are the sculpted granite silhouettes of **Isola di Molara** and **Isola di Tavolara**. Tavolara, a limestone mountain island 4km (2.5 miles) long and just 1km (0.5 mile) wide, towering to the height of 565 metres (1,850ft), can be reached either by private boat (enquire among the local fishermen) or by one of the small ferries which leave from Porto San Paolo.

To the west soar the shimmering red-and-white granite peaks of the mountains of the interior, while in the foreground groves of holm oaks and cork oaks stretch out before them, rising above an undergrowth of myrtle, arbutus and buckthorn. Here and there blackened stretches resembling a lunar landscape are the result of fires which regularly afflict Sardinia during the summer months.

COSTA SMERALDA

This stretch of coastline in the northeast of the island was transformed over half a century ago into the most exclusive tourist resort in the Mediterranean.

I
f you drive directly north from Olbia Airport you will reach the place where Sardinia is at its most beautiful, the **Costa Smeralda ❶**, or Emerald Coast. Here the sea shimmers in hundreds of shades of aquamarine, your lips taste of salt, and your hair is tousled by a breeze fragrant with the scent of the *màcchia*, a heady mix of forest, aromatic rosemary and lavender.

High, wind-eroded cliffs, wild mountain terrain, 80 stunning bays and a string of idyllic coves make this 55km (35-mile) coastal strip in northwest Sardinia one of the most attractive holiday destinations in the world. It is also one of the most exclusive. It was discovered at the start of the 1960s by His Highness Karim Aga Khan. Although scarcely out of his teens at the time, he was able to see the untamed potential of this craggy shoreline. Along with his wealthy friends, he set about creating a holiday resort for people just like him. In his own words: "This is obviously a place for people with above-average material possessions – I wouldn't even want to have the others here as guests".

Cardinal rule

The Aga Khan's **Consorzio Costa Smeralda** was a non-profit organisation which committed itself to a harmonious relationship between nature and man. One cardinal rule was that no villa, hotel or apartment block could be visible above the tops of the typically small holm oaks and tamarisks. All telephone wires and electric cables run underground, while waste water from the villas, the hotels and even the yacht harbour is processed by the most expensive treatment plant in the world. If a boat-owner is caught emptying his chemical toilet into the harbour or into some lonely bay, he can expect

Main Attractions
Porto Cervo
Cala di Volpe
Porto Rotondo

Fabergé shop in Porto Cervo.

hefty fines and, if he reoffends, banishment from the marina.

In recent decades, land prices on the Costa Smeralda have soared incessantly. In 2003 Tom Barrack, of the US property development group Colony Capital, outbid a coalition of Sardinian and Italians and bought Smeralda Holding, owner of a portfolio of properties on the coast including the Porto Cervo marina, for the pricely sum of €290 million. But he suffered a major setback when Sardinian law stymied his plans for a series of new hotels; indeed, legislation passed in 2004 prohibits development within 2km (1.25 miles) of the coast. Barrack did not lose out however: in 2012, he sold Smeralda Holding for €750 million to Qatar Holding, so what previously belonged to the Aga Khan is now owned by the emir of Qatar. The new owners have ambitious plans for four new hotels and a water park.

Boats and festivals

Rustic craftsmanship with character.

A private yacht is the ultimate status symbol on the Costa Smeralda. Excluding *ferragosto* (15 August), when Italian high society swoops in from Milan and Rome, hiring a boat or obtaining a mooring in the harbour is easy enough – but paying for it might be more of a deterrent.

The Costa Smeralda **marina** was completed in 1975, and altogether there are 650 berths for boats between 12 and 55 metres (38–176ft) in length. The best skippers in the world converge here – nowhere else in Europe will yacht owners have so little difficulty finding experienced yachting crews to help them win one of the Costa's many regattas.

Every fortnight in summer there are major competitions, including the Premio Offshore: the race for the fastest motor boats (known as "cigars"). Less glamorous, but all the more entertaining and convivial for it, is the spectacle of Is Fassonis Regatta. This takes place on the first Sunday in August as the sun sets over the water at Santa Giusta. The boats used for the race are Phoenician in origin and made of the cane husks found around this area.

Beaches and golf

If you don't have access to a private yacht then you can still visit some of the beautiful bays on the Emerald Coast. You can enjoy diving in style: head for the sheltered **Petra Manna Beach** or **Capriccioli Bay** on windy days. You will need a boat, however, to get to the gorgeous **Spiaggia Rosa**, where the soft sand has a rose tint (also see page 141 for details of the Maddalena Islands).

The sea is not the only attraction of the Costa. International golfers regard the **Pevero Golf Course** ❷ (above the Cala di Volpe hotel; www.peverogolfclub.com) as one of the loveliest and most challenging (18 holes, par 72) in the world. It was designed by golf-course architect extraordinaire Robert Trent-Jones on a raised spit of land; from each hole players enjoy spectacular views of the coast and the sea. There is also an excellent restaurant and a luxurious indoor and outdoor swimming pool. Those who are not content with the swimming, sailing and golfing facilities can practise their tennis on one of the nine courts at the plush **Porto Cervo Tennis Club.**

Porto Cervo

Little happens in **Porto Cervo** ❸, the focal point of the Costa Smeralda, before late afternoon, but at sunset the beautiful people flock for a sundowner on the **Piazzetta** or to shop at the designer boutiques at the **Sottopiazza.**

The atmosphere at Porto Cervo is glamorous but a little surreal, with luxury shops on one side and spectacular private yachts on the other. Anyone can wander around the pristine streets, but only the super-rich can afford to stay for longer than a drink or a bite to eat.

There are few cultural attractions in this area; culture is not the main appeal here. However, the pretty **Stella Maris church** built on a hill above the marina is worth a visit. Designed in 1968 by architect Michele Busiri Vici, the whitewashed church contains the *Mater Dolorosa*, a painting by El Greco, a valuable 16th-century organ from Naples, a German

Detail on Stella Maris church, Porto Cervo.

BERLUSCONI'S PARTIES

The Costa Smeralda is a sanctuary for the very rich and the sometimes famous; access is restricted, so it is one of the few places where they can holiday without every ripple of flesh being captured by the paparazzi. It's popular with the incredibly rich Americans, Arabians and Russians, but the headline-makers and glitterati provide the real razzmatazz: P Diddy, Rod Stewart, the Clintons and Claudia Schiffer all hang out here, and Princess Diana and Dodi moored his father's yacht off the coast before their death. However, it is another frequent visitor who has put Costa Smeralda in the headlines. Former Italian prime minister Silvio Berlusconi has a house in La Maddalena further up the coast, and also held infamous "parties" in Porto Cervo and on huge yachts moored close by.

altar cross from the same period, and two outsize Polynesian shells which serve as baptismal fonts.

Eating and drinking

You can eat and drink pretty well on the Costa Smeralda, but one thing is quite clear: apart from a few notable exceptions it is no mecca for gourmets. Fish, eel, *spaghetti aragosta*, roast suckling pig from the barbecue and smoked wild boar ham are popular options on the menu, and everything is accompanied by warm *pane carasau*.

The Terrace Bar at Hotel Cervo, overlooking the piazza of Porto Cervo, serves as a meeting place for the whole resort and is popular for *aperitivi*.

However, in terms of nightlife, Porto Cervo doesn't have much to offer. To the south on Romazzino Bay – where many of the swankiest pads are found – is the chic **Sottovento**, an expensive and exclusive nightclub (www.sottoventoclub.it). North of Porto Cervo towards Baia Sardinia lies Ritual, the training

ground for the new generation of the Costa's millionaires. Those who prefer more peace and less stress should take their after-dinner *digestivo* in **Il Portico** on the Piazzetta. The bar is very attractive and decorated in Moroccan style.

For more pleasant beaches, try the sheltered **Cala di Volpe** ❹ and Cala Liscia Ruja.

Alternatively, you can continue south to **Porto Rotondo** ❺ (a miniature Porto Cervo), only 20 minutes from Porto Cervo by car, or 10 by boat. Built in 1963, though less attractive architecturally, it is also a stylish resort. It lies in a little bay, with tiny piazzas, a handful of designer boutiques, a small harbour and two white sandy beaches. In summer the cafés and restaurants are usually crowded with visitors. The pretty granite church of San Lorenzo, up the steps leading off the central Piazzetta San Marco, was designed by the architect Andrea Cascella. An open-air theatre which holds concerts during the summer months is nearby.

Porto Cervo Marina.

GALLURA AND THE NORTH

This itinerary takes in Gallura's dramatic coastline, the islands of Maddalena, the town of Stintino and then travels through the interior of the region.

Main Attractions
Arzachena
Giants' Tombs
Palau
La Maddalena
Isola Caprera
Santa Teresa di Gallura
Costa Paradiso
Castelsardo
Stintino
Tempio Pausania
Luras
Perfugas
Ozieri

*Giants' tomb
at Arzachena.*

A journey through the Gallura, in the northeast of Sardinia, is a full and varied experience. The island's most extensive oak woods surround Monte Limbara and the little town of Tempio Pausania, and the shores of the Costa Paradiso form part of one of its loveliest stretches of coastline. What's more, at Arzachena there are two of Sardinia's best-preserved *tombe di giganti* (giants' tombs).

Gallura's principal characteristic is defined by the granite rocks that determine its landscape. The countryside is punctuated with *stazzi* (traditional houses). These are low, elongated buildings usually formed by three aligned rooms: the central room is both the entrance and dining room, with a bedroom on each side. Placed at the centre of a vast land, *stazzi* are surrounded by the necessities of family life (a kitchen garden, an orchard, vineyard and maybe a small patch of wheat) and grazing ground for cattle. Built from the 18th century by shepherds that were looking for new lands to settle, they slowly transformed themselves into farms, which are still inhabited.

The Golfo di Arzachena

The fashionable atmosphere of the Costa Smeralda fades as one drives away from Porto Cervo, but the first place of any size on the Golfo di Arzachena is the elegant seaside resort of **Baia Sardinia**. Just across the bay, however, the small fishing port of **Cannigione** has a more down-to-earth feel.

The steep cliffs surrounding **Arzachena** ❶ lend the little town the appearance of a village in the Dolomites rather than one on a Mediterranean island. However, the rapid development of the Costa Smeralda over the past decade has brought economic benefits and considerable change to the town and neighbouring regions. In the vicinity are many interesting prehistoric settlements.

Arzachena's archaeological sites

For some 3,500 years the Gallura was inhabited by groups of semi-nomads and shepherds, and around Arzachena are a number of important remains from the time of the Nuraghi. Archaeologists now call this civilisation Arzachena Culture. The main prehistoric sites – Li Muri, Li Lolghi and Lu Coddu Ecchju (in Italian, Li Longhi and Lu Coddu Vecchju) – can be reached by taking the SS 427 towards Calangianus for about 3km (2 miles), then the right turn towards Luogosanto; a dirt track is signposted to "Coddu Ecchju".

At **Lu Coddu Ecchju** (tel: 335-127 6849; Easter–Oct 9am–8pm, rest of year by appointment) is one of the best-preserved *tombe di giganti* in existence. A stela, 4 metres (13ft) high and subdivided into two sections – a square unit and a half-arch – stands sentinel in front of the grave. Through the semicircular opening at ground level, which repeats the contours of the stela, sacrificial offerings could be presented to the dead person. Flat stone slabs positioned vertically form a semicircle demarcating the ceremonial and sacrificial arena.

On a hill a few kilometres further on, also marked by a signpost on the Luogosanto road, are the stone box graves of **Li Muri** and **Li Lolghi** (Lu Coddu Vecchiu; tel: 338-378 7751; Easter–Oct 9am–7pm, rest of year by appointment). These witnesses to the Nuraghic epoch were found each to be holding a single corpse buried in a squatting position. The graves themselves were surrounded by concentric circles of stones. The *tombe di giganti* of Li Lolghi comprise 14 huge slabs of granite, under which lay 100 bodies.

The traveller approaching the region via the SS 125 from Olbia will find the **Nuraghe Albucciu**. It is signposted about 3km (2 miles) before Arzachena. The nuraghe itself is not constructed in the familiar tower form – it is one of the very few corridor nuraghi in Sardinia. Close by stands the **Temple of Malchittu**, which formed part of the settlement. The **Roccia Il Fungo** (Mushroom Rock) is a weathered granite rock near Arzachena.

Figs and wild fennel drying in the sun.

Garibaldi memorial on La Maddalena.

GIANTS' TOMBS

Built in the Bronze Age, there are 321 *tombe di giganti* (giants' tombs, namely megalithic gallery graves) in Sardinia, all of which are aligned south to southeast to ensure their residents would catch the rising sun which symbolised rebirth. Whilst many have the appearance of large cairns, flat stone slabs positioned vertically form a semicircle demarcating the ceremonial and sacrificial arena. The best examples still have their stela: the large slab, up to 4 metres (13ft) high, which commonly has a semicircular doorway cut into it. These stelae were adorned with carvings: Lu Coddu Vecchju has the most ornate carvings. The inside chamber, which lies north to northwest to catch the setting sun, is a square or rectangular burial unit.

GIVSEPPE GARIBALDI

LA MADDALENA

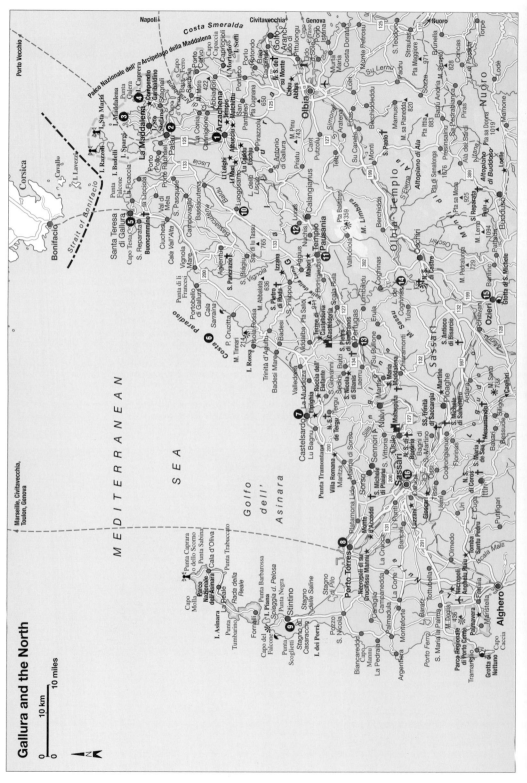

Gallura and the North

Like the spectacularly shaped Roccia dell'Elefante (Elephant Rock) near Castelsardo and the Roccia l'Orso (Bear Rock) near Palau, it features on many postcards.

Palau

Continuing along the SS 125, you pass first through the little port of Palau and then through **Capo d'Orso**, where a weathered cliff formation, the Roccia L'Orso, resembles the eponymous bear. **Palau ❷** itself is a little coastal town dominated by its harbour, from which ferries leave regularly for Caprera and La Maddalena. It is easy enough to find boats to take you to any of the offshore islands (just ask around at the quay; the fishermen will advise), but at Palau Mare in Palau's Via Nazionale you can hire everything you might need to explore the archipelago independently.

La Maddalena

The island of **La Maddalena ❸** is the largest in size – almost 50 sq km (19 sq miles) – in the archipelago, and the only one with an urban centre,

also called La Maddalena. Lying only a few kilometres from the mainland, together with the other islands of the archipelago, it represents what remains of the land link that once existed between Sardinia and the island of Corsica.

La Maddalena has enjoyed a higher profile thanks to Silvio Berlusconi having one of his infamous holiday villas here. The former Italian prime minister had even intended to host the 2009 G8 summit on this peaceful and secure island, but it was eventually held in L'Aquila.

The town of La Maddalena has a prosperous, laid-back charm, with 18th-century pastel-hued villas surrounding graceful piazzas. Highlights include chic shopping on Via Garibaldi, a bustling daily indoor market (mornings) at Piazza Garibaldi and the parish church of **Santa Maria Maddalena**, which contains two silver candlesticks and a crucifix donated by Horatio Nelson in 1804, as thanks to the island's residents during the admiral's lengthy campaigns against Napoleon's fleet.

The town of La Maddalena.

The belltower of the church of San Vittorio in Santa Teresa di Gallura.

Dramatic rock formations envelop the Capo Testa.

Driving around the island on the Strada Panoramica, there are plenty of opportunities to stop, take photos and admire the weathered, other-worldly sculptural shapes of huge granite boulders. Between stops and walks along stunning beaches you can visit the **Museo Archeologico Navale Nino Lamboglia** (Maritime Museum; Giardino, Strada Panoramica; tel: 0789-790 633; May–Sept Tue–Sun 9.30am–12.30pm and 3.30–6.30pm, Oct–Apr mornings only) which contains the remains of a Roman cargo ship dating from the 2nd century BC.

Other islands in the archipelago

The fame of the other large island, **Isola Caprera ❹**, is largely due to its famous resident, Giuseppe Garibaldi (1807–82), for whom it was home for many years, the refuge to which he always returned, and the place where he died. Garibaldi created a model farm on the island; his memorial museum, the **Compendio Garibaldino** (tel: 0789-727 162; www.compendiogaribaldino.it; Tue–Sun,

summer 9am–8pm, winter 9am–1pm), has the air of a place of pilgrimage, and is well worth visiting.

The Maddalena archipelago is formed by seven major islands, of which **Budelli** is also well known thanks to its **Spiaggia Rosa** (Pink Beach), made famous by the 1965 film *Il Deserto Rosso* (Red Desert), directed by Michelangelo Antonioni. Its sparkling rosy-hued grains of sand (the ancient remnants of a protozoan sea creature) were so attractive to visitors that they would grab a handful to take home – so much so that today the grains are protected by law.

The stop-off point on the island of **Santo Stefano** is the Spiaggia del Pesce beach; most of the rest of this former US military base is still off limits. Thanks to their advantageous strategic position, the islands often played an important military role in the past and a controversial one at that. The island of Santo Stefano was from 1972 a US nuclear submarine base, set up as a technical and logistical base to monitor Soviet activity. The US navy base was dismantled in 2008, an indication of the shift in relations between Europe and Russia. The Italian navy remains in La Maddalena, albeit with a much reduced presence.

Back on the main island

Santa Teresa di Gallura ❺ lies at the northernmost tip of Sardinia. Its harbour is the starting point for ferries across to Corsica. The twin approach roads – the SS 133 from Tempio and the SS 200 from Castelsardo – both pass through attractive countryside. The most noteworthy sights here are the bizarre rock formations along the cliffs near **Capo Testa**. From the **Torre Longosardo** there is a spectacular view of the wild and often inaccessible coast of the Gallura, whose waters and seabeds provide ideal conditions for deep-sea diving and the white cliffs of Bonifacio. Also in the vicinity of Capo Testa are two quarries dating from Roman times.

Paradise coast

The road from Santa Teresa to Castelsardo has one of Sardinia's most stunning stretches of coastline. The steep precipices typical of the northern coast force the road inland. Running parallel to the coastline, it follows a serpentine course through untouched *màcchia*. The reddish peaks of the Monte Pitrighinosu and the Monte Puntaccia stand on the horizon.

The sparsely populated area between the SS 200 and the SS 133 has a wild charm. Along the lonely stretch of road to **Tempio** you will see cork oaks, their trunks, with patches of freshly peeled reddish bark, gnarled and misshapen by the wind. Some 10km (6 miles) past Santa Teresa, the **Spiaggia di Rena Maiore** and the **Cala Vall'Alta** are good places to stop for a swim.

The best-known stretch of coast here is the lovely **Costa Paradiso** ❻, which consists of several little *villagi* (holiday villages), hidden away in dense thickets. Inevitably, development comes at a price. Legislation in 2004 has halted building within 2km (1.25 miles) of the coast, but for a region heavily dependent on tourism

Sandy cove on the island of La Maddalena.

and largely owned by rich foreigners, this law is repeatedly challenged.

The two smaller beaches of the **Baia Trinità** are open to the public; overlooking them is the **Isola Rossa**. From here there is also a long sandy beach stretching almost as far as the rocky promontory overlooking the town of Castelsardo.

Castelsardo

Perched on a cliff, **Castelsardo ⑦** offers a mixture of Sardinian folklore and kitsch. It was founded in 1102 by the Genoese Doria family. First known as Castel Genovese, the settlement's name was changed after the Spanish conquest to Castel Aragonese; in 1796 the King of Sardinia gave it the present name of Castelsardo.

Nowadays, during the summer months at least, the town is usually too full of tourists to make a visit here entirely pleasurable, but the castle hill has managed to retain its attractive atmosphere and it is worth venturing up its steep, narrow alleys.

The fortress at its summit houses the **Museo dell'Intreccio**

The harbour at Porto Torres.

Mediterraneo (Via Marconi; tel: 079-471 380; July–Aug 9am–midnight, June and Sept 9.30am–1pm and 3–9pm, Nov–March Tue–Sun 9.30am–1pm and 3–5.30pm, Mar until 6.30pm, Apr–May 9.30am–1pm and 3–7.30pm, May until 8.30pm), which displays a collection of basketwork and weaving. Other attractions in the town include the **Cattedrale di Sant'Antonio Abate**; inside is a 16th-century altarpiece, *Madonna with Angels*, by a 15th-century painter known as the master of Castelsardo.

If you're in Castelsardo at Easter, you'll witness Lunissanti (Holy Monday), generally regarded as one of the best Easter festivals on the island, when people dressed in hooded costume proceed through the torch-lit streets. Interspersed with ancient rituals and traditional songs, the ceremony has retained all its original medieval character.

Outside the town, on the twisting road to Perfugas, lies the **Roccia dell'Elefante**, a curiously shaped outcrop of rock which resembles a young elephant with its trunk raised.

Along the coast

Continuing south, the SS 200 follows the outline of the coast once more. Some 15km (9 miles) from Castelsardo it arrives at the **Punta Tramontana**. By taking the route via **Sorso** and **Sennori**, you can quickly reach Sassari. The SS 200, however, carries on along the coast through the *pineta* (pine forests), beyond which lies the **Platamona Lido**, the favourite beach of the inhabitants of Sassari. Over 20km (12 miles) long, the beach stretches as far as the industrial port of Porto Torres. Its backdrop of pine groves makes for an attractive setting, but the proximity of Sassari has somewhat marred its beauty. Campsites alternate with discotheques and beach cafés.

Porto Torres

It makes no difference from which side you approach **Porto Torres** ❽; it is an unattractive little town dominated by vast oil refineries. Since Roman times it has been famous as the home of seafarers; even in those days the inhabitants conducted lively trade with the mainland. Nowadays container ships and tankers have taken over. The principal port in northern Sardinia, Porto Torres is one of the main gateways to the island, with ferry links to Civitavecchia and Genoa.

The town has impressive remains from its early Roman history – ruins of the original trading post and the former Turris Libisonis, the Roman colony founded in 27 BC. Near the present railway station lie the **Terme Centrali** (Roman Baths), with mosaics dating from the 3rd–4th century AD. There is also a seven-arched bridge from the same period and a museum, the **Antiquarium Turritano** (Via Ponte Romano 99; tel: 079-514 433; Tue–Sun 9am–8pm) that contains finds from archaeological excavations in town and on its outskirts. The **Basilica di San Gavino** (7am–noon, 4–7.30pm) was completed in the year 1111; it houses the tomb of the martyr of the same name and is one of the most important Romanesque buildings to be found on Sardinia.

Following the main highway to Sassari, the SS 131, you will arrive at the

Hand-crafted Sardinian shepherds' knives make an excellent souvenir (although remember not to carry them in your hand luggage on your return).

THE SHEPHERD'S KNIFE

The shepherd's knife, a potent symbol of a lost pastoral world, is still a significant accessory; although they may not be strictly necessary for their work, many a Sardinian factory worker or bank employee considers his knife as part of his identity. Designed for daily use, these days shepherd's knives have become sought-after collector's items.

Sa resolza or sa resordza (the Sardinian shepherd's knife) comes from the Latin word *rasoria*, referring to knives with a swivelling sheath, and only the very finest knives have their blades protected by a sheath of wood or horn. The test of a good knife, if you are a man, is to spit on the back of one's hand, rub hard and then check whether the knife will give a close shave.

The very best knives with a classic pointed blade *a foll'e murta* – "like a myrtle leaf" – are made by true master craftsmen who will only work to order. As recently as 50 years ago, such knives were commonly produced in pastoral communities all over the island – Arbus, Guspini, Gavoi, Fonni, Santu Lussurgiu and Pattada, to name a few. Nowadays, however, good-quality knives are really only produced in the traditional manner in the last two of these villages. Knives from Pattada are considered to be the ultimate in Sardinian craftsmanship.

Cork is obtained from the stripped bark of cork oak trees which grow in the region.

sanctuary of **Monte d'Accoddi**, (9am–6pm), an early altar shaped like a truncated pyramid with a large access ramp. Similar to a Mesopotamian ziggurat, it dates to approximately 2500 BC. It is the only structure of this kind to be found in the Mediterranean area.

Up to Stintino

The most northwesterly point of the island is a small triangle of land bounded by the towns of Porto Torres to the north and Alghero to the south. The drive from Porto Torres to Stintino passes through fertile, sparsely populated farmland; unfortunately vast chemical complexes dominate much of the landscape.

Stintino ❾ is a small, unaffected place consisting of holiday cottages, a few hotel complexes and two marinas. Founded at the end of 1800 by fishermen and shepherds forced to abandon the island of Asinara, the town is a major tourist destination. The **Pelosa beach**, at Rada dei Fornelli between Capo del Falcone and the island of Asinara, is regarded as being among the most beautiful beaches in Sardinia. In August, the Regata della Latina, with vintage boats and colourful yachts, is worth seeing.

The island of **Asinara** was expropriated in 1885 to set up a hospital and a penal colony. In its recent history the Fornelli prison on the island was used to confine Italian *brigatisti* and *mafiosi*. The penal colony was closed in 1997 and the island became a national park, the **Parco Nazionale dell'Asinara**. Although access is still restricted, you can arrange a guided tour of the island to see the wildlife (contact the tourist office, see page 249).

Just before Stintino lies the Tonnara Saline, formerly an important tuna fishing station which has now been converted into a complex of holiday homes. The former mining village of **Argentiera** has little miners' cottages and a preserved main shaft.

Northeast Gallura

Parts of Gallura consist of gentle countryside punctuated by large heaps of granite blocks, inselbergs (granite

THE CORK OAK

Cork harvesting is still an important part of the Gallura regional economy, as visible in the forests around Calangianus. French traders introduced industrial cork processing to Sardinia in the 1830s. Spread across what remains of the once-magnificent woodland that cloaked the island is a species of oak tree found only in the Western Mediterranean: the *Quercus suber* or cork oak. Extensive woods of cork oaks are found in Giara di Gesturi and Gallura. The various dialect names for the cork oak – *suberju, suelzu, suveliu, suergiu, suaru* or *cortigu, ortigu, orteghe* – are derived from the Latin *suber* or *corticulum* – "cork" or "bark".

The thick cork bark protects the tree from damage, cold, heat and drying out. A cork oak can produce bark until it is about 125 years old if the peeling is done correctly. Peeling requires skill and experience to avoid harming the bright-red cambium, the growing surface for the next layer of cork. When stripping is done properly, the bark is peeled from a cork oak for the first time when the tree is around 15 years old. A tree will be peeled about eight times during its lifetime, usually at intervals of nine to 12 years, or until the quality of the cork declines below an acceptable level. The sections of

stripped bark are transported to the cork factories in Tempio or Calangianus, where they are graded according to quality. The poorest quality is processed straight away into cork waste for the building industry, where it is used as insulation material. The elastic cork from later peelings is left to mature in the open air for at least six months. During this process the sun and rain, heat and cold removes most of the red powder and other impurities from the cork's pores and makes it lighter in colour. The cork is then soaked in vats of hot water for an hour, which removes the tannic acid and causes the cork to swell up so that it gains the requisite elasticity. Bottle corks are then stamped out from the sheets of bark, which are pressed flat as they dry.

The cork industry is worth hundreds of millions of euros to the Sardinian economy but the trend towards screw tops means cork is less in demand, resulting in falling prices and a decline in farmed cork oak. Environmentalists and Sardinians are urging the wine industry to show corporate responsibility towards this sustainable, environmentally friendly natural resource, and is seeking government action to preserve the economic viability of cork production.

towers) and cork tree woods. To the southwest of Arzachena, the village of **Luogosanto ⑩** (350 metres/1,148ft above sea level) is typical of the region, in a verdant setting surrounded by pinkish-grey rocks. Continuing south, **Aggius** lies at the foot of the impressive granite mountains (Monti di Aggius) and is connected via a panoramic road to the **Valle della Luna**, a vast plain with an incredible scenery of weathered granite blocks, piled one on top of the other.

The chic little town of **Tempio Pausania ⑪** lies at the heart of the Gallura, at the foot of the granite peak of **Monte Limbara**. Irrespective of the direction from which you approach this area, you cut through dense oak forests unlike any to be found elsewhere in Sardinia. Tempio Pausania itself lies at an altitude of 555 metres (1,820ft), giving it the air of a mountain resort – an impression underlined by the town's atmosphere. Worth a visit are the 15th-century cathedral and **Museo Bernardo de Muro** (daily 8am–2pm and 4.30–7.30pm; free), dedicated to

the famous tenor who was a native son of the town.

About 10km (6 miles) east of Tempio is **Calangianus**, the cork capital of Sardinia. Nearby is **Luras ⑫**, which is worth stopping at to see the **Museo Etnografico** (tel: 368-337 6321; www.galluras.it; daily), a three-storey traditional house crammed with objects from the locality. The recreated traditional Sardinian bedroom is deeply evocative of a time now lost.

Leaving Tempio and travelling towards Sassari, the road No.127 crosses the Coghinas river, the natural border between Gallura and the subregion of Anglona, and reaches **Perfugas ⑬**. The oldest man-made lithic tools of Sardinia, dating back to the Palaeolithic period, have recently been found in this area. The **Museo Archeologico e Paleobotanico** (Via Nazario Sauro; tel: 079-564 241; Tue–Sun, June–Sept 9am–1pm, 4–8pm, Oct–May 9am–1pm, 3–7pm) displays many of the prehistoric and Nuraghic objects found in the region.

Mural of Stintino fishermen catching tuna during the matanza.

Lakeside picnic

Following side roads through a mountainous area, you will reach the **Lago del Coghinas** , the second-largest lake in Sardinia. It was dammed in 1927 and provides one of the island's main supplies of drinking water. The journey is delightful if you don't mind the serpentine nature of the road. A good place to have a picnic is at the site of the Romanesque church of **Nostra Signora di Castro** (daily) because of its position dominating the plain and Lake Coghinas. It was built in the second half of the 12th century and was the seat of the bishopric of a medieval hamlet until 1505. Passing through **Oschiri** and taking the SS 199 you will finally arrive in **Ozieri** ⑮, a prosperous and attractive little town with some handsome neoclassical houses, lying on a fertile plain supporting crops and cattle farming.

Prehistoric finds

Not far from Ozieri lies the **Grotta di San Michele** (tel: 079-787 638; guided tours Tue–Sun summer 9am–1pm and 3–6pm, winter 9am–1pm and 2–5pm), the scene of some of Sardinia's most important archaeological finds. The name of the town was given to the prehistoric period which they represent, which is now known as the Ozieri Culture. Part of the excavated material can be seen in the **Museo Archeologico** (Convento delle Clarisse; tel: 079-785 1090; Tue–Sat 9am–1pm, 4–7pm, Sun 9.30am–12.30pm), housed in the 17th-century cloisters of the convent annexe of the church of San Francesco.

In the same square is an interesting 16th-century noble house. The **Cattedrale dell' Immacolata** (daily) has a neoclassical facade and an interior with Gothic vaults. There is also an important polyptych, the *Madonna di Loreto*, the work of a 6th-century Sardinian artist known as the master of Ozieri. The nearby village of **Pattada** is the best place to buy a genuine hand-crafted shepherd's knife. If you are not yet tired of winding roads you could tackle the lonely, sinuous and unforgettable stretch of road from **Buddusò** to **Bitti** and **Nuoro**.

Cheeky mural on a cake shop (pasticceria).

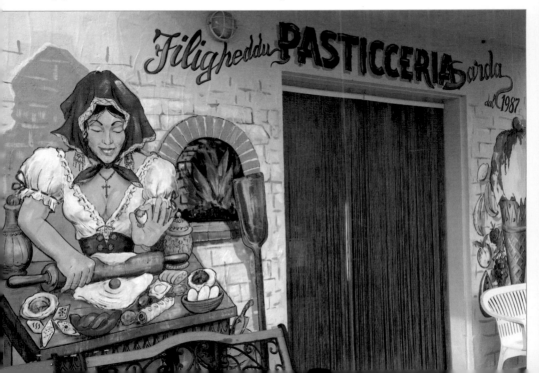

SASSARI

If you arrive in Sassari at the end of a tour of Sardinia, you will probably feel as if you have returned to the Italian mainland without actually crossing the sea.

Sardinia's second-most important city, **Sassari** ⑯ has a long history of raids and conquests, but also of stubborn resistance which perhaps shows in its urban, worldly countenance. In fact, a great deal of mainland blood flows through the veins of its inhabitants. In the early 13th century the merchants of Genoa and Pisa – both cities of international importance in medieval times – transformed an insignificant peasant village in the hinterland of Porto Torres into a flourishing commercial town.

Even today, the citizens of Sassari are proud of being a "community of shopkeepers". Trade enabled them to free themselves from the dependence on Porto Torres which had dogged their existence since Roman times. Their only regret is that throughout their long history they have never quite managed to oust Cagliari from its position as the most important town on the island. During the 17th century it was a close-run thing, as Sassari almost managed to overtake its arch-rival in the south. In 1617 the University of Sassari received its charter, three years before that of Cagliari. Such was the town's prosperity that private citizens donated enough money to build or renovate nine churches and monasteries. However, the plague in 1652 and the subsequent fall in population shattered the hopes of Sassari's inhabitants. It seemed that thereafter their town was fated to remain the perpetual runner-up.

The modern city

Today, with its population standing at nearly 130,000, Sassari is again able to show that it is at least as good as the capital. Three of the most famous Sardinian politicians of post-war times – Communist Party leader Enrico Berlinguer, and former presidents Antonio Segni and Francesco Cossiga – were all natives of Sassari.

Pretty Sassari square.

Bust of Giuseppe Garibaldi.

In the sphere of arts, too, Sassari succeeded in finding its own individual style. Many of the churches are the work of local stonemasons, known as *picapedras*, who gave the basic architectural styles imported from the mainland a popular, Sardinian touch. This tendency also applied to the sculptors of Sassari, who during the 17th century adorned the town's numerous new churches and monasteries with countless statues and altars. They also carved the *candelieri*, enormous wooden pillars shaped like candles which every year on 14 August are carried through the Old Town from the Piazza Castello to the church of Santa Maria di Betlem (St Mary of Bethlehem) by the members of the various craftsmen's guilds. The

I Candelieri (Feast of Candles), whose origins appear to lie way back in the 13th century, has remained an authentic folk festival, drawing many expatriate Sassaresi home each year.

During the *Cavalcata Sarda* (usually held in May), however, the local population prefers to leave the town to foreigners and tourists. The Cavalcata, one of Sardinia's best-known festivals, draws from surrounding villages and features a horseback parade of riders in traditional costume who later take part in a daring horse race. Over the weekend, folk groups perform traditional songs and dance in the Piazza d'Italia.

The Piazza d'Italia

The spacious **Piazza d'Italia** Ⓐ, covering an area of precisely 1 hectare (2.5

acres), is framed by elegant 19th-century buildings such as the **Palazzo della Provincia** and the neo-Gothic **Palazzo Giordano**. For an entertaining look at Sassari life, visit the square during the evening *passeggiata*. Some 150 years ago, sheep still grazed on this piazza, in whose numerous banks and administrative buildings the financial and political fate of the town is now decided. Until well into the 19th century there seemed no necessity to expand the urban area beyond the limits set by the 13th-century city walls. For 600 years, under the Spanish and the Piedmontese, the entire area was compressed within an area of only 30 hectares (75 acres).

Providing a link between the Old Town and the newer districts is the **Piazza Castello**, which lies to the north of Piazza d'Italia. In the 1870s, whilst new buildings in the architectural style of the Italian mainland were sprouting up on the Piazza d'Italia, on the Piazza Castello they were demolishing the fortress after which it is named. The castle was built in 1330 by the Aragonese; for centuries afterwards it served as a symbol of foreign rule and oppression. Recent archaeological excavations have revealed two **Barbican** passageways which are now open to the public (tel: 331-238 9208; guided tours: Tue 10am–1pm, Wed–Sat 10am–1pm and 4.30–7.30pm, Sun 10am–1pm).

Two museums

The military barracks attached to the castle house the **Museo della Brigata Sassari** Ⓑ (Piazza Castello; tel: 079-208 5308; Mon–Fri 8am–4.30pm, Sat 8am–1pm; free). The museum is dedicated to the Sardinian regiment, famous for their bravery, who endured heavy losses during World War I fighting against the Austrians. The museum's collection has a reconstruction of sandbag trenches alongside military items and poignant memorabilia from the conflict.

There is one more essential site to see before making a tour of the historic Old Town: the **Museo Nazionale G.A. Sanna** Ⓒ (Via Roma 64; tel: 079-272 203; www.museosannasassari.beniculturali.it; Tue–Sat 9am–3pm; first Sun of each month free). Housed in

Piazza d'Italia is surrounded by neoclassical buildings.

the immaculately ordered galleries of a handsome neoclassical villa, the museum presents a summary of the most important aspects of the island's archaeology. The **ground floor** is dedicated to a complete vision of the island's prehistory and history up to medieval times; a room is dedicated to the prehistoric altar of Monte d'Accoddi (about 2500 BC), followed by showcases that display objects coming from *tombe di giganti* (giants' tombs) and natural caves (from the Neolithic to the Bronze Age, 6000–1800 BC). The **upper floor** focuses on the Nuraghic civilisation and includes a collection of 2,000–3,000-year-old bronze statues, among which is the realistic bronze ox found in the sacred well of Perfugas. There is also a collection of imported Etruscan and Greek pottery and equally fascinating pieces of gold and silver Carthaginian and Roman jewellery, which is still worn with traditional Sardinian costumes.

The heart of the Old Town

Through the middle of the Old Town runs the **Corso Vittorio Emanuele**

II, built upon the old Porto Torres–Cagliari Roman road. The town's long-standing residents still call it the Plath de Codinas (the Street of Stone) because it was once lined with elegant palazzi and the residences of wealthy merchants. At no. 35 is the **Teatro Civico**, a grand 19th-century neoclassical theatre built upon the medieval Palazzo di Città – it now houses the City Museum (Mon–Sat 9am–2pm and 4–8pm, May–Oct until 9pm) dedicated to the history of Sassari with backstage glimpses of thespian life.

Apart from the Corso, the citizens of Sassari have given other streets and squares local dialect names. The **Via La Marmora**, which runs parallel to it, is lined with crumbling stucco facades known to locals as the Carra Longa; leading off the Corso is the Carra Pizzinna (today's Via Battisti), which links up with the Carra Manna (the Piazza Tola). The dialect names – "little bushel" and "large bushel" – refer to the fact that these official market measures were once in use here. Rising above **Piazza Tola ❿** is

Sculptural detail on Sassari's Duomo.

the monument to the influential historian Pasquale Tola (1800–74), who sits above the market stalls. Tola's bequeathed book collection forms the core of the **Biblioteca Comunale di Sassari** (Piazza Tola 1; information about exhibitions and cultural events tel: 079-279 380), housed in the imposing 16th-century Palazzo d'Usini on the piazza.

The most popular street in the Old Town is the **Via al Rosello E**. The silversmiths after whom the alley was named are a rare species today. You'll see the odd cobbler and carpenter at work, latter-day representatives of a once-thriving craft tradition. The picturesque Via al Rosello leads to a spring and the **Fontana di Rosello F**, the island's most famous monumental fountain, reopened in 2015 after restoration (tel: 079-200 345; Tue–Sun, 9am–5pm, May–Aug until 7pm). The 12 stone lion's heads adorning the Renaissance fountain are surrounded by statues symbolising the four seasons. The statue in the middle of the fountain represents a divinity called Giogli, and a statue

of San Gavino rides a horse at the arched summit.

Returning via the **Ponte Rosello** you'll come to the **Nuovo Mercato**, the New Market, where fresh fish from the Gulf of Asinara is on sale every morning. To the west is the elegant church of **Sant'Antonio Abate G** (daily). Dating from the early 1700s, this Baroque church, with its harmonious proportions, dominates the tree-lined Piazza Sant'Antonio.

Sassari's cathedral

Continuing along the Via al Rosello and across the Corso, you will come to the Cattedrale or **Duomo di San Nicola H** (daily). The towering, ornately carved Baroque facade (*c.*1700) was added to a Gothic structure which was itself built onto an 11th-century Romanesque church. After exploring the restored Gothic interior, head to the Museo del Tesoro in the sacristy which contains fine statuary, reliquary, silverware and other pious treasures. There are many churches near the Duomo: opposite stands the desecrated Manneristic Chiesa di San Michele.

A statue in the Giardini Pubblici overlooking the pleasant grounds.

Inside Santa Maria di Betlem.

MUS'A ARTWORKS

Opened in 2008, the Museo Sassari Arte displays a fascinating collection of artworks dating from the medieval period right up to the mid-20th century. Here are a few highlights to look out for. Among the religious paintings on the ground floor *(piano terra)* is a 13th-century cross with intriguing geometric patterns and a *Madonna con Bambino* (1473) by Bartolomeo Vivarini (examine the dainty hands). A mesmerising mix of the sacred, allegorical, saintly and erotic fills rooms III–IV of the first floor *(primo piano)*. Francesco Solimena's (1657–1747) *La Resurrezione di Lazzaro* is all brooding Baroque drama. The mythological, religious and pastoral combine in dreamy Arcadian scenes in Sala IV, while portraits of the Italian aristocracy line Sala V. Next door, nymphs frolic amid the plump flesh and ecstatic gestures of gods Venere (Venus), Giove (Jupiter) and Semele. The second floor *(piano secondo)* rooms (XII–XIX) feature the Ottocento and Novecento, starting with the works of Sardinian Giovanni Marghinotti (1798–1865) – full of delicate portrait features and romantic heroism – to the emotive etchings of Mario Delitala (1887–1990), who explored sacred and folkloric themes (Via S. Caterina–Piazza del Comune–Via Canopolo; tel: 079-231 560; www.pinacotecamusa.it; Mon–Fri 9am–1.30pm, Tue 9am–1.30pm and 3–5.30pm).

The Baroque façade of the church of Sant' Antonio Abate.

Statue of Vittorio Emanuele II on Piazza d'Italia.

Art, churches and a park

On Piazza del Comune is the grandiose **Palazzo Ducale** (Ducal Palace), built for the Duke of Vallombrosa from designs of Valino between 1775 and 1805. It has housed the town hall since the early 20th century. Now it's also home to a branch of the City Museum, the **Duke's Rooms and Cellars** (tel: 079-2015 122; Tue–Sat 10am–1pm and 5–8pm, Sun 10am–1pm). Excavations in 1985 and 2006 unearthed five cellar rooms probably dating back to the 16th century.

Following the main road in front of the palace is the Jesuit College of Canopoleno built between 1559 and 1605, together with the annexed church of San Giuseppe. In 1617 it became the first university in Sardinia. The Jesuit college now houses **MUS'A**, **Museo Sassari Arte ❶** (Via S. Caterina–Piazza del Comune–Via Canopolo; tel: 079-231 560; www.pinacotecamusa.it; Mon–Fri 9am–1.30pm, Tue 9am–1.30pm and 3–5pm), an important collection of around 400 artworks exhibited over three floors.

On the far side of the broad expanse of the **Piazza Mazzotti** rises the church of the Convento Cappuccini, which houses a number of altars carved by local artists.

Across the **Corso Vico**, outside the city walls, stands the church of **Santa Maria di Betlem ❿** (daily), with its striking silver dome. This much-venerated church is where the huge 3-metre (10ft) wooden candles used in the *I Candelieri* festival are stored. On 14 August they are carried here in procession. Inside the cloister is a 14th-century fountain which once supplied the town with water.

Passing along the **Via Maddalena** and the **Via Turritana** in the Old Town, where there is a succession of modest inns and restaurants, you will arrive in the bustling **Via Brigata Sassari**, named after the heroic Sardinian brigade which saw action during World War I. Continuing across the semicircular **Emiciclo Garibaldi ⓚ**, dominated by the statue of Giuseppe Mazzini (1805–72), the politician instrumental in the unification of Italy in 1861 – you will soon reach the **Giardini Pubblici ⓛ** (Municipal Park), a refreshing place to cool down and unwind.

On the sea walls at sunset, Alghero.

ALGHERO TO ORISTANO

There is much to explore along the western coast of Sardinia: nature reserves, caves, hiking trails, Romanesque architecture, splendid towns, Roman remains and, of course, beaches.

Main Attractions

Alghero
Grotta di Nettuno
Valle dei Nuraghi
Bonorva
Santu Lussúrgiu
Nuraghe Losa
Oristano
Tharros
Is Arutas
Bosa

Strongly influenced by Spanish culture, **Alghero** ❶ has the most Spanish feel of any Sardinian town. The city is generally considered to have been founded in 1102. However, long before the dawn of the Christian era the Phoenicians set up a trading post on this exposed bay in western Sardinia. In the early Middle Ages Arabs kept a base here from which they set out on their raids of southern France. It was not until the 12th century that settlers fortified the little peninsula on which the Old Town remains huddled to this day.

Spanish loyalty

It was at this time, too, that the place received its somewhat inauspicious name, Alghero, which translated means "full of algae". For 250 years the Doria family from Genoa was in power here, but in 1353 they were forced to cede the town to the forces of Aragon. With the first Aragonese-Catalan officials came Catalan settlers. Following an uprising against harsh Aragon rule, the resident Sardinians and Ligurians were all driven out of Alghero, and were replaced from 1372 by settlers from Barcelona, Valencia and Mallorca.

Alghero was transformed into an urban fortress in which only citizens loyal to the regime were allowed to live. The town was closed in on all sides by walls, towers and bulwarks (the fortifications on the landward side were demolished during the 19th century to provide work for the inhabitants of a nearby penal colony). The citizens were not allowed to travel further than about 3km (2 miles) beyond the city boundaries, as far as a number of churches in the surrounding countryside. The dominant influence in Alghero was from the Iberian peninsula, and the Catalan language is very much alive and thriving.

Fortified Alghero.

Alghero to Oristano

SARDINIAN

SEA

0   10 km

0   10 miles

N

Palmadula
La Corte
Barcali
Sassari
Osilo
N. S. di
Bonaria
127
Chiaramonti
Luzzani
Caniga
S. Maria
la Palma
Porto Ferro
L. Baratz
Tottubella
Gioscari
Bunnari
M. Pilosu
677
672
132
291
Tissi
Ossi
Muros
Bagni di
S. Martino
SS. Trinità
di Saccargia
Martine
Usini
Codrongianos
S. Michele
di Salvenero
Ploaghe
S. Antioco
di Bisarcio
Parco Regionale
di Porto Conte
M. Doglia
436
Necropoli
Anghelu Ruju
Olmedo
Uri
Florinas
597
I.
Piana
M. Timidone
361
Palmavera
Tomba
Santu Pedru
Fertilia
Putifigari
Ittiri
S. Maria
de Sea
N. S.
di Coros
Mesumundu
S. Maria
de Coros
Ardara
4
Porto
Conte
Tramariglio
Grotta di
Nettuno
Maristella
Rada di
Alghero
Alghero
1
Banari
Siligo
M. Santo
733
Mores
Mtreddu
Capo Caccia
292
S. di Valverde
Sassari
L. Cuga
L. Bidighinzu
Thiesi
Bessude
Bonnanaro
Sa
Coveccada
5
Poglina
Speranza
Villanova
Monteleone
Pedra Ettori
718
L. del
Temo
Romana
Borutta
Cheremule
Torralba
S. Pietro di Sorres
N. S. de
Cabu Abbas
S. Antine
Tres
Nuraghes
Necropoli di
Pottu Codinu
Monteleone
Rocca Doria
M. Traessu
719
Bonu Ighinu
Oes
Giave
Cossoine
Rebeccu
Necropoli di
S. Andrea Priu
M. Mannu
802
Montresta
Mara
S. Nicolò
di Trullas
Bonorva
7
Padria
Semestene
Pozzomaggiore
Altopiano di Campeda
I. sa Pagliosa
Capo
Marargiu
Argentina
S'Ulia
292
131
Badde
Salighes
Pta Palai
Villa
Piercy
1200
Nuoro
Nuradeo
131
Lei
Silanus
Catena di Marghine
Bosa
26
S. Pietro Extramuros
Sindia
Monte Muradu
Bortigali
9
I. Rossa
27
Suni
S. Barbara
S. Sabina
Bosa Marina
Tinnura
Abbazia di
S. Maria di Corte
129
Necropoli di
Filigosa
Macomer
8
Biron
Medolo
Magomadas
Sagama
Porto Alabe
Tresnuraghes
M. S. Antonio
908
Dualchi
Noragugume
Sennariolo
Scano di Montiferro
Borore
S. Marco
Cuglieri
S. Leonardo de
Siete Fuentes
S. Ignazio
Sedilo
Punta di Foghe
25
Foche
Monte
Ferru
S. Leonardo
Altopiano di Abbasanta
Nuoro Olbia
Norbello
Aidomaggiore
10
292
M. Urtigu
1050
Santu
Lussurgiu
S. Agostino
Abbasanta
Ombedo
Zuri
M. Ferru
11
Losa
12
13
S. Caterina
di Pittinuri
Fattoria
Pilli
Bonarcado
Ghilarza
14
Boroneddu
Tadasuni
S'Architu
Cornus
24
Seneghe
Lugherras
Paulilatino
Ardauli
Cala su Pallosu
Narbolia
Milis
15
Ulà
Tirso
Is Arenas
Rocca Tunca
16
Il Pozzo di
S. Cristina
S. Chiara
Capo Mannu
Porto Mandriola
Stagno
de is Benas
Putzu
Idu
S'Urachi
S. Vero Milis
Bauladu
Oristano
Busachi
Cala
Saline
Cala
Saline
Sale Porcus
Narbolia
Riola Sardo
Zeddiani
Tramatza
Villanova
Truschedu
Tirso
388
I. di Mal
di Ventre
Parco Nazionale
Capo sa Sturaggia
Mari Ermi
Is Arutas
della Penisola di Sinis
Stagno di Cabras
Nurachi
Zerfaliu
S. Lussurgiu
Fordenginus
Allai
Punta
is Arutas
21
23
Donigale
Fenughedu
Siamaggiore
Massama
Solarussa
Ollastra
Simaxis
M. Grighini
673
Samugheo
S. Salvatore
Cabras
Solanas
Simaxis
Siapiccia
Siamanna
I. Catalano
Isola Mal di Ventre
18
Stagno
di Mistras
Torre
Grande
Madonna
d. Rimedio
17
Oristano
Sili
S. Giusta
Palmas
Arborea
Villaurbana
Ruinas
S. Giovanni di Sinis
22
Tharros
Capo S. Marco
19
Foce
del Tirso
S. Giusta
Stagno di
S. Giusta
Tumbol
Mogorella
Villa
S. Antonio
Asuni
Golfo di
Oristano
Arborea
Sant' Anna
Is Bangius
Pau
Escovedu
Senis
Ales
Albagiara
Zeppara
S'Ena Arrubia
Capo Frasca
Arborea
Cagliari
2
3
6

Alghero Old Town

The Old Town of Alghero covers barely one-tenth of today's total city. It is, however – apart from the beaches and hotels located beyond the city limits – the only part of the town worth exploring. Surrounded on three sides by towers and fortifications, the best introduction to the town can be gained from a walk along the old **battlements**.

Setting out from the massive round **Torre dell'Espero Reial** (the Tower of Royal Ambition), you can stroll past the lively **Piazza Sulis** in the southeast, fringed by cafés and trees, to the half-ruined but still impressive Forte de la Magdalena lying right beside the harbour in the north. En route is the octagonal **Torre de Sant Jaume** (St James's Tower) and the circular **Torre de la Polvorera**, which is situated on the northwesterly tip of the peninsula. From the fortifications along the **Lungomare Marco Polo** there are spectacular views across the Bay of Alghero as far as Capo Caccia. Finally, via a narrow battlement walk,

you reach the 16th-century **Forte de la Magdalena**, where fishermen repair their boats. Locals take their evening stroll along the three-sided seafront promenade, especially the **Lungomare Colombo** to the south, which is overflowing on public holidays. The fascinating alleys of the Old Town, tall and narrow like dark mountain gorges, lead off the promenade. The Old Town itself is best entered through the **Porta a Mare**, the Sea Gate, on the north side. Another entrance is in the **Porta a Terra**, the original main entrance to town. The door still bears the stone coat-of-arms of the crown of Aragon and used to be closed at dusk.

Duomo di Santa Maria

The **Duomo di Santa Maria** (Cathedral of Our Lady; Mon–Tue and Thu–Sat, June–Aug 10.30am–1pm, 7–9.30pm, Apr–May and Sept–Oct 10.30am–1pm and 4–6.30pm) is reached by crossing the long, funnel-shaped main square – the **Piazza Civica**. Its style evolved over 200 years, from the mid-16th to the

View of the Duomo di Santa Maria.

The battlements of Alghero Old Town.

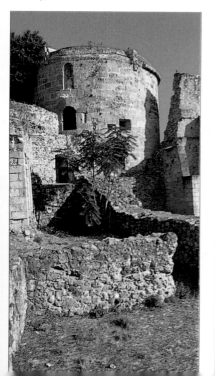

UN'ISOLA LINGUISTICA

Although you become accustomed to the coexistence of two languages in Sardinia – Italian and Sardinian with its myriad of dialects – the situation in Alghero is considerably more complicated; it is often referred to as *un'isola linguistica* – a linguistic island. Here you will hear Catalan in addition to Italian, which virtually all Sardinians speak perfectly even if it is not their mother tongue, and the archaic-sounding Sardinian, which is comprehensible only to the initiated.

The visitor will often hear local inhabitants using Catalan in conversation, and will notice that it is used with increasing frequency on the streets, in the squares and, for some reason, in relation to buildings of interest to tourists. Perhaps the local inhabitants think Prassa del Pou Vel, Carrer de Bonaire and Les Quatre Cantonades sound more inviting than **Piazza Civica**, **Via Umberto** and **Via Carlo Alberto**.

In the general wake of all stronger minorities, the citizens of Alghero have revived an interest in their Catalan roots, founding parties to promote the interests of their minority culture and various folklore groups to breathe new life into their traditional folk music. It is not surprising, therefore, that the town's most famous culinary speciality is Catalan-style lobster.

Alghero is famed for its fresh seafood. Stop at the market in Via Sassari for lobster, sea urchins and squid, or try the local restaurants.

Sunset over the west coast.

mid-18th century; unsurprisingly, the result, a late Baroque-Manneristic superstructure on top of the late Gothic main building, lacks unity. Attached to the Duomo is the **Museo Diocesano d'Arte Sacra** (tel: 079-973 3041; www.mosaicoalghero.com; Jul–Aug Mon–Sat 10.30am–1pm and 6–9pm, Apr–June and Sept–Oct Thur–Tue 10.30am–1pm and 5–8pm, Jan–Mar Fri–Sun 10.30am–1pm and 4.30–7.30pm, Dec Thu–Tue 11am–1pm and 4–7pm) inside the church of Nostra Signora del Rosario. On display is a collection that forms the town's liturgical treasure.

In front of the cathedral, on either side of the **Via Sant'Erasmo**, lies the former Jewish quarter; the Jews formed an essential part of the community in every trading centre of international importance during the Middle Ages and often rose to positions of influence. In the middle of the 15th century, with the necessary permission of the King of Aragon, Alghero's Jews raised the required finance for the construction of the **Torre des Hebreus** (The Jewish Gate).

It provided a second point of access to the town on the landward side; until well into the 19th century it was closed every evening at dusk with the traditional cry "All those outside must stay outside!".

Fanning out behind the cathedral are the most elegant streets of the Old Town: **Via Umberto**, in which the aristocracy and clergy resided under the rule of Spain and Savoy, and the **Via Carlo Alberto** (Carrer Major), now filled with upmarket shops. Dominating the end of the street is the sumptuous Baroque **Chiesa di San Michele** (daily), built by the Jesuits. Its coloured majolica dome rises above the exquisitely restored monastery complex of San Francesco (built during the 14th and 16th to 17th centuries); during the summer months the Romanesque cloisters form an atmospheric setting for classical music concerts. Some of the alleys of the Old Town have a distinctly southern flair, with a less restrained feel reminiscent of Naples. This is for good reason, as for centuries Alghero was the capital of the Mediterranean coral industry, and attracted Neapolitan fishermen specialised in the hazardous business of fishing for coral.

The combination of this influx from Campania, linked to the Catalan influence, has given the townspeople their characteristic bonhomie. Nowadays only a small proportion of the coral used in the decorative items on display originate off the Sardinian coast. The coral reefs have long been depleted.

Excursions from Alghero

Moving north from the town and passing the Bombarde beach, you come to the Nuraghic complex of **Palmavera** ❷ (tel: 079-994 4394; Apr–Oct 9am–7pm, Nov–Feb 10am–2pm, Mar 9.30am–4pm; guides available). This is surrounded by a village of round huts that includes one used as a meeting house, with a stone bench along its perimeter that could seat over 40 people.

Continuing along the same road, the bay of Porto Conte, the ancient Roman **Portus Ninpharus**, appears in front of you. It's the only true natural port in Sardinia, where Charles V's fleet was harboured on its way to Tunis; it is closed on one side by the promontory of Capo Caccia, which houses the **Grotta di Nettuno** ❸ (summer 8am–7pm, winter 9am–2pm). To get to the grotto you can either take a *traghetti navisarda* (tel: 079-978 961; www.navisarda.it) motor boat (pricey), sailing boat (magical) or bus (cheapest and most comfy when the water is choppy), all from Alghero port. Once inside the cave, the tour brushes the seawater lake, Lago La Marmora, through atmospheric chambers filled with multicoloured rocks hewn into otherworldy stalactite and stalagmite forms, with names like Grand Organ and Cupola.

North of Porto Conte is the inaccessible **Cala dell'Inferno** (Hell's Bay), set in a limestone cliff shaped by erosion and surrounded by *màcchia* bush. From Porto Conte to the north it is easy to reach Argentiera and Stintino.

Taking the road through Sassari, you reach the **Via Carlo Felice**, the SS 131, which passes through a region full of historical interest and several Romanesque churches. The majority of them were constructed between the 12th and 14th centuries by Tuscan master craftsmen – often at the behest of the wealthy mainland merchants who imported large quantities of minerals, coral, hides, cattle, cheese, salt and cereals from Sardinia.

From Ardara to Borutta

About 15km (8 miles) further along the road is the village of **Ardara** ❹, a fascinating stop for anyone interested in the house of Hohenstaufen (a dynasty of German kings in the 12th and 13th centuries). Here, in 1239, in the **Santa Maria del Regno** (the Black Cathedral; daily) – built of black basalt in about 1100 – Enzo, the son of the Hohenstaufen Emperor Frederick II, celebrated what was to prove a short-lived marriage to Adelaida. Since his wife's dowry included a sizeable proportion of the island, in the form of the *giudicati* of Torres

TIP

A magical way to experience the natural wonders of Capo Caccia – including trips to the Grotta di Nettuno often accompanied by dolphins – is aboard the handsome *Andrea Jensen* sailing boat which sails from Alghero (tel: 3389-708 139; www.ajsailing.com; charge includes lunch).

Boats at sunset in Alghero's harbour.

SPOTTED COW CHURCH

Santissima Trinità di Saccargia (Church of the Trinity of the Spotted Cow; daily), one of the finest Romanesque churches, stands near the village of Codrongianos, 15km (9 miles) from Sassari. According to legend, a gentle, pious cow played a significant role in the church's foundation – though, with its distinctive walls of alternating layers of dark basalt and light limestone, in fact it resembles a zebra more than a cow. Inside, the apse contains the only extant cycle of 13th-century frescoes in Sardinia. Only 3km (2 miles) away is the 12th-century **Chiesa di San Michele di Salvènero** (daily), which retains some of its Romanesque-Pisan charms despite alterations at the beginning of the 20th century.

Rock of Ages: Sardinia's Karst Caves

The enormous variety of rock types makes Sardinia a dream destination for geologists and cavers, and creates the landscapes that appeal to the rest of us.

Karst formations – which are shaped by the action of water on soluble bedrock – cover a relatively small area of Sardinia (about 6 percent of the island, mainly along the coast) compared with the more extensively occurring metalliferous rocks and granite. But it's the karst formations and their eerie underground worlds that are the main attraction for most travellers.

Sardinia's karst limestone was created almost 500,000 years ago (Palaeozoic Era). Erosion by sea action has created an amazing range of grottoes, each with an individual character, making them attractive to geohydrologists, palaeoclimatologists, biologists and everyday punters. A Golfo di Orosei boat trip with an expert local guide is a chance to swim in many such magical sea grottoes.

The study of Sardinia's caves didn't start until the 1950s. In 1954 a British team of explorers discovered and investigated the Grotta di Nettuno on the Capo Caccia, a formation of red limestone rising 180 metres (600ft) above the sea. Today, over 100,000 people a year clamber into the bowels of the earth via the Escala Cabirol, the so-called Deer's Steps. Many more visit by fishing boat from Alghero harbour. The cave contains a small lake (La Marmora), which provides a perfect miniature example of the vast underground lakes of Europe. Passing through the chambers you witness strangely shaped stalactites and stalagmites formed by the drip-dripping of mineral-rich water over millions of years. It is thought that these, along with other caves on the island, had religious significance during the Ozieri period.

Sardinia's caves were mostly discovered by accident: some by engineers seeking karst springs to increase the island's water supplies, others by miners after lead and zinc, and even some by workers collecting seabird excrement for use in fertilisers. In the 19th century, General Alfonso La Marmora made a study of the cave network. Scientifically based speleology has been applied to Sardinia only since the end of World War II. Only a small number of caves have been studied, but for the visitor there are plenty of underground worlds to explore.

Stalactite formations of the Grotta di Ispinigoli, near Dorgoli.

and Gallura, Enzo proclaimed himself King of Sardinia. He soon abandoned both his wife and the island (he seems to have been unable to stand life on this rough and lonely island for any length of time), but he refused to relinquish his royal title, which he held until his death in a dungeon in Bologna, where his enemies kept him prisoner for 23 years.

In the same cathedral is Sardinia's largest retable: a polyptych measuring 10 by 6 metres (32 by 20ft), painted in 1515 by Giovanni Muru, hanging behind the main altar and formed by various wooden panels.

Romanesque churches

From Ardara, continuing east on the SS 597 there are two other important Romanesque churches: **Sant'Antioco di Bisarcio** (daily), built in 1065–1153, with an unusual asymmetrical facade, and **Nostra Signora di Castro** (daily 9am–noon) situated in a panoramic position.

Heading south from Ardara, after 20km (12 miles) the highway rejoins the Carlo Felice Superstrada at the farming village of **Bonnanaro** ⑤. The effects of the steady migration from the land during the past decades have been particularly noticeable here. The settlement has given its name to an advanced culture (the Bonnanaro Culture, 1800–1600 BC) which preceded the Nuraghic period. It must have been an austere civilisation based on the bare essentials of life – in keeping with the harsh, unyielding nature of the island interior – and yet, according to archaeological evidence, it was sufficiently sophisticated for the performance of complicated surgical operations such as trepanation, the drilling of the skull.

Another Romanesque church lies in the vicinity of Bonnanaro. **San Pietro di Sorres** (daily), in the village of **Borutta**, stands dramatically perched at a height of 520 metres (1,665ft) on a little plateau. Its location amid the bleak limestone landscape is breathtaking.

Situated on a limestone plateau nearby is a largish village, **Thiesi**, whose inhabitants make a living from arable and livestock farming.

In this area are some of the best-preserved Megalithic remains on the island.

"Royal palace" at the Nuraghe di Santu Antine.

In the heat of summer, you will see lizards darting into rock crevices as you approach.

Nuraghe di Santu Antine.

A mural on the building of the local middle school by Aligi Sassu, a well-known artist of Sardinian extraction who lived in Thiesi, represents *S'annu de s'attaccu* – "the Year of the Attack" – 1800, when the Duke of Asinara launched an attack on the villagers who refused to deliver his feudal dues. This illustrates the part played by chauvinism and exploitation in Sardinian history. Those of the island's politicians who support Sardinian autonomy accuse the Italian state of these same attitudes.

Valley of Nuraghi

From Thiesi, a road crossing pretty countryside passes under the Carlo Felice Superstrada and leads into the **Valle dei Nuraghi** ❻ near **Torralba**. The name sounds as though it is a slogan coined by the tourist office, but it is authentic. The hollow contains a large number of mysterious Megalithic Nuraghic constructions. The finest, the **Nuraghe di Santu Antine** (www.nuraghesantuantine.it; daily 9am–8pm; charge includes admission to Museo dei Nuraghi), stands in the middle of the valley. Its main tower, now some 17.5 metres (56ft) high, may well have measured as much as 20 metres (68ft) before the top courses of stones were dismantled during the 19th century to build the village well in Torralba.

The nuraghe is of a highly complex construction; built of layers of basalt blocks, it includes – apart from the 3,500-year-old main tower – three lower and less ancient subsidiary towers arranged in a clover-leaf shape. In later times, the local population was so impressed by the nuraghe that it called it Sa Domu de Su Rei, the Royal Palace. Strangely enough, the king referred to was actually the Roman emperor Constantine, who is revered throughout the island as a courageous fighter of holy wars and a protector of the Sardinian people.

You can discover more about the Nuraghe Santu Antine – its labyrinthine interior structure of walls, corridors and rooms as well as the remarkable construction of the main tower, which consists of 28 courses of stone blocks, mounted upon each other without the use of mortar – at Torralba's **Museo dei Nuraghi** (tel: 079-847 481; www.nuraghesantuantine.it; daily 9am–8pm), where excavated items and other interesting exhibits are on display.

Also famous for its nuraghe, as well as its attractively coloured hand-woven carpets, is **Bonorva** ❼, a small agricultural market town lying further to the south. One of the most famous sites is the **Sant' Andrea Priu** necropolis (daily), a prehistorical ipogeic tomb formed by 18 rooms that in Palaeo-Christian, Byzantine and medieval times was used as place of worship. Frescoes discovered on the walls are in the process of being restored. Other ancient ruins lie at an altitude of approximately 650 metres (2,080ft) on the **Su Monte** plateau. Here the Nuraghi must have made their last desperate stand against the incursions of the Carthaginians.

Macomer

In 1478 yet another Sardinian dream of maintaining the island's independence was shattered near the little town of **Macomer** ❽, which lies some 15km (10 miles) further southwards. The soldiers of Leonardo Alagon, Margrave of Arborea, were defeated by a vast army sent by the new rulers from Aragon. It was this Spanish victory that broke the last remaining pocket of resistance on the island. Macomer lies on a trachyte ledge which slopes away to the south. The panorama from the town sums up the island's geological history. It stretches from the basalt plateau in the foreground to the granite and limestone mountains of the interior on the horizon.

The town itself has a welcoming atmosphere: as an ancient trading centre and road junction, Macomer has a long tradition of hospitality. The area was settled in ancient times by the Nuraghi, who were followed by the Carthaginians and the Romans. The roads radiating from Macomer follow tracks used since time immemorial: east through the village of **Silanus** ❾, with the Byzantine-Romanesque **Chiesa di Santa Sabina** and the nuraghe of the same name, and west through **Sindia** with its nearby Romanesque-Burgundian Cistercian abbey church to Bosa.

Spring water and extinct volcanoes

Alternatively one can take the road to Santu Lussúrgiu, which runs through the hills to the southwest of Macomer; after 15km (10 miles) of lonely countryside one reaches the hamlet of **San Leonardo de Siete Fuentes** ❿, whose *siete fuentes* (seven springs) rise in a shady park. In summer people come to take the waters, which have a mildly diuretic effect. The parish church, the Chiesa di San Leonardo, built of dark-coloured trachyte rock, dates from the 12th century. It was originally constructed in Romanesque style, but extensive Gothic additions were built at a later date.

Along the barren rocky cliffs of the Monte Ferru is an extinct volcano, and the region's topography shows scars of past eruptions. In fact, the market town of **Santu Lussúrgiu** ⓫ spreads out across a former crater.

Limoncello, a popular Sardinian liqueur made with lemon zest, is usually served as an after-dinner drink.

Rooftops of Santa Lussúrgiu.

The warm water for the Roman baths at Fordongianus flows from the local hot springs.

Rugged Sardinian landscape.

Livestock farming is the main source of livelihood for the inhabitants, and its handicrafts are closely linked with sheep rearing: the women weave rugs and blankets from the wool, and the men produce the sharp knives which they need for shearing in the spring. The town also has a reputation for excellent woodcarving, a skill which in days gone by occupied the shepherds in the long days and weeks as they grazed their flocks.

From Santu Lussúrgiu to Abbasanta the road descends the barren slopes of the Monte Ferru and then passes between an endless succession of *tancas*. These plots of land demarcated by stone walls are an essential characteristic of the Sardinian countryside, giving it a geometric chequerboard appearance. When the land was parcelled out during the 19th century to enable more peasants to become landowners, the construction of these walls marked a revolution in land use. For thousands of years – since the earliest days in the island's history – the Sardinians enjoyed common land that was worked by the community as a whole. From this point on, however, this quasi-communist concept of property ceased to exist.

Abbasanta churches and a museum to Gramsci

In the tiny village of **Sant'Agostino**, modest cottages and guesthouses for pilgrims, known as *muristenes*, are clustered round a solid basalt church. The same dark stone was used for the buildings forming the heart – the oldest part – of **Abbasanta**. This village possesses a pseudo-Renaissance parish church which lends it a certain dignity.

Ghilarza ⑫, which today forms part of the Abbasanta built-up area, appears to have a much more urban air, an impression due in part to the large number of churches within the town limits. They include **San Palmerio**, **San Giorgio**, **Santa Lucia** and the **Carmelo**. In addition there are several picturesque medieval country churches in the vicinity.

The small **Casa Museo di Antonio Gramsci** (tel: 0785-54164; www.casa gramscighilarza.org; Sat–Sun 10am–1pm, 3.30–6.30pm) on the Corso Umberto in Ghilarza provides an insight into the life of the Marxist writer, philosopher and politician. Gramsci was born in 1891 in the village of **Ales**, attended the school in Ghilarza for 10 years and died in 1937 in Rome after enduring a lengthy prison sentence for his anti-Fascist views. His writing left a lasting philosophical and political legacy – not least in the resurgence of the Partito Communista Italiana (PCI) following World War II.

From Ghilarza it's a stone's throw to the tiny hamlet of **Tadasuni**, where the local priest has founded a museum of traditional Sardinian musical instruments, the most complete of its kind.

Zuri and Roman baths

The village of **Zuri** ⑬ is also worth a visit. During the 1920s, when the Omodeo Dam was under construction, the entire settlement was moved to its present site. Not only the inhabitants but also the lovely Romanesque-Gothic parish church of **San Pietro** was relocated: the pink trachyte blocks were painstakingly dismantled, one by one, and then reconstructed here.

The village of **Fordongianus** to the south offers the only possibility to visit the ruins of Roman thermal baths where hot water still flows (tel: 0783-60157; summer 9.30am–1pm and 3–7pm, winter 2.30–5pm). The name comes from the Latin Forum of Traiani, an important Roman settlement which controlled the movements of the local population from the mountains to the east. Not far below, **Samugheo** has an important Textile Museum, the **Museo Unico Regionale dell'arte Tessile** Sarda (tel: 0783-631 052; http://murats.it; Wed–Sun, summer 10am–1pm and 5–8pm, winter 10am–1pm and 4–7pm), showcasing the skills of the local artisans.

Nuraghe and water temples

Before leaving this densely populated region on the edge of the basalt plateau of Abbasanta, it is well worth making a slight detour to view the well-preserved **Nuraghe Losa** ⑭ (tel: 0785- 52302; www.nuraghelosa.net; 9am–one hour before sunset), located some 3km (2 miles) southwest of

Sheep provide the milk for Sardinia's most famous export – pecorino cheese.

For something different, visit Tadasuni's museum of traditional musical instruments.

MUSICA SARDA

Tadasuni's priest, Don Giovanni Dore, founded its **Museo degli Strumenti della Tradizione Sarda** (Museum of Traditional Sardinian Musical Instruments; Casa Parrochiale, Via Adua 7; by appointment only, tel: 0785-50113).

His indefatigable enthusiasm led him to make a study of the sophisticated construction techniques employed in the seemingly primitive musical instruments of Sardinia – above all, the *launedda*, the shepherd's flute, the *serraggia* fiddle and the *tumbarinu* drum.

Don Dore's demonstrations provide the best introduction to the island's musical tradition. Although this music is still performed at folk festivals, the archaic tone patterns make it largely inaccessible to the uninitiated.

Architecturai detail in Oristano.

Red-tiled rooftops of Oristano.

Abbasanta. The ivy-clad ruins exude a nostalgic air; naturally enough, in this volcanic area, the walls are constructed of dark basalt blocks. The main 12-metre (40ft) high tower dates from the middle Bronze Age (approximately 14th century BC) but has been built upon many times since – as have the later subsidiary towers and exterior walls.

The Nuraghe Losa, the fortress of Santu Antine near Torralba, and the settlement Su Nuraxi near Barumini are all quite different constructions, and represent excellent examples of the nuraghe – some 7,000 in all – which can be found all over Sardinia. Some are in good condition, but many are decayed almost beyond recognition. The nuraghe lend the landscape an aura of archaic melancholy, in which all attempts at progress seem out of place. All the more powerful, therefore, is the impact of the Nuraghe Losa, standing on a small rocky outcrop just a stone's throw from the noise and frenzy of the traffic ploughing up and down the Carlo Felice superstrada below.

Visitors are frequently surprised by the obvious parallels between the religious rites of the Nuraghi and those of present-day Christianity. Three thousand years ago, the Nuraghi used to gather to celebrate their festivals around **Il Pozzo di Santa Cristina** (Water Temple of Santa Cristina; tel: 0785-55438; summer 9am–1pm and 3–7.30pm, winter 9.30am–1pm and 3–6pm), which lies a few miles south of **Paulilatino** ⓯ on the stretch of the Carlo Felice between Abbasanta and Oristano.

The elegantly constructed well shaft of the ancient sacred spa is surrounded by walls which archaeologists believe to be the remains of former pilgrims' huts called *muristenes*. Housed in a handsome 19th-century *palazzina* in the centre of town, the **Museo Archeologico-Etnográfico** (Tue–Sun summer 9am–1pm and 4.30–7.30pm, autumn and winter 3–5.30pm, spring 3.30–6.30pm; entrance with Water Temple ticket) has a collection of finds from Santa Cristina as well as artefacts recreating the pastoral lives of peasants. The rural **Chiesa di Santa**

Cristina, situated not far from the ruins of the nuraghe spa temple, is similarly encircled by simple dwellings for worshippers. Here, as so often on Sardinia, there is no clear distinction between the pagan and the Christian. To sample the potent mixture of the secular and the sacred, and the warmest Sardinian hospitality, it is best to visit during the town's ancient feasts, that coincide with the planting and harvest of crops: the nine-day rites of Santa Cristina in May or San Serafino in October.

On the road to Oristano, one more detour remains – a short side-trip to **Milis** ⑯. On the edge of the village stands the Romanesque **Chiesa di San Paolo**, dating from the 12th–13th centuries. The houses are surrounded by the citrus orchards which the French poet Paul Valéry described in his *Sardinian Journey*.

Oristano – the small capital

Regardless of the direction from which you approach the town of **Oristano** ⑰, it is easy to fall under the impression that you are entering an overgrown village rather than the capital of Sardinia's smallest province. The town has become the focal point of western Sardinia, a region it governed during the period of the medieval *giudicati*. Until well into the 15th century the town was the capital of the judicature of Arborea, which was subjugated by the rulers of Aragon later than the other three *giudicati*. It is possible that the Aragonese were in no particular hurry when it came to conquering this province – the ruling family of Arborea was itself originally of Catalan descent, although they had been resident on Sardinia for many years. The dominant personality of the house of Arborea was the *Giudichessa* Eleonora, who died in 1404.

Historic centre

Eleonora's seat of government is commemorated in the main square, **Piazza Eleonora d'Arborea**; during the 19th century it was also decided that a somewhat pompous statue should add to the tribute. Surrounded by figures of lions, Eleonora strikes an elegant pose. Today, people gather

Statue of Eleonora d'Arborea in the piazza of the same name, Oristano.

here, especially in the evening, to meet their friends and lovers, lick ice creams, exchange gossip or just to see and be seen.

Dominating the Piazza Eleonora is the **Palazzo Comunale** (town hall). It is a former Piarist monastery, whose (desecrated) church, with an unusual oval ground plan, now serves as the local council chamber. A stone throw's away, at Piazza Eleonora 19, is a tourist information point (tel: 0783-36831; Mon–Thu 8.30am–1pm and 3pm–6pm, Fri 8.30am–1pm). Despite the increase in population to over 31,000 over the past 30 years, Oristano has none of the sophisticated flair of Cagliari, Sassari or even Alghero, but its compactness adds to the charm of the centro storico.

From **Piazza Roma** you enter the pedestrian area in the historical centre, once completely surrounded by medieval walls of which today only the **Torre di Mariano II** (Torre di San Cristóforo), built 1291, remains. It once served as the main gate to the city. The small pedestrianised area has new, upmarket shops.

Lining Via Parpaglia are elegant buildings, including Palazzo Arcais, with its wrought-iron balconies, and Palazzo Parpaglia, which houses the **Antiquarium Arborense** (tel: 0783-791 262; www.antiquariumarborense.it; Mon–Fri 9am–8pm, Sat–Sun 9am–2pm and 3–8pm). This museum features a wonderful art gallery, with some interesting 16th-century altarpieces in Catalan style, and a large and wide-ranging archaeological collection, including Roman, Neolithic and Nuraghic artefacts from the excavations at Tharros and Sinis. There is also a large reconstruction of Tharros in the 9th century AD.

The cathedral

The **Cattedrale di Santa Maria Assunta** (summer 8am–1pm and 4–7pm, winter 7am–1pm and 3–6.30pm) was built in a mixture of architectural styles; of the original complex, dating from the 13th century, only the Gothic Cappella di Rimedio in the right aisle remains. Parts of a Romanesque ambon, created by Pisan craftsmen and used as a chapel balustrade,

The Cattedrale di Santa Maria Assunta in Oristano.

are now displayed in the first chapel of the right aisle. Nino Pisano, whose name indicates that he, too, was a native of Pisa, carved the coloured Gothic wooden statue of *The Annunciation* in the cathedral, as well as a statue of St Basil standing in the nearby church of St Francis. Nino Pisano was a craftsman who lived and worked during the 14th century, when Pisa was still anxious to maintain its links with the *giudicato* of Arborea and its capital.

The Spanish influence

Next to the Duomo is a good example of 18th-century architecture, the **Seminario Tridentino** (daily), and along the same road is the church of San Francesco, with a neoclassical facade, where you will find the *Crocifisso di Nicodemo* (Crucifix of Nicodemus) in a side chapel. The colourful wooden crucifix is generally considered to be one of the finest examples of Spanish sculpture.

Following in the footsteps of the Pisans and other Tuscans, who had been instrumental in encouraging the skills of Romanesque church builders on the island, the new Spanish colonial rulers began to show their determination to excel in the realm of the arts as well. The best way of establishing contact with the people and buying their loyalty was undoubtedly via the churches and the art treasures they contained; they enabled them to impress and surreptitiously influence the masses.

Also clearly of Spanish origin is the **Sartiglia** (www.sartiglia.info), a spectacular competition for mounted riders which takes place on the last Sunday before Lent and on Shrove Tuesday. Cervantes describes a *Sortija* of this kind (even the name is very similar) in his world-famous picaresque novel, *Don Quixote*. The event is a riding competition between two leading riders and their attendants, masked and wearing typical Spanish dress, with lace mantilla and top hat. Lances at the ready, they are required to gallop at and pierce a hanging star. Magical powers are ascribed to the two leading riders, who are known as *componidoris*. It is said that the success

There are plenty of opportunities for horse-riding in this region.

Much of the countryside in the west is planted with vineyards.

Wild flowers grow amongst the thick, shrubby vegetation of the màcchia.

of the next harvest can be predicted from the number of times they manage to strike the star.

Around Oristano

Seven kilometres (4 miles) west of Oristano, built on a once marshy isthmus, is **Torre Grande** , an Aragonese tower which lends its name to the beguiling beach beside its cylindrical hulk. A 2km (1-mile) promenade lined with cafés and *gelaterie* makes it popular with families and couples.

To the south of Oristano the **Campidano** is a vast alluvial plain, in part still covered by coastal marshes and lagoon. The fertile alluvial soil and the abundance of water make this a very important region for Sardinian agriculture, and excellent vegetables, rice and wines are produced here. In the inner part of the plain, villages have an agriculturally based economy, while fishing is the major activity for communities living near the lagoons, for example Santa Giusta and Cabras.

Prickly pears grow in abundance.

The cathedral of **Santa Giusta** , 3km (2 miles) south of Oristano,

was built when Pisan influence on the region was at its zenith, not only in politics but also in the arts. Standing imposingly on a hill, the 12th-century trachyte basilica, a jewel of Pisan Romanesque architecture, with Arab and Lombard elements, served as a model for many churches in Sardinia. The interior, with its triple nave, is supported by granite and marble columns which are far older than the church itself: they were lifted from the Carthaginian-Roman settlements of Tharros and Othoca (a common practice at the time). Latest archaeological investigations indicate that Othoca, once a prosperous town, must have been located on the site of the present village of Santa Giusta.

Bird paradise under threat

Santa Giusta lies between two coastal marshes which are havens for island wildlife. The first, the **Stagno di Santa Giusta**, covers an area of some 900 hectares (2,200 acres) and is well stocked with fish. There are, however, many pressures on the

---

AN ENDANGERED SPECIES

Environmental lobbyists have been vociferous in their criticism of the traffic-ridden coastal road, since they fear its impact on an area which has served as nesting territory and sanctuary for many species of coastal and seabirds.

They fear, too, that increased numbers of tourists will drive away the huge but rare griffon vulture from this habitat. The griffon vulture *(Gyps fulvus)* is the last remaining of three large vulture species that lived on the island up to the mid-20th century. Numbers have been decimated in recent years, largely because of the use of hunters' poisoned baits. From a population of 1,000 in the 1940s, the number of birds recorded in 2007 was a mere 60 individuals. Some 90 pairs have been reintroduced and are now living in five different areas of Sardinia and the population is on the rise, while in all of the rest of Italy the species has completely disappeared. The conservation project aimed at saving the bird from extinction also concentrates on supplementing the food supply and creating protected areas. A study was also carried out to test the feasibility of a programme of semen collection and cryopreservation of the griffon vulture. Hopefully these efforts have ensured that the sight of the griffon vulture's colossal wingspan soaring over the Sardinian cliffs will not be consigned to memory and photographs.

wildlife, especially from heavy industry and the fishing sector. In 2009, the Sardinian regional government authorised a culling of cormorants wintering in Oristano's lakes (stagni). This measure was in contravention of European law and has enraged environmentalists.

The second lake, the **Stagno Pauli Maiori** (Big Swamp), is in fact smaller than Santa Giusta. It lies to the east, with its dense reeds, interspersed with tamarisk, providing a home for mallards, coots, marsh harriers, bitterns and the rare purple heron. Ruddy shelduck, which are already extinct in mainland Italy, can still be spotted in parts of the **Stagno di Cabras ⓴**, a lake lying to the west of Oristano. Its vast size – 2,000 hectares (5,000 acres) – helps to make it one of the most fascinating ecological wetlands in the whole of Europe.

Although it is directly linked to the sea, the lake displays a relatively low level of salinity; for this reason, the flamingos prefer the saltier waters of the **Stagno di Mistras** to the west. In autumn they settle in their hundreds

– even thousands – when they migrate from the Camargue in the south of France to spend the winter months in Sardinia. A wealth of unexpected discoveries awaits nature-lovers in the region surrounding Oristano. You can hire a local guide for a tour of the Stagno di Cabras. Until recently, the fishermen here used *fassonis* – narrow, one-man boats made of reeds similar to those that are still used on parts of the Nile and Lake Titicaca.

Silent churches

Those heading from Cabras to **San Salvatore ㉑** will feel themselves transported into another world as they approach the village isolated between the lagoons. For most of the year the village-sanctuary is utterly deserted, but it comes to life during the summer months when tourists arrive, and at the beginning of September when pilgrims from the surrounding villages come to take part in the nine-day *Sagra di San Salvatore* (Festival of the Redeemer).

During the festival they live in *cumbessias* (pilgrims' houses) praying,

FACT

The old Sardinian proverb *"Portant de Tharros sa perda a carros"* (They carry stones away from Tharros on carts) alludes to the recycling of the town's old walls to construct new buildings.

Beach of Capo San Marco.

The Corinthian columns at Tharros, the symbol of the town.

eating and sleeping in the company of the other visitors over a period of several days. The statue of Christ is borne in procession from Cabras to the church of San Salvatore, accompanied by youths in white robes, running barefoot.

It is noteworthy that here, too – as in Santa Cristina near Paulilatino – a Christian place of pilgrimage coincides with a pagan holy site. Beneath the present building lies a *hypogaeum* (ancient burial chamber; tel: 347-818 4069; irregular times, call for details) constructed by the first inhabitants of the area, the Nuraghic, as a water temple. Carthaginians used the three underground cellars as storerooms for their wares (the flourishing trading centre of Tharros lay only 5km/3 miles away); the Romans used them as a dungeon, and from the 4th century AD the Christians turned them into a catacomb church, which they decorated with monochrome wall paintings with divinities related to water worship: Venus, Mars, Eros, nymphs; the Punic writing of the word *rufus*, meaning "heal", is also frequently seen.

Interior of San Giovanni di Sinis.

Not far from San Salvatore, the church of **San Giovanni di Sinis** also has a long history. A simple 6th-century building was extended into a triple-naved edifice during the 9th–11th centuries, or possibly even earlier; the barrel vaulting of the roof rests on short, massive pillars. The stone blocks needed for the conversion were brought from nearby Tharros. From the 11th century onwards the once-magnificent Phoenician and Carthaginian trading city served only as a quarry – not only for the extension of San Giovanni in Sinis, but also for **Christano**. Here magnificent medieval buildings were constructed using marble and stone blocks already hewn into the appropriate shapes and often decorated with splendid carvings.

Tharros

At the southernmost tip of the Sinis peninsula lie the evocative remains of the Punic-Roman town of **Tharros** ㉒ (tel: 0783-370 019; archaeological site: summer 9am–7pm, winter 9am–5pm). It was founded by Phoenician merchants during the 8th century BC, who built their protected mooring spot upon an earlier Nuraghic village. It achieved incomparable prosperity before passing to Carthage in 510 BC, who transformed it into a naval base and Punic city. It passed into the hands of the Romans after the First Punic War (241 BC), who extended it considerably, adding basalt pavements, sewers, temples and aqueducts.

During the 8th and 9th centuries the inhabitants started to leave the town – possibly because of the Saracen raids which were an almost daily occurrence, but conceivably also because of the malaria which had reached epidemic proportions in a marshy district of the peninsula. Later, during the 11th century, when an attempt to resettle Tharros ended in complete failure, the new and rapidly growing town of Aristanis (Oristano) finally wrested supremacy from its declining neighbour. Its stones were thereupon plundered to build churches and other buildings in the new town across the gulf.

Sinis peninsula

The Sinis peninsula lies between Capo Mannu in the north and Capo San Marco in the south. The beach of **Is Arutas ㉓**, northwest of San Salvatore, consists of glittering round grains of quartz, and is now a protected zone after visitors started to take sand home as a souvenir. Nearby **Sa Mesa Longa** is a popular beach with families – a long rocky platform calms the surf here, creating a beautiful marine pool for paddling and swimming. Further to the north, by the **Capo sa Sturaggia**, the coast becomes steeper as it plunges seawards down yellowish-brown cliffs. Here the flocks of cormorants reign supreme, building their nests on the rocky crags.

A short distance further on is **Putzu Idu**, which has become a popular place to buy a holiday home for people living in Oristano, although the inauguration of the **Parco Nazionale della Penisola di Sinis** (Sinis Peninsula national park) has put an end to the uncoordinated building proposals which threatened the area.

Exploring Tharros.

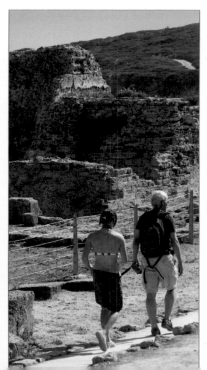

THARROS'S PLUNDERED PUNIC TREASURES

It was a Punic custom to bury the dead with rich funeral gifts: exquisite gold jewellery, precious stones, valuable glasses and fine pieces of pottery. Many such items can be seen in the principal archaeological museums of the island, especially in the Museo Archeologico Nazionale in Cagliari (see page 102) and the Museo Nazionale G.A. Sanna in Sassari (see page 153). But as organised excavations did not begin until recent times, some archaeological treasures inevitably fell into the hands of plunderers. An English aristocrat, Lord Vernon, removed the contents of 14 graves during the 19th century; and neither Charles Albert (1798–1849), the King of Savoy and Piedmont-Sardinia, nor the French novelist Honoré de Balzac (1799–1850), could resist the temptation to take a few precious "souvenirs" home with them. Of the magnificence of former days, only ruins and the remains of walls are left – the best-preserved dating from Roman times. Visitors with little experience of archaeological sites may find it difficult when confronted with these ruins to imagine a living town with temples, public baths, streets, shops and a colourfully mixed population. But anyone can appreciate the magnificent setting of the ruined city on its narrow peninsula jutting out into the Gulf of Oristano.

TIP

Weekend visitors to Bosa
Marina shouldn't miss
the opportunity to enjoy
spectacular coastal
views from the terrace of
the Torre Aragonese (Sat
3–6.30pm, Sun
10.30am–1pm and
3–6.30pm).

*Seaside activities on
Putzu Idu's beach.*

Santa Caterina di Pittinuri is an unpretentious modern seaside resort situated on an attractive rocky inlet, near which interesting examples of coastal erosion, such as the rock arch **S'Archittu**, are in evidence. Near the town lie the ruins of **Cornus ㉔**, probably founded by the Carthaginians during the 5th century BC.

During the First Punic War the native Sardinians and the Carthaginian immigrants, among whom relations had not always been convivial, joined together in an anti-Roman alliance – but this did not prevent their being defeated by the legions of Rome. Cornus remained a town of some importance even in Roman times; in about AD 1000 it was nonetheless abandoned by its inhabitants, who probably found a new place to live in Cuglieri, 15km (10 miles) away.

The road to **Cuglieri ㉕** climbs along the sides of Monte Ferru. The town has been the seat of old religious orders, a bishops' headquarters and the site of an important seminary. In days gone by there were no fewer than three monasteries in this farming village, and in **Scano di Montiferro** nearby. The region also has other remains bearing witness to even older civilisations: *tombe di giganti* and the ubiquitous nuraghi, of which there must have been three (hence the name) in **Tresnuraghes**.

From here it is worthwhile climbing down to the crystal-clear sea and the enchanting coastal strip. The leafy branches invariably lying on the village streets of **Flussio** and **Tinnura** tend to remind visitors of preparations for Palm Sunday. In fact, they are fronds of bog asphodel grass, spread out to dry before being woven into attractive basketwork, which is then offered for sale in the doorways of the houses along the main street. Passing through Suni, with its characteristically squat houses, the road continues downhill into Bosa.

Bosa

The little town of **Bosa ㉖** lies on the banks of the Temo, the only navigable river in Sardinia. Thanks to its attractive urban architecture and the gentle green of the surrounding countryside, Bosa is one of the most attractive towns in Sardinia.

It was founded by the Phoenicians and settled by the Romans before being ruled by a succession of Tuscan nobles. The town has two major districts: Sa Costa and Sa Piana. A residential area grew up and formed a link between the two districts; the main characteristic of Sa Piana is that the buildings are rather higher and the alleys narrower than in any other town on the island.

The district of the town known as **Sa Costa** clings with a succession of parallel rows of houses to the side of an 80-metre (260ft) hill, the summit of which is crowned by the **Castello Malaspina di Fosdinovo** (tel: 0187-680013; www.castellodifosdinovo.it; guided tours on the hour: May–Sept Wed–Mon 11am–noon and 4–6pm, Oct–Apr Sat 3–5pm, Sun 11am–noon and 3–5pm), which was built by the Malaspina family in 1112 and later extended by the rulers of Aragon. This district has no church

of its own, since the residents were dependent on the castle in religious as in other affairs. They were permitted to use the castle chapel, **Nostra Signora di Regnos Altos**, where in recent years a cycle of 14th–15th-century frescoes of the Catalan school was discovered. If the church is open, climb to the top of the ramparts for a magnificent view. Beneath the maze of cobblestone alleys and stairs which make up the streets of Sa Costa, the former free town of **Sa Piatta** sprawls across the plain by the river. The **Corso Emanuele II** contains some elegant patrician houses and the imposing **Cattedrale** (7am–12.30pm and 3–7pm), which has a 16th-century marble statue of *Madonna col Bambino*.

There is a small, picturesque river port by the bridge over the Temo river, and beyond the bridge extend the unusual terraced houses of **Sas Conzas** – former tanneries which present a fascinating example of industrial architecture of a bygone age.

In idyllic isolation on the left bank of the Temo, 2km (1 mile) from the

Bosa is beautifully situated on the River Temo.

town centre, stands the Romanesque-Gothic **Chiesa di San Pietro**. Constructed in the 11th century, the church formerly served as the cathedral of Bosa. As the presence of the necropolis indicates, it occupies the site of the Roman town.

Be sure to take a gentle stroll up to the fortress – wandering aimlessly through the Sa Costa district before climbing a further 111 steps between olive, fig and almond trees to the summit of the castle hill. In the alleys of Sa Costa black-clad women produce beautiful embroidery and sell it outside their homes – although the women are supposed to sell all their exquisite needlework to cooperatives, which then sell it at set prices in the tourist towns. Along with gold and silver filigree work, coral jewellery and woodcarving, this so-called *filet de Bosa* is eloquent proof of the craftwork tradition still practised here.

The nearby seaside resort of **Bosa Marina** ㉗ has a beach of darkish sand containing a high proportion of iron which is said to possess healing properties in the case of rheumatic illnesses. Today the beach is a more popular venue for windsurfers, and equipment can be hired locally in the summer months.

About 10 minutes' drive from Bosa is the pleasant hillside village of **Magomadas**, where you can enjoy a good lunch at Riccardo (see page 233).

From Bosa a road leads northwards in the direction of Alghero. It passes through an austere landscape with eroded slopes and strangely formed trachyte rocks. Skirting round the villages of **Montresta** and **Villanova Monteleone**, it then descends to the plain of Alghero via a series of vertiginous bends and switchbacks.

Since the 1960s Bosa and Alghero have also been linked by a new coastal road. Nonetheless, the stretch of coastline made accessible by this road arouses a wonderful sense of solitude more intense than almost anywhere else on the island; driving or hiking through the region is a real pleasure.

Fisherman and his boat on the River Temo.

THE SOUTHWEST

From beautiful, remote countryside to sand dunes and beaches via prehistoric settlements and former mining towns – this area is an eclectic mix.

Map on page 184

Main Attractions

Chia
Isola di Sant'Antioco
Isola di San Pietro
Grotte di Is Zuddas
Iglésias
Arbus
Piscinas
Arborea
Sanluri
Su Nuraxi

The southwest mixes natural beauty in its beaches, dunes and geological marvels – including limestone caves and a "Geopark" – with the relics and scars of a fascinating history. Costa del Sud and Costa Verde sand dunes and granite outcrops are still largely untouched, bar a few lavish resorts and golf courses, while the splintered rocks of Isola di Sant'Antioco and Isola di San Pietro possess lots of charm and seafood. At Carbónia and Iglésias, rich seams of lead, zinc, silver, copper and iron have been mined for millennia by successive foreign rulers. Vestiges of exploitation, conflict and culture left by Neolithic Ozieri, Nuraghic, Phoenician, Roman, Spanish, Fascist and Italian hegemonies can be explored on hilltops and museums, and down mine shafts.

The alluvial plains known as the Campidano divide the southwest from the rest of the island – and are crossed by two motorways (*autostrade*): the north–south A131 and the A130 west to Iglesias.

Leaving Cagliari on the SS 195, heading southwards towards the **Capo Malfatano**, you pass the lagoon of the **Stagno di Santa Gilla ❶**, an area of international importance which has managed to survive despite creeping industry and aircraft noise. The lagoon and ancient Macchiareddu salt flats extend over 4,000 hectares (9,800 acres) and have been used since Nuraghic times for the production of sea salt.

Roman city

About 30km (18 miles) from Cagliari is Pula, and on a small peninsula nearby stands the Roman town of **Nora ❷**. The oldest Phoenician inscription was found here, dating from approximately 1000 BC. In 238 BC Nora was chosen as the capital of the Roman province of Sardinia,

Mosaic floor, Nora.

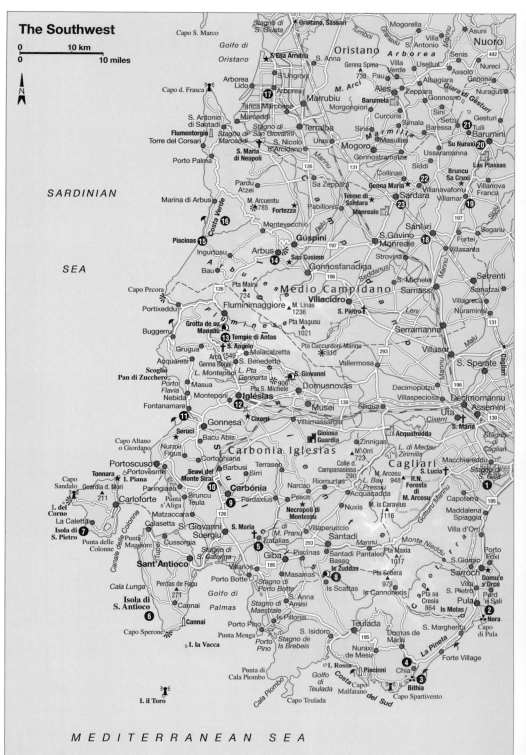

The Southwest

0 ____ 10 km
0 ____ 10 miles

N

largely due to its favourable location and a fine natural harbour. From the 5th century AD the town sank into insignificance, to be reawakened after centuries of oblivion by archaeological excavations during the 1950s. They revealed what is thought to be a Phoenician temple to the fertility goddess Tanit, a 2nd-century Roman temple, a theatre and on the *sa punta 'e su coloru*, the Cape of Snakes, a Phoenician-Carthaginian holy place.

It is possible to take a free guided tour (also in English) of Nora's remaining excavations contained within an **archaeological site** (tel: 070-921 470; 10am–sunset). On the beach at Nora is the church where the 350-year-old May procession of *Sagra Sant' Efisio* ends. According to tradition, the underground crypt preserves the remains of the saint.

Stunning coastal route

In contrast to the north of the island, the south coast of Sardinia has not as yet suffered from overdevelopment. However, there are signs of billionaire investments at the world-class **Is Molas** golf course and the massive Forte Village complex. This resort lies between Santa Margherita and Bithia, taking advantage of the 10km (6-mile) stretch of sandy beach, **La Pineta**.

Bithia ❸ is accessible via the nearby village of Chia, where you can see the Saracen Tower built in the 17th century to defend the island against the Turks. It is also the site of a Phoenician-Roman township with a temple complex, where a likeness of the archaic deity Bes, originating in Egypt, was discovered.

In **Chia ❹** there are fine granite sand dunes that can reach up to 24 metres (75ft) and upon which ancient juniper trees grow. The wild, unspoilt topography recalls the landscape of the west coast of Scotland, but on closer exploration of the flora and fauna – lots of yellow broom instead of thorny gorse sprouting amidst the familiar granite outcrops, and bulbous exotic insects instead of midges – reveal its true Mediterranean character. A dip into the warm, shallow emerald and deep-blue waters off **Spiaggia Campana** and gorgeous **Spiaggia Su**

Ancient Roman remains found at Nora.

The church of Sant'Antioco stands on the site of a 6th-century church.

Relaxing in the shade in Pula.

Giudeu make it a wonderful place to relax, bathe and snorkel.

The coastal road now becomes the Strada Panoramica della Costa del Sud, and goes past **Capo Spartivento** with views over largely unspoilt southern coastline, through a sparsely populated area to a lighthouse and then on to the **Capo Malfatano**. The rocky headlands are emphasised by additional watchtowers, such as the 17th-century **Torre Piscinni**, which was built over a Roman quarry.

Near the little hamlet of **Porto di Teulada** the road leaves the coast, skirting the **Monte s'Impeddau** (267 metres/876ft), a vast area used by NATO forces for target practice. Near **Sant'Anna Arresi**, which holds an annual international jazz festival (www.santannarresijazz.it), a little side road leads back towards the coast, to the seaside resort of **Porto Pino**. There are the many coastal marshes hereabouts: the **Stagno de Is Brebeis, Stagno di Maestrale, Stagno Baiocca**, and the **Stagno di Santa Caterina** shortly before you arrive in Sant'Antioco. Ornithologists flock here to watch flamingos, herons and cormorants. In the old ghost village of **Tratalias** ❺ stands the Pisan-Romanesque church of Santa Maria (Tue–Sun 9am–1pm), built in 1213 in grey trachyte.

Isola di Sant'Antioco

At 109 sq km (42 sq miles), the volcanic **Isola di Sant'Antioco** ❻ is the largest island lying off the coast of Sardinia, and the fourth-largest in Italy. It is reached via a causeway; just before entering the village of Sant'Antioco itself you can see the remains of an old **Roman bridge**. Sant'Antioco is a bustling little port with a picturesque old town centre and pine tree-shaded main street, the **Corso Vittorio Emanuele**. During the Phoenician era (9th and 8th centuries BC), **Sulcis**, as Sant'Antioco was called, was one of the most important port cities in the Mediterranean area, dispatching ores mined in the region. The **Museo Archeologico** (tel: 0781-82105; www.archeotur.it; daily 9am–7pm) has displays of recent excavations. More relics lay in the catacombs beneath the parish church. On the way to the necropolis, in an early 20th-century farmhouse in Via Mazzini, is the **Ethnographic Museum** (tel: 389-050 5107; www.archeotur.it; daily Apr–Sept 9am–8pm, 1–15 Oct 9am–1pm and 3.30–8pm, mid-Oct–Mar 9.30am–1pm and 3–6pm).

Not far away lies the **Tophet** (Via Castello; www.archeotur.it; daily 9am–7pm), the ritual ground of the Phoenicians where their deceased children were cremated. Countless urns containing children's ashes stand on the archaeological site close to the vast **Necropolis**.

During the First Punic War, Sulcis acted as a Carthaginian naval base, which in turn led to harsh retaliatory measures by the forces of the Roman empire. Under the emperors the town regained much of its former importance, but it was plundered on several occasions by the Saracen hordes. During the 16th century virtually all the inhabitants abandoned the city. Only in the 19th century did it rise again from oblivion, a trend which has continued as a result of the local tourist industry.

Calasetta

More attractive is the little port of **Calasetta**, which lies on the northernmost tip of the island. Founded around 1770 to house the Ligurian fishermen arriving from Tabarca in Tunisia, the chequerboard street layout and low, two-storey houses recall the Arab influence. The parish church in the main piazza has a belltower of Arab derivation, and the local popularity of couscous is a culinary relic of this time.

If you are on the island in May or early June and have the stomach for it, take a boat trip to witness the *matanza*, the bloody but dramatic ritual in which tuna fish are harpooned and hoisted on board by hand. During the *matanza*, a complicated system of nets is erected in order to lure the fish into the *camere della morte* (death chamber), in which the sea turns crimson with blood as the tuna are killed. Processing takes place in the *tonnara* (tuna factory) on the **Punta Maggiore**. The entire procedure attracts large crowds of onlookers every year.

For a less gruesome spectacle, make a visit to the **Museo d'Arte**

EAT

A mix of Ligurian, Sardinian and Tunisian influences goes into *cucina Calasettana* creation *pilau* (couscous with crustaceans) and *pè di porcu* (pig's trotters).

Sea view from Sant'Antioco.

TIP

The *Matrimonio
Mauritano* (Mauritano
wedding) on the first
Sunday in August in
Santadi represents a
genuine example of
traditional Sulcis country
life: a wedding ceremony
celebrated according to
centuries'-old customs.

Contemporanea (tel: 0781-840 717;
June–Sept Tue–Sun 6–9pm, Oct–May
Sat–Sun 10am–1pm), housing the Lei-
nardi collection of Constructivist and
abstract works.

Isola di San Pietro

Calasetta is also the starting point for
the crossing to the pretty **Isola di San
Pietro ❼**. Its area of 50 sq km (20 sq
miles) makes it the third-largest of the
offshore islands. The only place of any
significance is **Carloforte**, a pleasant
town overlooking the port founded
in 1738 under the King of the House
of Savoy, Charles Emmanuel III. As in
the case of Sant'Antioco, the island
was settled by Ligurians; during the
16th century many of them were kid-
napped and borne off to Tunisia, but
were later set free. The island has volcanic rock formations and pillars such
as the Punta delle Colonne and Capo
Sandalo, and myriad species of birds,
among them Eleonora's falcon, named
in honour of Eleonora d'Arborea who
first declared that the bird should be
protected in the 14th century. For years
Sardinian conservationists have been

lobbying to have the island declared
a national park. Apart from a *grotta* in
the south, San Pietro can also offer the
visitor a *tonnara* (tuna factory) in the
north of the island.

The inland route

Leaving Cagliari in a northwesterly
direction on the SS 130, pass **Elmas
Airport** and continue towards Iglésias
and Sant'Antioco. To the west in the
mountainous area is **Monte Arcosu**
(Sat and Sun, June–July 8am–7pm,
Sept–June 9am–6pm, Aug by appointment only), the largest World Wildlife
Fund Reserve in Italy, covering 3,000
hectares (7,400 acres). It is one of the
last habitats for the Sardinian deer.

About 15km (10 miles) from the
capital lies the pretty village of **Uta**,
and some way outside the village lies
the church of Santa Maria (built in AD
1140), a most beguiling Romanesque
country church. A few miles south of
Siliqua stands the 13th-century **Castello di Acquafredda** (www.castello
diacquafredda.it; daily 10am–6pm), on a
volcanic outcrop overlooking the Cix-
erri river.

*Statue of statesman
Quintino Sella, in
Piazza Sella,
Carbónia.*

OZIERI REMAINS

North of the village of Villaperuccio is the
Necropoli di Montessu (daily, summer
9am–1pm and 3–8pm, winter 9am–1pm
and 2–5pm), the most important rock
necropolis in Sardinia. Dating from the
late Neolithic period of Ozieri Culture
(end of the 4th to beginning of the 3rd
millennium BC), it contains almost 40
domus de janas, the so-called "houses
of the fairies", some of which retain their
original red and yellow walls. Trachyte or
granite menhirs litter the mountains
Monte Narcao and Terrazzu. More creepy
domus de janas chambers can be seen
at **Marchiana** and **Sa Grutta**. The Museo
Archeologico in nearby Santadi (Via Umberto I; tel: 0781-954 203; www.museoar-
cheologicosantadi.it; daily winter 9am–1pm
and 3–5pm, summer 9am–1pm and
5–7pm) is filled with prehistoric finds,
including ceramics from Montessu.

The scenic SS 293 winds around the Colle della Campanasissa, Villaperuccio and Monte Pranu. Abandoned stations of the narrow-gauge railway criss-cross this mining region of the **Sulcis**. Visitors can park by one of the stations and walk along the routes of the former tracks. Near **Nuxis** stands a rare example of Sardinian Byzantine architecture: the country church of **Sant'Elia** (daily), dating back to the 8th century. West of here is the Montessu Necropolis.

The territory of **Santadi** belongs to the part of the island which emerged from the sea in the Lower Cambrian era. The abundance of limestone and schist have created natural caves rich in weathered rocks and crystal formations. Particularly worth a visit for their fine stalagmites and stalactites are the **Grotte di Is Zuddas** ❽ (tel: 0781-955 741; www.grotteiszuddas.com; daily, times vary, check website), 8km (5 miles) south of Santadi.

The economy of the region is based on sheep rearing and agriculture, as is demonstrated by the existence of numerous *furriadroxius*: small rural hamlets created by shepherds in the 18th century in order to protect their flocks from Saracen incursions. **Casa Museo Sa Domu Antiga** at Santadi (Via Mazzini; tel: 0781-955 955; Tue–Sun summer 9am–1pm and 4–7pm, winter 9am–1pm and 3–6pm) recreates the interiors and courtyard activities of typical Sulcis peasant dwellings.

Fascist architecture

The former mining town of **Carbónia** ❾ was built in just two years following Mussolini's 1936 Abyssinian campaign and subsequent international sanctions. The town is a typical example of Fascist architecture, with broad streets converging on the main square, **Piazza Roma**, where the buildings are heavy and imposing.

The sulphurous "Sulcis coal" produced was supposed to ensure self-sufficiency but was virtually useless. Sulcis's mining history is related at the **Museo del Carbone**, housed in the former mine Grande Miniera di Serbariu (tel: 0781-62727; www.museo delcarbone.it; mid-June–mid Sept daily 10am–7pm, mid-Sept–mid-June Tue–Sun 10am–6pm), which ceased

Carloforte on the island of San Pietro.

activity in 1967. Also worth a look is the **Museo Archeologico Villa Sulcis** (Via Napoli; Apr–Sept Tue–Sun 10am–7pm, Oct–Mar Wed–Sun 10am–5pm), where finds from local *domus de janas*, such as bronze statuettes and jewels, are on display.

In stark contrast to Carbónia's Fascist architecture is the important nearby archaeological site at **Monte Sirai** (Apr–Sept Tue–Sun 10am–7pm, Oct–Mar Wed–Sun 10am–3pm). The former Nuraghe settlement was destroyed during the 7th century by Phoenicians from Sulcis (Sant'Antioco), who then constructed a fortress here. Today you can explore atmospheric remains of an acropolis, houses and a necropolis. Views of the industrial havoc wrought throughout the countryside plunge you back into the present. From the nearby harbour of **Portoscuso** you can take a boat to the Isola di San Pietro.

Miners' towns

Continuing along the road in a northerly direction, strike off westwards towards **Fontanamare** ⑪, soon after the **Gonnesa** turning. Driving

In the Old Town of Carbónia.

through the district surrounding the reedy estuary of the **Torre Gonnesa**, the road eventually reaches the sea. Of the former coal port very little remains today; abandoned buildings and slag heaps take on the appearance of prehistoric ruins.

The mountains and coastline of the Sulcis and the Iglesiente show the scars of centuries of exploitation. From Fontanamare there is a breathtaking corniche leading to the mining villages of **Nebida** and **Masua**. The **Scoglio Pan di Zúcchero**, a vast rocky outcrop ("sugarloaf"), rises dramatically from the sea on the horizon. In this area there are many mines or part of mines which can be visited with specialist guides (contact Igea, tel: 0781-491 300; www.igeaspa.it), including: Porto Flavia in **Masua**, where minerals were taken from tunnels directly to ships for export; and Galleria Henry, in **Buggerru**, which clings to a cliff above the sea on Planu Sartu plateau.

The most important town in the southwest of the island is the mining town of **Iglésias** ⑫ (derived from *ecclesia*, Latin for church), at the heart of the zinc- and lead-quarrying district. Founded in the 13th century, it was a significant silver-mining centre; the community was even awarded the right to mint its own coins. The Old Town was built according to a chequerboard plan; it is clustered around the Gothic-Romanesque **Cattedrale di Santa Chiara** (Fri–Wed) on Piazza Municipio, and filled with attractive townhouses with wrought-iron balconies. The **Museo delle Arti Minerárie** (tel: 0781-350 037; www.museoarteminueraria.it; June–Sept Sat–Sun 6.30–8.30pm, other times by appointment) has over 8,000 rare stones and fossils discovered during mining excavations alongside some intriguing mining equipment.

Spectacular mountain road

The Iglésias to Oristano road (SS 126), with its hairpin bends, views over vast oak forests and dizzying drops, requires careful driving but is well worth the effort. This underpopulated region can compete with Barbagia in terms of remoteness and beauty. At the top of the pass, at the **Arcu Genna Bogai**, a

valley vista frames the pillared **Tempio di Antas ⑬** (summer daily 9am–1pm, 3–8pm, winter Sat–Sun 9am–1pm), where Sardus Pater was worshipped. A Roman place of worship during the 2nd century AD, it was built on the site of a much earlier Punic temple. According to Sardinian mythology, Sardus Pater is the original ancestor of the island's inhabitants. He reputedly came from Africa to populate the island, but the origins of the deity can be traced back to a Punic god. Today, only six of the pillars and the partially restored floor plan of the temple remain; its undeniable attraction is derived primarily from its enchanting site.

Following the course of the Rio Antas on the SS 126, you pass the **Grotta di su Mannau** (tel: 0781-580 411; www.sumannau.it; Apr–June daily 9.30am–5.30pm, July–Oct daily 9.30am–6.30pm, winter by appointment only) and the small town of Fluminimaggiore. At the village of **Arbus ⑭** to the north, the **Museo del Coltello** (Museum of Knives; Via Roma; tel: 070-975 220; www.museodelcoltello.it; Mon–Fri 9am–12.30pm and 3.30–7pm; free) displays *s'erburesa*

MINING

Some regions of Sardinia consist of rocks considerably older than other mountains in the Mediterranean, which means much richer mineral deposits.

Sardinia's southwest (Sulcis and Iglesiente), southeast (Gerrei and Sarrabus) and Nurra in the northwest, consist of rocks with rich mineral deposits, especially lead, zinc, silver, copper and iron.

Around 4,500 years ago settlers began to extract and smelt metals (copper, lead and silver), then the Nuraghic civilisation prospered from their trading links and skills in metalworking. Evidence of the degree of mining activity in Phoenician, Carthaginian and Roman times can be found in the tools and oil lamps discovered in mine shafts, as well as in vast slag heaps such as the one at Campo Romano near Iglésias. Under the Roman empire, Christians were often exiled to the mining areas of the Iglesiente. Under Pisan rule, silver casting around Iglésias (Monteponi, Campo Pisano) became prevalent. During the 13th century Iglésias, the former city of Uilla Ecclesiae, received its charter as a "silver town" with exemplary mining regulations and municipal rights under Pisan law, including that of minting its own

coins. In 1343, 20 years after their conquest of Sardinia, the rulers of Aragon imported Sardinian mineworkers to Spain in order to improve the silver-mining industry.

Sardinian mining creaked back to life in the 19th century – thanks to increased mechanisation and the use of explosives. Piedmontese Mining Laws of 1848 permitted foreign investors to circumvent the property rights of Sardinian landowners.

Sardinia's mining heyday waned at the turn of the last century, with falling prices and declining productivity. Mussolini ignited an artificial boom with the intention of making Italy strong and independent. It was a sham: Carbónia was founded to produce sulphurous lignite (with a combustion rate scarcely above that of peat), dubbed "Sulcis coal" by Musscolin's propaganda machine.

Visitors to Buggerru will have difficulty imagining that the mining town of 100 years ago – complete with public services and a concert hall – was the first town on Sardinia to have electricity. Indeed, there is hardly a trace left of the living and working conditions which in 1904 led to bloody unrest and the first general strike in Italy's history.

The parish church at Villamar.

Inside the Grotta di San Giovanni.

knives – hand-crafted clasp knives from the town – and has a reconstruction of a blacksmith's workshop.

San Cosimo is a well-preserved *tombe di giganti* by a little road leading from Arbus to Gonnosfanadiga. Heading west from the SS 126 before you reach Arbus, a side road leads down to the mining communities of **Ingurtosu** and **Naracáuli**, consisting of miners' quarters (open but not secure) and management headquarters (closed to the public).

The dirt road continues down to the stunning sand dunes of **Piscinas** ⓯ that cover about 30 sq metres (almost 12 sq miles). The 100-metre (330ft) high dunes of fine sand are being continually reshaped by the mistral, a strong north wind that blows in from France. This unique ecological niche is an ideal habitat for many animals, including foxes, wild cats and rabbits, whose footprints you can usually spot in the early mornings.

On the Costa Verde

A small winding road leads from Gúspini along the ridge to **Montevecchio**. The lead and zinc mines here closed in 1960 but it's possible to explore the 1876 Liberty-style pit and view a mineral collection (tel: 070-973 173; www.minieramontevecchio.it; guided tours: times vary, check website). Continuing on you reach the **Costa Verde** ⓰; the name refers more to the hinterland than to the coastal margin itself, for its massive sand dunes recall a desert rather than a green and pleasant land. From **Marina di Arbus** the coastal strip is open to vehicles in both directions. Despite a law passed in 1990 forbidding development of this particular coastal strip, small fishing villages have sprouted ugly holiday complexes.

Arborea

Heading north again, you negotiate 30km (20 miles) of arduous bends to reach the **Golfo di Oristano**, behind which lie the **Stagno di Marceddi** and the **Stagno di San Giovanni**. Back on the SS 126 is **Arborea** ⓱, originally called Mussolinia after Il Duce. Arborea was laid out along new-town principles in 1928 in order to populate

SAN GIOVANNI GROTTO

The **Grotta di San Giovanni** (daily) near **Domusnovas** carves through the oldest rocks in Italy, which are over 500 million years old. A road, some 900 metres (3,000ft) long, follows the course of the river through the stunning grotto. At the end of the tunnel there is a restaurant, a bar and a picnic area. Within this vast **Foresta Demaniale Marganai** territory, at 720 metres (2,360ft) above sea level, is the Giardino Montano Linasia, 9,000 sq metres (96,900 sq ft) brimming with native plants and many other rare species. Its museum, Casa Natura, contains collections of fossils, minerals and archaeological finds (May–Sept Tue, Thur, Sat and Sun 9am–12pm and 4.30–7.30pm, Oct–Apr Sat–Sun 9.30am–1pm).

the plain of Oristano, which had been made agriculturally viable by the construction of irrigation canals. It was decided to introduce settlers from Venetia and the plain of the Po; they defied the endemic malaria and transformed the region into fertile land. The little town possesses a few fine Art Nouveau villas and an equestrian sports centre called Horse Country.

Su Nuraxi

Following the SS 131, take the exit to **Sanluri** ⑱ where, in 1409, the Aragonese troops led by Martin the Young won the battle that put an end to Sardinia's independence. The Castello di Eleonora d'Arborea houses the **Museo Risorgimentale Duca d'Aosta** (tel: 070-930 7105; July–mid-Sept Sun 10am–1pm, 4.30–9pm, Tue–Fri 4.30–9pm, mid-Sept–June Sun 9.45am–1pm, 3–7pm). The museum contains 19th-century military exhibits and Napoleonic memorabilia. On the upper floor is the **Museo della Ceroplastica**, displaying miniature 16th-century wax sculptures. Also in Sanluri is the **Museo Storico**

Etnografico (Via Cappuccini; tel: 070-930 7107 by appointment), attached to the Convento dei Cappuccini.

On the way to Barumini is the small village of **Villamar** ⑲. The parish church contains a large polyptych, painted in 1518, situated behind the main altar, which was the most important work of the Sardinian painter Pietro Cavaro. Just after the village, a road on the left leads to the Nuraghic site of **Bruncu Sa Cruxi** (daily).

Su Nuraxi ⑳ (tel: 070-936 8128; daily 9am–dusk; guided tours every 30 minutes), about 1km (0.5 mile) to the west of Barumini, consists of a large Nuraghic fortress dating from the 13th to the 6th century BC, surrounding a massive round 15th-century BC defensive tower with a well. This Unesco World Heritage site, excavated in 1949, reveals fascinating layers of construction including 200 small circular huts, Carthaginian and Roman remnants and a canal system.

Wild animals and springs

South of Su Nuraxi, the appropriately named Marmilla (from the word for

Ask at the local tourist office for horse-riding centres.

Castle ruins at Las Plassas.

bosom) rises out of the plain. Perched on top is an ancient fortress marking the frontier between the former *giudicati* of Arborea and Cagliari. The ruins of the castle of **Las Plassas** date from the 12th century. Between Barumini and Las Plassas is the **Sardegna in Miniatura park** (tel: 070-9361 004; www.sardegnainminiatura.it; Apr–Oct daily 9.30am–7pm), where the island's most important archaeological sites and monuments are reproduced in 1:20–25 scale.

Just to the northwest of Barumini is **Tuili ㉑**, an unspoilt village, perfect for a stroll soaking up the island's old way of life. Seek out the polyptych of San Pietro, painted by the Master of Castelsardo (1500) in the parish church.

The **Giara di Gesturi**, a volcanic high plateau to the north, is famed for its 500 wild horses (*cavallini*); the isolated table mountain is covered by myriad large and small rainwater ponds that in the spring are covered by various *ranunculi* (aquatic plants), creating a unique and enchanting landscape. The plateau has also become home to a variety of birds, some of which are migratory. It is possible to hire a guide to take you on a horseback tour of the area.

In the town of **Villanovaforru ㉒**, the **Museo Archeologico Genna Maria** (Viale Umberto; tel: 070-930 050; www.gennamaria.it; Tue–Sun, Apr–Sept 9.30am–1pm and 3.30–7pm, Oct–Mar 9.30am–1pm and 3.30–6pm) displays Nuraghic artefacts found in the nearby nuraghe complex of **Genna Maria**, 1km (0.5 mile) west of the town.

Sardinia has a number of springs which have been exploited for thermal cures. The town of **Sardara ㉓** was famous in Roman times for its healing spas, and today they are used in the treatment of rheumatic illnesses. Sardara also contains an important sacred spa from the era of the Nuraghi; it rises near the **Chiesa di Sant'Anastasia**. The new **Museo Civico di Sardara** (Piazza Libertà; tel: 070-938 6183; Tue–Sun, June–Sept 9am–1pm and 4–7pm, Oct–May 9am–1pm and 5–8pm) displays material ranging from pre-Nuraghic pottery to objects belonging to the *Giudicati* period.

The Unesco World Heritage site of Su Nuraxi.

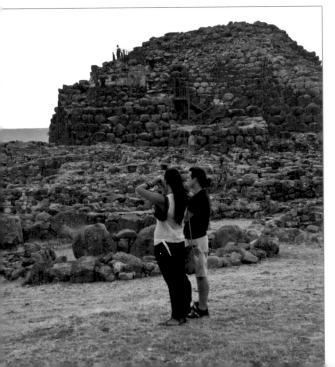

LA GIUDICESSA

Eleonora d'Arborea, born in Catalonia in 1347, is celebrated as a Sardinian national heroine. Her strong leadership, under the title *Giudicessa*, and forward-thinking laws make her an iconic figure on the island. Firstly she took the helm after her brother Hugo was assassinated and then her husband was captured and imprisoned in Cagliari's towers of Pancrazio and Elefante. Eleonora refused to acknowledge the sovereignty of the Aragonese, uniting virtually the whole of the island in her resistance, during a fierce four-year tussle in the 1380s. In 1392 she was responsible for the famous *Carta de Logu*, a comprehensive and enlightened legal code which governed the lives of the islanders well into the 19th century.

The Roman temple at Antas.

THE ART OF THE MURALES

As a form of public art, murals communicate directly to a wide audience. In Sardinia they are becoming an artistic tradition.

Brilliantly coloured murals (*murales*) on satirical, political or social themes are a popular form of expression in Sardinia and can be found in many villages around the island. The tradition of mural painting in Sardinia dates back to the 1960s and reached a peak in 1975 in the town of Orgosolo in the Barbagia, when the local art teacher Francesco del Caslon and his students decided to fill the town with murals on local and universal themes. The Italian Association of Painted Towns was formed to preserve and publicise towns with murals and to promote cultural and creative links between the regions. Perhaps the most famous touristic murals are to be found in the village of San Sperate, about 8km (5 miles) northeast of Uta, which contains works by the local artist Pinuccio Sciola. The murals here are not as vibrant, numerous or political as they are in Orgosolo. Instead they are painted in the muted tones of the Sardinian countryside and represent bucolic and domestic scenes.

Fonni's murals are less overtly political than those of Orgosolo.

Another Orgosolo mural illustrating shepherds' strength of feeling against industrialisation.

Mural of a religious procession in Fonni.

Goats in Orgosolo.

MURALS IN ORGOSOLO

If you're travelling in the Barbagia region, make a detour to Orgosolo to see some of the town's 150 murals. On Via Deledda there are characters drawn from the books of Grazia Deledda. Along Via Gramsci is a mural depicting the life of the politician, one of the founders of the Italian Communist Party; at No. 60 another depicts the tragic events leading to the end of the Baader-Meinhof Group and at No.166 is a mural showing shepherds protesting against not being able to leave their pastures fallow in the spring with the slogan "*Vardamos o non vardamos?*" (To keep or not to keep?). Opposite is a mural with the message "The young want to work, not shoot" – a reference to the town's reputation for banditry. Further on is a mural protesting against noise pollution. On Via Mercato on the walls of the library are paintings by local artists; in front of the parish church is a scene from a bandit hunt, while other murals indicate strong opposition to war and militarism.

Nuoro mural on the rights of women.

Mamoida mural showing Mamuthones in the traditional costume of masks, cow bells and goatskins.

Anti-war mural in Orgosolo: "Fertilisers, not missiles".

Lago di Gusana, near Gavoi, and beyond.

THE BARBAGIA

In the heart of the island, this region of rugged mountains, raw beauty and isolated villages characterises the essential Sardinia.

The Barbagia, which runs almost parallel to the mountain range of the Gennargentu, is the highest of the sub-regions of Sardinia. The name is of Roman origin and is derived from the Latin *Barbaria* or *Barbaricum*. The Roman conquerors described as Barbarians any people whose culture was based neither on the Roman nor the Greek civilisation, and whose social order and lifestyle were markedly different from their own (the people here resisted Roman colonisation for longer than those in any other Sardinian region). It was probably a *giudice* from the *giudicato* of Arborea who first subdivided the region into five sections: Barbagia di Ollolai, di Seui, di Seulo, di Belvì and Supramonte.

Prehistory and history

Remains of antiquity, bearing witness to the early settlement of the area, can be found here as elsewhere in the form of the nuraghi, which date from the 15th to the 2nd century BC. Unlike those to be found elsewhere on Sardinia, most of Barbagia's nuraghi, *tombe di giganti* (giants' graves) and *sas pedras fittas* (massive standing stones) are remarkably well preserved. Examples of the last stand at Gavoi-Lodine, not far from the original Byzantine cemetery of Nostra Signora d'Itria, as well as Grillu (near Fonni) and Ovodda. Archaeologists reckon they

Sweet chestnuts.

were worshipped as late as the 6th century AD, before local inhabitants and their chieftain Ospiton were converted to Christianity by Pope Gregory I.

Other stone relics worth visiting are the *domus de janas* (fairy dwellings), dating back to the Neolithic age (3500 BC). Legend maintains that they were inhabited by fairies or virgins; they took the form of small houses or caves hewn from the bedrock and measured about 1–2 metres (3–5ft) in height.

Ancient scientific and historical texts describe the inhabitants of the

Main Attractions
Barumini
Aritzo
Tonara
Desulo
Sorgono
Fonni
Gavoi
Mamoiada
Nuoro
Bitti

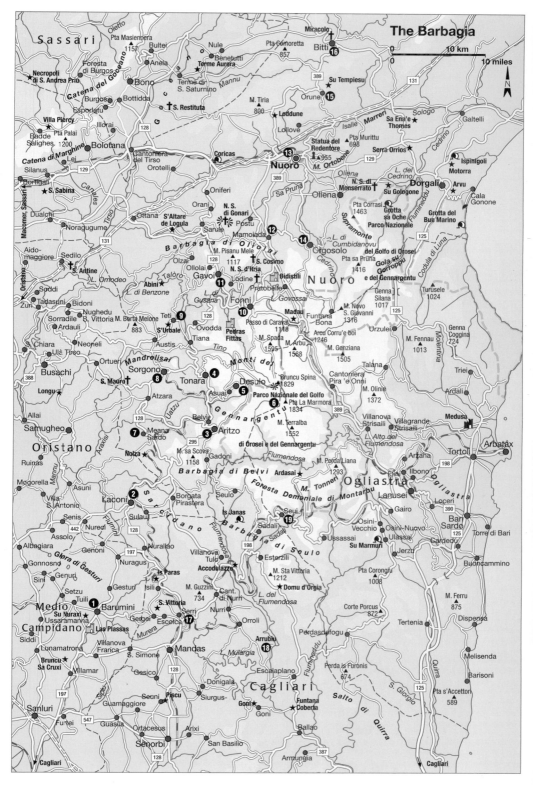

The Barbagia

0   10 km

0   10 miles

N

Sassari

Oletto
Pta Masiemera
1157
Bultei
Nule
Benetutti
Terme Aurora
Pta Cumoretta
857
Bitti **16**

Necropoli
di S. Andrea Priú
Foresta
di Burgos
Anela
Catena del Goceano
Bono
Terme di
S. Saturnino
Miracolo

Su Tempiesu
131

Burgos
Bottidda
S. Restituta
M. Tiria
800
Orune **15**

Esporlatu
Illorai
Lodune
Lollove
Isalle
Marreri
Sa Ena'e
Thomes
Galtelli

Villa Piercy
Pta Palai
1200
Lei
Bolotana
Cantoniera
del Tirso
Coricas
Statua del
Redentore
955
Pta Murittu
698
Sologo
Ispinigoli
Motorra

Badde
Salighes
Catena di Marghine
128
Orotelli
Nuoro **13**
M. Ortobene
Oliena
Serra Orrios
L. del
Cedrino
Dorgali
Arvu

Silanus
Lei
129
Oniferi
Sa Pruna
389
N. S. di
Monserrato
Su Gologone
Cala
Gonone

Portidali
S. Sabina
Canales
Tirso
Ottana
Orani
N. S.
di Gonari
Postu
Sarule
Oliena
Pta Corrasi
1463
Grotta
sa Oche
Parco Nazionale
Grotta del
Bue Marino

Dualchi
Noragugume
131
S'Altare
de Lógula
Mamoiada **12**
Orgosolo **14**
L. di
Cumbidanovu
Supramonte
del Golfo di Orosei
Gola su
Gorroppu
e del Gennargentu
Codula di Luna
125

Aido-
maggiore
Sedilo
S. Antine
L. Omodeo
Olzai
Ollolai
Barbagia di Ollolai
M. Pisanu Mele
1117
S. Cosimo
Lodine
N. S. d'Itria
Bidistili
Cedrino
Pta sa Pruna
1416
Genna
Silana
1017
Turusele
1024
Genna
Coggina
724

Soddì
Tadasuni
Bidoni
Nughedu
Abini
Taloro
Gavoi **11**
Pratobello
Govossa
Nuoro
M. Novo
S. Giovanni
1316
M. Fennau
1013

Zuri
Sorradile
Ardauli
B. Vittoria M. Berta Melone
883
Teti **9**
S'Urbale
Fonni **10**
Madau
Funtana
Bona
Passo di Caravai
1118
Arcu Corru'e boi
1246
M. Arbu
1568
M. Genziana
1505
Urzulei
M. Fennau
1013
Genna
Coggina
724

S. Chiara
Ulè Tirso
Neoneli
Ovodda
Tiana
Pedras
Fittas
Tino
M. Spada
1595
Talana

388
Busachi
Ortueri
Sorgono **8**
Austis
Mandrelisai
Monti del
Desulo
Asuai
Bruncu Spina
1829
Cantoniera
Pira 'e Onni
M. Olinie
1372
Triei
Ardali

Longu
Allai
S. Mauro
Atzara
Tonara **4**
Aritzo **3**
Desulo
Parco Nazionale del Golfo
Gennargentu
Pta La Marmora
1834
Medusa

Samugheo
Ruinas
Oristano
Meana
Sardo **7**
Belvì
Nolza
M. sa Scova
Gadoni
1158
295
M. Terralba
1552
di Orosei e del Gennargentu
Flumendosa
389
Villanova
Strisaili
Villagrande
Strisaili
Alto del
Flumendosa
Artana
Ilbono
Ogliastra
Tortolì
Arbatax

Mogorella
Asuni
Laconi **2**
Su
dano
Borgata
Pirastera
Seulo
Is Janas
Sadali
Barbagia
di
Seulo
Foresta Demaniale di Montarbu
M. Tonneri
Barbagia di Belvì
Ardasai
M. Perda Liana
1293
Ogliastra
Lanusei
Gairo
Osini-
Vecchio
Osini-Nuovo
Ulassai
390
Bari
Sardo
Loceri
Torre di Bari
Candelo

Villa
S. Antonio
Senis
442
Nureci
Assolo
Nurallao
197
Nuragus
Villanova
Tulo
198
Seui **19**
Su Marmuri
Jerzu
125

Albagiara
Gonnosnó
Giara di Gesturi
Genoni
Nuragus
Accodulazze
Esterzili
Pta Corongu
1008
Buoncammino

Sini
Genuri
Setzu
Tuili
Barumini **1**
Gesturi
Isili
Is Paras
M. Guzzini
734
Cant.
di Nurri
Villanova
Franca
M. Sta Vittoria
1212
Domu d'Orgia
L. del
Flumendosa
Corte Porcus
872
Tertenia
M. Ferru
875
Dispensa

Medio
Campidano
Su Nuraxi
Ussaramanna
Las Plassas
S. Vittoria
Serri **17**
Gergei
Escolca
Nurri
Orroli
Perdasdefogu
Perda is Furonis
674
Melisenda
Barisoni

Siddi
Lunamatrona
S. Simone
Murera
Mandas
Mulargia
Arrubiu **18**
S. Giorgio
125
Pta s'Accettori
589

Bruncu
Sa Cruxi
Villamar
Gesico
Donigala
Escalaplano
Cagliari
Pta Corongu
Armungia
387

Sanluri
Furtei
547
Villanova
Franca
Guasila
Seuni
Piscu
Siurgus
Salto
di
Quirra

197
Ortacesus
Arixi
Goni
Funtana
Coberla
Ballao
Quirra

Senorbi
San Basilio
128
Goni
Cagliari
Cagliari

Barbagia as "the people from Ilion" or "the descendants of Iolaos", who bravely fought against the Carthaginian and Roman hordes in an attempt to preserve their freedom and independence. One derivation of the name indicates a link with Troy ("Ilion"), and refers to a maritime people originally from Asia Minor who had come to Sardinia in order to found their own colony. The other harks back to Iolaos, the legendary Greek hero who is purported to have reigned over a Greek colony with the assistance of the sons of Hercules.

Romans, Christians and Saracens

When the island came under Roman rule in 238 BC, the new conquerors, while trying to bring the entire island under their sway, encountered determined resistance in the Barbagia. Under the rule of the Emperors Tiberius and Justinian a large number of exiled Romans were dispatched to quell the Barbaricini. During the 6th century AD the Barbaricini were converted to Christianity. Pope Gregory I sent Felix and Cyriacus to the Barbagia to spread the Gospel throughout Sardinia. The Barbaricini embraced the new faith with fervour. It seems possible that their passionate enthusiasm for the new beliefs encouraged them to desecrate the symbols of their former religion, as other Sardinian tribes before them had done.

During the Saracen invasion many Sardinians fled deep into the interior of the island in the face of the brutality of the advancing foe, finding refuge with the Barbaricini and thus augmenting their numbers. Although contemporary sources provide no information on the matter, it seems possible that the inhabitants of the Barbagia, true to their reputation as indomitable warriors, may have played a decisive part in the crushing defeat of the Saracen Prince of Mogeid-al-Amiri, referred to in ancient chronicles as Museto. After the victory over Museto (AD 1015–16), the history of the Barbagia becomes progressively more integrated into that of the island itself.

It passed through the period of the *giudicati*, became the scene of violent

Notices of deaths in Fonni.

The Barbagia people converted to Christianity in the 6th century AD.

struggles and was ruled in turn by the Genoese, Pisans, Aragonese and Spanish. In the face of the frequent unjust tricks played on them, the people of the region never abandoned their guard and maintained a rebellious attitude. This can be witnessed in an episode dating from 1719, when a sudden doubling of taxes prompted the Barbaricini, and in particular the citizens of Olzài, to revolt against Spanish rule.

Mountain peaks

The Barbagia consists almost entirely of mountainous and hilly country, which rises towards the east as it approaches the massive ranges of the Gennargentu. Some of it is very bleak. Its highest peak is named after General Alfonso La Marmora (Italy's most senior general, 1804–1878). The summit of **La Marmora** reaches 1,834 metres (6,017ft) above sea level, while the neighbouring peak of **Bruncu Spina**, which for several months each year is capped with snow, is more than 1,829 metres (6,000ft). On a fine day with little cloud, the view from the highest peaks of the Gennargentu is

Mountain range in the Gennargentu.

overwhelming and confounds the sense of bleakness that the region so often inspires. In particularly clear conditions you can see as far as the Tyrrhenian Sea on the distant horizon.

The peak of **Monte Spada** lies in the region known as **Barbagia di Ollolai**. It marks the end of an extensive mountain range which stretches eastwards as far as the **Corru'e boi** (Cattle Horn) gorge and the pass of the same name on the main Nuoro–Lanusei–Ogliastra road. Then the highland area winds on further to Monte Novo S. Giovanni in the district of Orgosolo, where the Cedrino river rises, and on as far as the limestone escarpment by Oliena and the Lanaittu Valley, which marks the boundary between the administrative districts of Oliena and Dorgali.

Springs and rivers

Throughout the region there are springs fed by the mountain snows. Their fresh water is popular all over the island; healing powers are even attributed to some of them, such as the springs of **S'Abba Medica** near Gavoi, or the spring water from the

---

RETURN TO THE LAND

Migrant workers and traders who sought employment in the more prosperous regions of the island, such as Nuoro, Cagliari, Sassari or mainland Italy, often return eventually to their native mountains, where they invest part of their savings in the construction of a new house or the renovation of an old building. Today, vegetable fields, vineyards and orchards which had been allowed to lie fallow since the 1960s are being revived by owners who have become disillusioned by jobs in the service industries or in one of the factories in the faraway towns.

The future also looks rosy for the groves of oak and chestnut trees and the large areas planted with hazelnut bushes, oak and pine woods, groves of cork oaks and the *màcchia*, where heathers, rosemary, thyme, rock roses, arbutus trees, mastic shrubs and black-berried myrtle flourish. The mastic shrub is the principal source of food for both goats and pigs; it is also used to yield an oil for household use. Myrtle berries and juniper are used to distil *mirto*, a schnapps. Not long ago there were entire woods of juniper bushes several hundred years old. Today the stands are much younger, although in the valleys of the Barbagia you may still come across an ancient specimen which is as big as a tree.

Guppunnìo spa and the **Regina Fontium** (Queen of the Springs) in Ollolai. The most famous healing spas are those of **Monte Spada** and **Campu Maiore** in Ortueri. People come to sample them from all over the island.

Three main rivers flow through the Barbagia: the **Flumendosa**, the **Talòro** and the **Araxisi**. The Flumendosa rises in the southern gorges of the Corru'e boi, collecting the water of the eastern Gennargentu and numerous smaller tributaries from the mountains of the Ogliastra before flowing into the Tyrrhenian Sea. The Talòro, a tributary of the Tirso – the island's biggest river – has its source in the Barbagia di Ollolai, expanding between the districts of Gavoi, Ovodda and Olzai to become the lake of the same name, after which it flows across the Plain of Ottana and the central Tirso Valley before joining the main river.

Holm and cork oaks

The Barbagia still retains some of the luxuriant vegetation, especially the forests, which at one time made Sardinia one of the greenest spots in the entire Mediterranean.

In the mountains, acorn-bearing oak trees still grow up to an altitude of 1,200–1,300 metres (3,800–4,200ft) above sea level. By far the most common species is the holm oak, some of which are hundreds of years old, followed by pedunculate and cork oaks. The latter supply the cork industry, a factor in the Sardinian economy since the 19th century (see page 146).

The cork, stripped from each tree every seven to eight years, is exported in a raw and processed state. The numerous forest fires which plague the region in the hottest summer months and uncontrolled overfelling have led to a drastic reduction in the tree stocks. At the beginning of the 19th century they were estimated at 66 million. The millenary woods of Sardinia were cut down by charcoal burners from the Italian peninsula and transformed into railway sleepers, charcoal for domestic heating or wood to feed steam engines. The protests of locals went unheard, and in a few decades the island's landscape had changed.

You will see evidence of the cork industry throughout the Barbagia.

Farming mural in Mamoiada.

The Barbagia is rich in wild flowers.

Sardinian honey is widely available.

Apart from the incalculable ecological and aesthetic damage, the fires have a deforesting effect which has led to a shortage of food for livestock. Oak trees are particularly important in the rearing of pigs, as they produce excellent meat for the manufacture of ham and sausages when fed on acorns.

Chestnut trees

Sweet chestnut trees in the region used to supply excellent wood for a variety of purposes, and still do to some extent. In the old days (and occasionally still today) craftsmen used it to make items for everyday use, such as doors or windows. Stylised yet functional objects are now popular, including benches with built-in storage chests (the front panel of which is almost always decorated with illustrations of birds, flowers, leaves or the landscape of the place of manufacture). Looms, spindles, distaffs and other items for the processing of wool are also crafted from chestnut. Tables, plate racks, kitchen furniture and beds were usually made of a softer wood, in particular that of the pear tree.

Plants and flowers

As far as flora is concerned, the Barbagia is especially well endowed: broom, oleaster, yew, ash, tamarisk, willow, elder, alder, poplar, holly and laurel grow in abundance. *Màcchia* shrubs – blackthorn, myrtle, arbutus and numerous other species – are one of the reasons that many visitors come to this part of Sardinia and scientists from Italy and abroad come to study the environment.

Many of the plants bear berries or wild fruits with a slightly bitter taste, for instance, the sloe. Others, such as the arbutus, produce delicious fruits; it is from the blossoms of the arbutus that bees collect nectar for the famous, pungent-tasting Sardinian honey. The fruits are red and are about the size of a morello cherry. They are eaten raw or made into jam, and are known for their laxative effect. In former times it was common for locals to distil them to make a schnapps-like drink.

Chestnut woods and hazelnut bushes are chiefly found around Desulo, Tonara, Aritzo and Belvì. The inhabitants of these districts include

MIELE di Millefiori
della Sardegna
Bresca Dorada

MIELE di Millefiori
della Sardegna
Bresca Dorada

BITTERSWEET HONEY

A piculture (bee-keeping) was once more widespread than it is today, but the increased number of uninhabited areas given over to protected flowering plants has led to a revival of the ancient occupation. As in the old days, walkers can once again delight in the unexpected discovery of a honeycomb tucked away in a tree hollow which one of the many swarms of wild bees has converted into a hive. You can pick up local honey in many villages. Particularly worth seeking out is the distinctively bitter *miele amaro corbezzolo*, which derives its punchy sweetness and bitter aftertaste from the *arbutus unedo* plant, called the strawberry tree in English. Honey features in many Sardinian desserts, including the classic sweet pastries *seadas*.

the fruits of the forest in their diet to some extent, albeit less than in days gone by. Nowadays much of the produce is exported to other regions of the island. Almonds and hazelnuts are the principal raw ingredient required by the confectionery industry for the production of *torrone* (nougat with nuts), eaten in great quantities during festivals. For generations it has been manufactured in Tonara, Aritzo and Belvì.

Among Sardinia's plants and herbs are thyme, rosemary, wild lavender, gorse with its characteristic yellow flowers and sharp thorns, brambles (laden with blackberries during September), pink and red rock roses, heathers and a wide variety of forest ferns. Seemingly endless fields of daisies, corn poppies and bog asphodel make for an unforgettable sight in spring and early summer.

Birds and beasts

A wide range of animals live in the Barbagia. Eagles, falcons, vultures, red kites, partridges, ring doves, thrushes, magpies, quail, turtle doves, snipe, blackbirds and buzzards all live and breed here. On the mountain slopes, where acorns and berries are plentiful, or even near vineyards and vegetable gardens, wild boar (*cinghiale*) may be seen. The Sardinian wild boar is a robust species which breeds easily in spite of damage to its environment. In recent years it has become a popular addition to the Sardinian menu. The most common wild animal on Sardinia and in the Barbagia used to be the mouflon, a wild short-fleeced mountain sheep. In former times it wandered the mountains in herds, but sadly today it is becoming increasingly rare. Only walkers crossing the crests of the Supramonte near Oliena and Orgosolo, or wandering through the heart of the Gennargentu may be fortunate enough to see this magnificent creature. It looks like a ram, but has the coat of a deer.

You are just as likely to encounter animals as cars on the road here.

A journey into the Barbagia

An expedition into the Barbagia is recommended to every foreign visitor; it is a truly wild spot which even many Sardinians haven't explored. That being

Mural near Orgosolo known as "the greedy landowner".

Festivals: La Festa or La Sagra

Festivals play a significant role in traditional village life in Sardinia, and they are celebrated with great gusto in the Barbagia, the most rural area of the island.

In the past, following a meagre harvest or a cata-strophic year, tensions were released in a *festa* or *sagra*. As well as being celebrations, they expressed confidence in the future and faith in a deity. Festivals were a means of expressing all the plans, ideals and dreams conjured up by human fantasy and an opportunity to give vent to a basic melan-choly. Nowadays, they still make up a crucial part of the Sardinian calendar of events.

Dance is an essential component of every cele-bration, and usually the musical accompaniment is provided by a single instrument, the accordion. Traditionally, the dancing takes place in front of a church or at country places of pilgrimage.

The Mamuthones of Mamoiada don carved wooden masks at festival time.

Giving thanks

Church festivals take place either at places of pilgrimage dedicated to the saint in question or to the Mother of God, or else in the villages themselves. They often honour a local patron saint, or another saint, or the Madonna. Some pilgrims recite their prayers in *novenae*, in a cycle of nine consecutive days. By this means they ful-fil a vow or thank God for His mercy. In the larger and major festivals, the faithful still sleep in the *cumbessias* (also called *muristenes*), which are peasant dwellings built in an arc or a circle around the church.

Many village and country festivals are still observed with great ceremony, sometimes even with pageantry. Wealthy men and women of good reputation assist the priest, and are given titles – although this is an image-building exercise for the organising families or clans.

Eat, drink and be merry

Entertainments include the game of Morra, the *ballu tundu*, the "national" dance of Sardinia, poetry competitions, guitar competitions and horse racing *(un palio)*. The entire contents of kitchen and cellar will be wheeled out as hosts try to outdo each other in their hospitality. *Torrone* (nougat) can be purchased, along with cow bells and a variety of small kitchen utensils of wood, copper or bog asphodel leaves manu-factured in Tonara, Desulo, Aritzo, Belvì, Isili, Ovodda or Ollolai.

Best festivals

The majority of festivals occur in springtime, when the shepherds and their flocks return from the plains of the Campidano or the Nurra, and in summer, when workers come home to see their families.

The most attractive festivals in the western Barbagia are the *Feste-Fiere* (the church dedica-tion festivals): in Samugheo this is dedicated to St Basil (13 August); *Ortueri* (8 September) cel-ebrates the nativity of the Virgin Mary; and in Sorgono the *festa* is for St Maurus Abate (1 June). In Sorgono the *Assunzione della Barbagia Vergine* (the Assumption of the Virgin Mary) and the Festival of the Redeemer *(Salvatore)* on 9 November are celebrated with due style. In the Barbagia di Seulo, the festivals of St Mary Magdalene, and that of Corpus Christi, in mid-June, and St John the Baptist (23–4 June) are legendary.

the case, travelling round the area is not as straightforward as the more tourist-oriented coast; the roads are winding, and sometimes little more than dirt tracks and road signs are limited.

The more adventurous can use public transport, but it is slow and unreliable – a private car will obviously give you a greater degree of independence. The SS 131 from Siniscola to Nuoro has been improved and is now of motorway standard, but has remained toll-free; by taking it, you can soon reach Nuoro, one of the possible starting points for a tour of the Barbagia. The following route, using **Cagliari** – with the largest harbour and the principal airport – as the point of departure, is only one of the many possibilities available. It is very difficult to organise a single itinerary that covers the Barbagia, because of the great morphological variability of the region. Deep valleys, high plateaux and mountain peaks and ridges, which are at times difficult to get over, take turns to provide the dominant geographical feature. In some places there is no asphalt road, only a dirt track to follow.

After leaving Cagliari on the Carlo Felice (SS 131), you will soon arrive at the right-hand turning of the SS 197 between **Serrenti** and **Sanluri**. Here a detour is recommended to the remarkable nuraghe complex of **Barumini ❶** and the **Giara di Gesturi**, a vast table mountain of basalt which is as geologically interesting as it is picturesque, and which is the home of wild Sardinian ponies (see page 193).

After about 10km (6 miles) on the SS 128 you reach the village of **Laconi ❷**, which is still in the **Sarcidano** but lies on the edge of the Barbagia. The largest town in the Sarcidano, Laconi enjoys an attractive situation. It is the birthplace of St Ignatius of Laconi, and the saint's meagre possessions are preserved in the house where he was born, **Casa Natale di Sant'Ignazio** (tel: 0782-86902; Thur and Sun 9am–noon). Apart from the 16th-century belltower, you can also visit Castello Aymerich; its magnificent park (8am–4pm, June until 7pm, July–Aug until 8pm) not only contains flowers native to Sardinia but also bay trees. horse chestnuts, pedunculate oaks, beeches

Take home some nougat (torrone in Italian), traditionally made in Tonara from walnuts. almonds, hazelnuts, eggs and fragrant Sardinian honey.

Winter sunshine and snow on the village of Atzara and surrounding countryside.

Driving around the Barbagia's tortuous roads is not for the faint-hearted.

Display of finery at Nuoro's Ethnographic Museum.

and cedars from the Himalayas and the Lebanon.

Some of the most important decorated menhirs of Sardinia have been found a few kilometres away from the village and have been gathered in the **Civico Museo delle Statue Menhir** (tel: 0782-693 238; http://menhirmuseum.it; Tue–Sun, Oct–Mar 10am–1pm and 3–6pm, Mar–Sept 10am–1pm and 3.30–7pm) in Pallazzo Aymerich in the Piazza Marconi.

The route continues northwards from Laconi and reaches **Aritzo ❸**. An important mountain resort surrounded by chestnut and hazelnut woods, the town still has some historic buildings, including a 17th-century Spanish prison and an Arangino "castle", which became a private home at the beginning of the 20th century. The town's **Museo della Montagna Sarda o del Gennargentu** (tel: 0784-629 801; Tue–Sun, June–Sept 10am–1pm and 4–7pm, Oct–May 9am–1pm and 3–6pm) has displays of craft, costume and domestic and agricultural machinery.

The *Sagra delle Castagne* (Chestnut Fair) held in the town at the end of October attracts people from all Sardinia. Aritzo is also the starting point for many excursions that can be done by four-wheel drive vehicles provided by local hotel owners or on foot, with a local guide. The **Tacco Texile** (975 metres/3,199ft), an unmistakable limestone rock at the top of a conical hill, is the destination of many walkers. Not far away is the village of **Belvì**, which holds its Cherry Fair in June and has a small but interesting **Museo di Scienze Naturali** (tel: 339-7531 025; daily 10.30am–1.30pm and 3.30–7.30pm).

Tonara, the home of nougat

The towns of Tonara and Desulo nestle in the western foothills of the Gennargentu massif, along the mountain route. These are some of the highest villages on the whole island. The town of **Tonara ❹** is known principally for its production of *torrone* (nougat), which is sold throughout the island at fairs. Honey is one of the prime ingredients of *torrone*, but it is also used to make the majority of Sardinian cakes.

CHANGING TIMES

The past few decades have seen some rapid changes in the customs and lifestyle not only of individuals but also of entire communities in Sardinia. This is as true of the Barbagia region as it is of other regions of the island.

Pasture land is not always in ample supply, but the grass and wild herbs available contribute to the taste – even the consistency – of the meat and the milk products of the sheep.

Gone are the days when every Barbagian shepherd wandered the countryside on foot with his dog. Today the large majority of shepherds use a car or a jeep for transport, be it for visiting their flock, transporting wood or food for their livestock, or delivering milk to the cheese factory – and lambs, kids or pigs to the butcher. Visitors may still occasionally see a mule or a donkey carrying goods. Indeed, at high altitude, in the remotest, most inaccessible places in the mountains, they are still very much irreplaceable.

Modernity has arrived even in the furthest corners of the Barbagia, as the inhabitants share in the latest creature comforts. Most houses are still of the traditional variety, with ancient moss-covered tile roofs, but many have been renovated to meet modern requirements.

Sardinian honey is prized for its quality and huge variety, largely determined by the diversity of wild flowers on the island, which give each honey its distinctive flavour. You can choose between perfumed citrus fruit honey, delicate asphodel or balsamic eucalyptus. The rare strawberry tree honey with its unique bitterness is highly sought after.

It is in the area surrounding the Gennargentu massif that Sardinia's traditional culture of sheep herding is most apparent. Visitors can still find a network of ancient footpaths, many of which are still in use by shepherds and their herds. These paths connected pasturelands and, in the 19th century, mountains, before they were deforested by charcoal burners. Today the paths are used by hikers to explore the Gennargentu massif. As the paths are not signposted, many people use local guides or walk the paths in groups. Hikers often come across *pinnette* (ancient round huts with thatched roofs) which are used by shepherds for shelter, especially during the lambing season when shepherds cannot leave their flocks.

Desulo and Punta La Marmora

The village of **Desulo** ⑤, at an altitude of 895 metres (2,900ft), is one of the few villages where you can still see some women wearing the traditional costume of the region. It is remarkable for its simplicity of design and use of bright colours: orange, red, blue and yellow. The Casa Montanaru houses an **ethnographic museum** (tel: 0784-619 624; by appointment).

Unscrupulous building development means the village has lost a good deal of its charm, but the main reason to visit is the splendid scenery. Many excursions start from Desulo; footpaths beaten by local shepherds lead walkers to **Bruncu Spina** (1,829 metres/6,000ft) and **Punta La Marmora** ⑥ (1,834 metres/6,017ft), the highest peak on the island. On the northern side of Bruncu Spina a ski lift has been in service since the 1990s. For several months of the year large quantities of snow fall on the summits and gorges of the Gennargentu, where it continues to lie for some time. Winter sports complexes and hotels are being

Peregrine falcons are just one of the birds of prey to be found in the region.

A lone tree among the rocky Barbagia countryside.

FACT

The Sardinian wild boar (*il cinghiale sardo*) is a smaller sub-species of the Eurasian *Sus scrofa* and typically has a length of 100–120cm (40–47ins), with a maximum weight of 70–80kg (154–76lb).

built in the area to attract skiers. There is no suggestion that the Gennargentu can compete with the more famous ski resorts of the Alps or the Appenines, but nonetheless this area provides winter fun for Italians and visitors looking for something different.

The Italian Alpine Club (CAI) built a shelter house on Punta La Marmora (Rifugio La Marmora) which is used as a landmark and for its good spring water by hikers, even though today only ruins remain.

Between villages grapevines and fruit trees grow. Here orchards reach as far as the eye can see: cherry and almond trees, plum, fig and pomegranate trees, olives, hazelnuts, walnuts and chestnuts are all cultivated.

Meana and Sorgono

The village of **Meana Sardo** ❼ is not usually part of regional itineraries. Pleasantly placed between mountains at 600 metres (1,969ft) above sea level, it preserves the feeling and quality of life of the Sardinian mountain people. A few kilometres above the village is **Nuraghe Nolza** (Nolza archaeological

area; tel: 0784-643 620; daily, summer 10am–1pm and 4.30–6pm, winter 10am–1pm and 2–5.45pm). In a dominating and extremely panoramic position, it is different from most nuraghi in that it was built using clay to cement the space between stone blocks – a revolutionary idea that caused instability and many structures to collapse. The nearby village of **Atzara** has a late Gothic parish church with a Romanesque belltower and side chapels decorated with precious wooden altars.

Sorgono ❽, part of the subregion of Mandrolisai, is in a valley surrounded by woods and orchards. It is a popular place to visit during the summer months because of its pleasant climate, which also allows for the cultivation of grapes for the famous Cannonau wine. Sights of interest in town include a 17th-century house, Casa Carta, with Aragonese windows.

Seventeen km (11 miles) outside Sorgono is the **Santuario di San Mauro**, one of the most interesting rural sanctuaries on the island. Built in the 16th century in an Aragonese-Gothic style, it has a Renaissance door

Procession in Fonni in honour of the Virgin Mary.

with a carved Gothic rose window above it. Inside is an impressive staircase and a single vault. Surrounding the church are *cumbessias* (pilgrim shelters) that were used as lodgings during the feast day of San Mauro, held on the first day of June each year.

The festival is still popular today, and its religious ceremony is accompanied by a fair at which local handicrafts and produce are sold: iron, copper, leather and terracotta goods, walnuts, hazelnuts, dried chestnuts and honey as well as different varieties of sweetmeats. During the 19th century the fair also provided an opportunity to purchase foreign-made goods like linen, woollens and leather items, silk, majolica, china, and thoroughbred horses.

Nuraghic finds

Before heading for Fonni via Ovodda, first visit the small archaeological museum in **Teti** ❾, the **Museo Archeologico Comprensoriale** (Via Roma; tel: 0784-68120; www.museoteti. it; Tue–Sun 9am–1pm and 3–5.30pm, summer until 6pm). The museum has a collection of objects found in the nearby Nuraghic archaeological site of S'Urbale, and a fascinating reconstruction of a round hut from 1000 BC with some sleeping niches and domestic articles inside.

About some 15km (9 miles) to the north of Teti, in a very isolated and difficult-to-find valley, are the remains of the large Nuraghic village of **Abini**. A number and variety of bronze votive figurines were found here, representing hero-warriors with four eyes or arms, that can now to be seen in the Archaeological Museum in Cagliari. Daggers, votive bronze swords and other small objects are displayed in Teti's Archaeological Museum.

Fonni – the highest village

At 1,000 metres (3,280ft), **Fonni** ❿ is the highest village in Sardinia. It is also one of the region's biggest centres and is popular with hikers and walkers, who use the town as a base for excursions into surrounding countryside and mountain peaks. The town's most interesting monument is the 17th-century **church of San Francesco** (daily),

Mamuthones masks ready for painting.

A local woman from Fonni.

Gavoi house.

also called the sanctuary complex of Nostra Signora dei Martiri. The complex is surrounded by porticoes and the interior of the church is remarkable for the 1,700 religious frescoes and late Baroque altars, and a curious statue of the Virgin Mary made from fragments of ancient Roman sculptures.

The fabrics and rugs of Fonni are well known for their fine workmanship, and the locals also produce excellent traditional sweets. These are all in evidence on Whit Monday (the first Sunday in June) and on 24 June for the festival of San Giovanni, when local people wearing traditional costumes parade through the streets on horseback and visitors from the surrounding villages join in pious tribute to the Virgin Mary. The festivals are well known throughout Sardinia and are described by Grazia Deledda in her novel *Canne al Vento.*

Sites around Fonni

A few kilometres east of Fonni is the **Arcu Corru'e boi** (1,246 metres/4,086ft), a pass between the inner Sardinia of the Barbagie, the Nuorese and the plains of the Ogliastra on the eastern coast. Before reaching the pass you will find the well-preserved Tombe di Giganti Madau (daily), noteworthy for the good condition of their burial corridors. Peer inside the long tunnels and you get an idea of how little has changed since they were built.

West of Fonni on the road heading towards Gavoi is the **Lago di Gusana**, a large artificial lake popular with canoeists and campers; you get an excellent view from the SS 128 as it hugs the right-hand shore.

From the lake the next stop on the route is **Gavoi** ⑪, an important centre dominated by the 16th-century church of San Gavino with a Gothic rose window in trachyte stone. Narrow alleys lead from the church square (Piazza San Gavino) lined with characterful old buildings. Gavoi is well known for its fiore sardo *pecorino*, made with sheep's milk.

From the village it is worth making a short detour to see the large sanctuary of **Madonna de Sa Itria** (daily) where, not far from the church, a

PREHISTORIC TOMBS

One of the best-known *tombe di giganti* (giants' tombs; types of megalithic gallery graves) in the Barbagia region is the **S'Altare de Lògula**, a few kilometres west of Sarule. The *tombe di giganti* are rectangular constructions of worked stone that range from 8–28 metres (26–92ft) in length.

These graves – which, according to legend contain men of enormous stature, the mythical first inhabitants of Sardinia – are often situated remarkably close to nuraghi or on the outskirts of a Nuraghic village. They are characterised by a vertical stela, whose size is proportional to that of the grave (the longest is more than 4 metres/13ft) and is placed over the entrance of the tomb. For more on giants' tombs, see page 139.

3.5-metre (5ft) high Neolithic menhir bears witness to the continuous use of the sanctuary as a place of worship throughout many millennia.

Continuing north from Gavoi through **Sarule**, **Orani** and **Oniferi** the road links up with the SS 131 from Abbasanta to Nuoro. Not far from the junction several *domus de janas* are set into the hillside. Part square and part concave, some of the individual chambers are linked to one another by means of low doorways or windows.

The pilgrimage church of **Nostra Signora di Gonari** (daily) lies between Sarule and Orani on an unmistakable wooded cone-shaped hill, from which talc is quarried. The building is unadorned and dates from the time of the *giudicati*. The festival of dedication, which is celebrated in appropriate style, falls on 8 September each year. During the Roman occupation Orani may well have been one of the most densely populated villages in the Barbagia. Many of Sardinia's artists, including the well-known contemporary painter Costantino Nivola, have hailed from Orani.

Festival in Mamoiada

In **Mamoiada** ⑫ (644 metres/2,060ft), a predominantly agricultural village producing vegetables, wine and fruit, one of the most original, fascinating and famous carnival processions in Sardinia takes place on Shrove Tuesday. The *Mamuthones* of Mamoiada, as frequently happens elsewhere in Sardinia, don special disguises for the carnival (in Orotelli they become *Thurpos*, in Ottana they are known as *Boes* and *Merdules*). The *Mamuthones* hide their faces behind black carved wooden masks and wear sheepskin or occasionally goatskin fleeces reaching down to their knees, with breeches of coarse velvet and the traditional shepherds' knee-high leather gaiters worn in the Barbagia until about 30 years ago. The *Mamuthones'* scary appearance is enhanced by the bunch of clanging cow bells weighing up to 50kg (110lb) hung over their shoulders and carried on their backs. They walk in procession accompanied by *Issohadores* (young escorts) in bright costumes and carrying leather lassos, which they use to capture astonished

FACT

When D.H. Lawrence arrived in Sorgono during his *Sea and Sardinia* trip he described the village as being similar to "some little town in the English West country".

Nuoro's flea market.

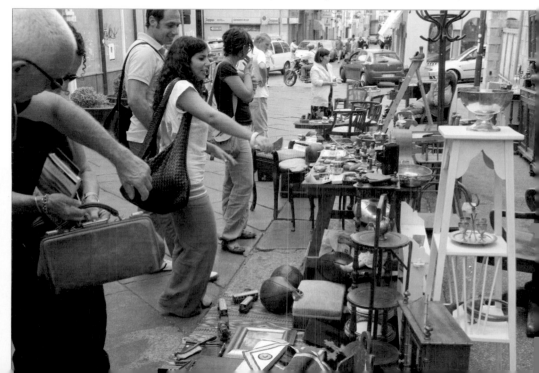

spectators or – better still – their beloveds from the crowds watching the procession.

A good place to experience the atmosphere of the festival out of season is at the **Museo delle Maschere Mediterranee** (tel: 0784-569 018; www. museodellemaschere.it; Tue–Sun 9am–1pm and 3–7pm), which displays a collection of traditional masks and a video about the carnival.

Another major festival in the town is held in honour of Saints Cosimo and Damian. It takes place in the little country church of the same name, which stands on a fertile upland plain near Mamoiada, directly opposite the picturesque Gennargentu massif.

Nuoro, heart of the Barbagia

Nuoro ⓭ lies under the same spell of enchantment as the Barbagia itself, caught between reality and myth, a passive witness to history and to the fate of its shepherds, peasants and poets. D.H. Lawrence reckoned there was nothing to see in Nuoro, though he did admit: "I am not Baedeker."

Image of a boy selling spoons and oars at Nuoro's Ethnographic Museum.

An expanding services industry and tourism have led to the town's rapid growth over the past 30 years. Today Nuoro has put on a guise of modernity, with the usual unsightly modern building developments that blight many Italian towns.

Since 1926 Nuoro has been the provincial capital again, as it was under the Sardinian monarchy. At the beginning of the 19th century approximately 3,500 people lived here. Today the population is between 35,000 and 40,000. No other town within the province can compete on a cultural level, although the economy, work situation, tourism and trade have resulted in greater fluctuations than were the rule in the not-so-distant past, when small independent businesses flourished by making and selling only the essential requisites of life. Traces of vanished peoples in the form of remains from the Nuraghic era and later epochs are to be found not only in the surrounding district but also close at hand: towards **Monte Ortobene** or in the direction of **Valverde** and **Badde Manna** (The Big Valley), from which one can see in the distance the plains and the mountain peaks of Oliena and Orgosolo. Nuoro's position as the centre and symbol of the entire Barbagia was assumed at the beginning of the 20th century; the region itself extends considerably beyond the boundaries laid down over the years, encompassing such places as **Orotelli**, **Orune**, **Bitti**, **Onanì** and **Lula** to the north.

Sites to see in Nuoro

Famous sons and daughters of Nuoro, such as the poet Sebastiano Satta, the Nobel Prize-winning novelist Grazia Deledda and many others are responsible for the town's amazingly rapid rise to cultural and social prominence. Travellers can visit the final resting place of Grazia Deledda in the eastern district of town, on the way to L'Ortobene: the **Chiesa della Solitudine** (Church of Solitude; daily).

The leading citizens of the town have created a museum in the house where the famous woman of letters was born. In the **Museo della Vita e delle Tradizioni Sarde** (Via Antonio Mereu; tel: 0784-257 035; www.isresardegna.it; Tue–Sun, Oct–mid-Mar 10am–1pm and 3–5pm, mid-Mar–Sept 10am–1pm and 3–6pm), also known as the Museo Etnografico, visitors can examine a varied and well-chosen collection of folkloric items from all over the island: traditional costumes for both men and women from various towns and villages, matching jewellery – valuable filigree work in gold or silver or of coral, and works of art by skilled goldsmiths whose families in many cases have plied the trade for generations. Apart from costumes, the museum displays a large number of exhibits illustrating the ancient craftsmanship of the island, which even today produces magnificent rugs and wall hangings, exquisite shawls, scarves and linen and silk embroidery. Also on display are a collection of traditional musical instruments; a room devoted to festival costumes and masks

and a section devoted to the sweets, cakes and breads found throughout the island. The museum complex is designed to evoke a Sardinian village.

Another museum well worth a visit in Nuoro is **MAN: Museo d'Arte di Nuoro** (tel: 0784-252 110; www.museoman.it; Tue–Sun 10am–1pm, 3–7pm, Apr–Sept until 8pm), housed in a 19th-century building between Corso Garibaldi and Piazza Sebastiano Satta in the Old Town. The museum displays a collection of Sardinia's best-known artists, featuring important painters such as Biasi, Ciusa and Nivola, whose brooding works document the islanders' tough rural lifestyle and modern upheavals. Look out for their contemporary art shows and archive works, which include some experimental video-art that usually raises a brow. It also organises various temporary exhibitions, often dedicated to art of the late 19th and early 20th century, poetry readings and jazz evenings.

There is also a compelling new **National Archaeological Museum**, close to the cathedral (tel: 0784-31688; Tue–Sat 9am–1.30pm, Tue and Thur

Nuoro elder.

Local produce for sale at Nuoro market.

VILLA PIERCY

Near Bolotana, 30km (18 miles) west of Nuoro, just off the SS129 to Oristano, is the restored home of Benjamin Percy, the British Victorian-era engineer who designed the Sardinian railway network. In 1862, fresh from his railway-building feats in Spain, France and India, the Welshman set to work on the Rete Ferroviaria Sarda, with the construction of the Cagliari–Porto Torres line, with offshoots to Sassari and Terran (Olbia). The work was completed in 1880.

Beyond the whitewashed colonial-style small turrets of Villa Piercy are the trappings of Victorian invention and good taste: mosaics, stucco-work, vibrantly painted ceilings and motifs, and an ingenious dumb-waiter system. For information about visiting the villa, contact tel: 347- 6512 084, www.assopassiflora.com.

3–5.30pm), which has dinosaur fossils found at Monte Tuttavista (Orosei) and Grotta Corbeddu (Oliena), significant Neolithic finds and a huge collection of Nuraghic bronze treasures unearthed at Sa Sedda 'e Sos Carros.

Further sights in the town centre include the neoclassical **Cattedrale di Nostra Signora della Neve** (Our Lady of the Snows; daily) built 1836–54 on the foundations of a considerably older, smaller place of worship. It houses a large number of valuable art treasures including a brooding painting from the studio of Luca Giordano, *Disputa di Gesù fra i Dottori*. Then there is the **San Pietro** district of town, birthplace of Grazia Deledda and Francesco Ciusa, and the **Chiesa delle Grazie** (Church of the Graces; daily) – both the old and new buildings – which owns a boarding school run by the Brothers of the order of Giuseppini d'Asti. The monks also take care of the pilgrimage chapel, which attracts large numbers of the faithful from surrounding districts, especially during the *Novene*, held in November each year.

Mural advocating peace on Orgosolo's police station.

Excursions from Nuoro

Two of the rural churches in the vicinity are worth an excursion: the church of **Nostra Signora di Valverde** on the wooded northern slopes of the Ortobene, from where there is a magnificent panoramic view right across to **Orune** and the lovely Valle di Marreri, and the **Cappella di Nostra Signora di Monte Ortobene**, lying about 8km (5 miles) from Nuoro at an altitude of some 1,000 metres (3,200ft) above sea level. It is accessible by car, public transport and on foot via a long and twisting road which climbs some 400 metres (1,280ft) above the town.

From the **Belvedere**, the observation platform on the Monte Ortobene, there is a breathtaking view of the dramatic scenery in all directions. Near the summit massive karst boulders sculpted into strange shapes by weather and wind teeter on ledges below a rousing bronze statue of *The Redeemer* with a shiny, much-venerated big toe: it is the work of the sculptor Vincenzo Jerace, dated 1901. During the last few days of August (26–30) each year, the *Sagra del Redentore* is celebrated in its honour. The festival is one of the most famous and impressive on the entire island, as it demonstrates not only the colourful costumes, the traditional dances and music, but also the deep and sincere piety of the Sardinian people. Nuoro is a good base for excursions into the surrounding countryside – to the towns and villages of Orotelli, Orune, Bitti, Siniscola, Orosei, Dorgali, Irgoli, Galtellì – all of which are described elsewhere in this book.

Oliena (see page 126) and **Orgosolo ⓮** in particular, which lie 10km (6 miles) and 16km (10 miles) respectively from Nuoro, are worthy of a more extended visit. Each of the little towns has both cultural and historic attractions as well as strong traditions of hospitality. Both lie on the Supramonte, the first limestone mountain range within the Gennargentu southeast of Nuoro. The murals in the village of **Orgosolo** are famous. Nowadays the original political message concerning the struggle against

powerful landowners and government repression is played down by the villagers. The film *Bandits at Orgosolo* (1961), directed by Vittorio de Seta, dubbed the town the bandit capital of the island, a label that has been hard to shake off. The bandit Graziano Mesina, known as the Scarlet Rose for robbing the rich to give to the poor, was born in Orgosolo.

Mountain walks

The **Supramonte**, which contains the communities of Oliena, Dorgali, Orgosolo and Urzulei, can be approached from a number of directions – albeit in general only by foot, on horseback or in a cross-country vehicle. In each of the four villages, but in particular in Oliena and Orgosolo, walkers will find everything to meet a trekker's needs. The Supramonte is clad in unspoilt holm-oak woodland. Broom grows between giant tree trunks felled by age or lightning, but from which fresh shoots are already beginning to grow. Others have been transformed into pillars of charcoal by some long-past or more recent forest fire.

This is olive country.

Archaeological finds from the nuraghe at Abbasanta.

TOP TREKS

Here are three spectacular walks in the limestone highlands. For the most demanding treks and technical climbs it is advisable to hire a walking guide accredited to the Associazione Italiana Guide Ambientali Escursionistiche. Sturdy boots with ankle support and other outdoor kit are essential.

Gola di Gorroppu: To explore the geological and botanical wonders of Europe's deepest (494 metres/1,620ft) and second-longest (5km/3 miles) gorge, La Gola di Gorroppu, set aside an entire day. Once inside the gorge there are dizzying views up vertical limestone walls where trees, shrubs, wild flowers and mouflon cling to the crumbling rock.

Cala Goloritzè: It takes 90 minutes of walking through centuries-old holm-oak woods to reach the transparent waters of Cala Goloritzè from the high plains of the Golgo Goloritzè. Limestone karst formations and sheer drops make it a dizzying spectacle. Climbers from all over the world come here to scale 120 metres (390ft) up the iconic spire Aguglia.

Punta La Marmora: It may not be the most demanding trek in the Sopramonte, but the classic three-hour ascent to Sardinia's highest peak (1,834 metres/6,000ft) offers great panoramic rewards.

In the half-shade of day or on bright moonlit nights they stand there like secret beings, monsters or devils from Dante's *Inferno*. Walkers be warned: grottoes and gullies open up without warning (across the millennia they may have swallowed up animals or even men); today speleologists are discovering their secrets.

The mountain itself is not high; its loftiest peaks scarcely reach 1,500 metres (4,921ft), with **Punta Corrasi** at 1,463 metres (4,800ft) and **Monte Ortu** at 1,340 metres (4,396ft). They lie on the northern boundary of the Supramonte, between Oliena and Orgosolo. In the southwest, within the district of Orgosolo, rise a number of ridges. They, too, are not particularly high, but, like the **Monte Novo San Giovanni**, they are steep and striking. Changing light conditions and the natural texture of the rock make the limestone shimmer – sometimes blue-grey or green, then silver, copper-coloured or chalky-white.

The way into the secret, enchanted world of this part of the Barbagia is via ancient footpaths or old,

Hikers taking the easy way down Punta Corrasi.

unmarked tracks made originally by the wild boar, mouflons, goats and pigs which even today roam through the dense undergrowth of woods and clearings in search of food. The impressions which visitors take home with them from the Supramonte are of relics from an Arcadian past: the cottages *(su pinnettu)*, built of largely untreated, massive trunks of oak, yew or buckthorn, the stalls for livestock and goats, the pigsties *(s'edìle)*, and the few nuraghi constructed of white blocks (Nuraghe Mereu), defying decay. And then there are the innumerable underground springs and rivers, crystal-clear especially in the caves, disappearing underground only to resurface either in **Su Gologone** in the Oliena Valley, or else in the heart of the Supramonte, maybe in the **Gorroppu**, the wild gorge of the same name.

The Nuorese

North of the Gennargentu mountains, the region of the high granite plateaux extends itself. It gets its name from the town of Nuoro. The **Nuorese** is a

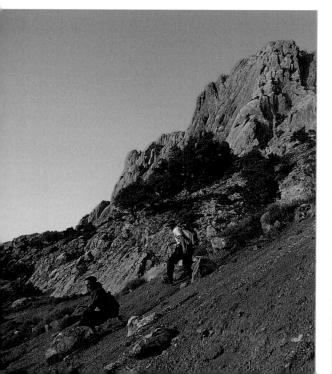

territory covered by vast cork and oak woods, inhabited in Nuraghic times, and today sparsely populated by shepherds living in isolated villages.

Orune ⓕ is one such village, situated at 765 metres (2,510ft) above sea level on the edge of the plateau and dominating the Isalle Valley. A few kilometres out of the village at the end of a specially built road (10 minutes' walk downhill on a path) is the sacred spring of **Su Tempiesu**, the most beautiful and refined water temple in Sardinia. It is architecturally unique – a small temple with perfectly cut stones, monolithic small trachyte arches that have only a decorative function – and dates from 1200 BC.

From the positioning of the springs it seems clear that the spring did not attract large of numbers of people, as in the case of the sanctuary of Santa Vittoria di Serri. The large number of Nuraghic springs and their distribution on the island demonstrate the great reverence the people had for water; so great that springs became sacred places of worship. For this reason, while the houses and even nuraghi seem to be primitive in their construction, in water temples a high level of craftsmanship in stone cutting and evocative and refined design is demonstrated.

Continuing north on the plateau, at 800 metres (2,600ft) above sea level, is the village of **Bitti** ⓖ, famous for the production of *pecorino* sheep's cheese and more recently for being the home town of the *Tenores di Bitti*. It is thought that the local dialect is the closest to resembling Latin on the island.

A large Nuraghic village called **Romanzesu** has recently been found on the granite plateau. The complex covers an area of 7 hectares (17 acres) and is characterised by buildings used for worship. A sacred well has been excavated, together with two *megaron* temples (rectangular temples preceded by a vestibule), a vast ceremonial space placed inside a large enclosure wall

and a structure of concentric walls, of unknown function. The dating of materials confirms that the site was in use from the 13th to the 9th centuries BC. The complex is particularly evocative, lying amid a cork-tree wood (summer Mon–Sat 9am–1pm, 3–7pm, Sun 9.30am–1pm and 2.30–7pm, winter Mon–Sat 8.30am–1pm and 2.30–6pm, Sun 9am–5pm). Moving towards the western border of the plateau, above the Tirso river, is **Benetutti**, a village well known for its thermal waters, one of the few thermal waters exploited in Sardinia. The most important spa is that of the Aurora or of San Saturnino on Benetutti, with sulphuric water and a temperature between 34–43°C (93–109°F).

The Barbagia of the south

The village of **Serri** ⓗ is best-known for its position near the Giara di Serri, a basaltic plateau on which the Nuraghic site of **Santuario Nuragico di Santa Vittoria** (Santa Vittoria archaeological area; daily, summer 9.30am–8.30pm, winter 9am–1pm and 2–6pm) is situated in a panoramic

TIP

Even experienced and fit trekkers go weak at the knees at the thought of **Il Selvaggio Blu**, the "Wild Blue" – one of the toughest and most technical long-distance routes in Italy. The six-day trek scales the dizzy heights and deepest gorges of the Sopramonte from Santa Maria Navarrese to Cala Gonone.

Peaches are cultivated on farmland around the Barbagia.

position. The archaeological complex is divided into three major sections: a temple area that includes a sacred well, a temple and a small church; a public area with a large courtyard for nuraghic festivals; and a market and living quarters that include a chief's hut. About 5km (3 miles) southeast of the town of **Orroli** is the **Nuraghe Arrubiu** ⑱ (area dell'Arrubiu; tel: 0782-847 269; daily, summer 9.30am–8.30pm, winter 9am–1pm and 2–6pm), one of the largest Nuraghic complexes in Sardinia dating back to the Bronze Age. It is formed by a tall central tower which today measures 16 metres (50ft) high, although it is thought to have been 21 metres (67ft) high when it was originally built. The tower is surrounded by a bastion with five towers, which is surrounded by a lower wall with eight towers. Nuraghe Arrubiu is situated on a high basaltic plateau (500 metres/1,600ft) near the edge of the canyon of the Flumendosa river, that here is more than 300 metres (960ft) high.

The Flumendosa is the second-longest river in Sardinia and flows to San Vito, on the eastern coast. Along its course it is interrupted by three dams that form as many lakes. The river creates a natural barrier with its deeply cut gorge between regions. The historic centre of **Sadali** was built around the 13th-century church of San Valentino, next to which a beautiful karstic spring bearing the same name erupts out of the rock as a 7-metre (23ft) waterfall. The surrounding area is bursting with water sources – not common in Sardinia – and it has created an otherworldly landscape in the limestone rocks. The **Grotte di Is Janas** (Fairy Caves; daily) are surrounded by a holm-oak wood. This section of the Barbagia is characterised by what is known as *Solitudini*, lonely, uninhabited expanses of land. The average population density in this region is fewer than 60 people per sq km (150 per sq mile) and can decrease in times of austerity.

The next village along the road is **Seui** ⑲. The town has a cluster of unusual collections under the title **Percorso Museale Sehuiense** (tel: 0782-539 002; Tue–Sun 9am–1pm and 3–5.30pm, summer until 7.30pm): the civic museum's art collection covers Baroque canvases to contemporary sculpture; La Palazzina Liberty has ornate, Liberty-style interiors; and nearby Casa Farci contains artefacts of Sehuiense life and the library of Filiberto Farci, co-founder of the Partito Sardo d'Azione.

Along the SS 198 from Seui is the unmissable **Foresta Montarbu** (Montarbu Forest), reachable by a long dirt road that winds into the vast, wild area, or by getting off the Trenino Verde at the stop for San Girolamo. Footpaths in the forest are well signposted and lead to Monte Tonneri, where it is possible to see deer and mouflons. The Perda Liana, about 1,293 metres (4,242ft) high from its base, is, together with Tacco Texile of Aritzo, one of the most characteristic peaks of the island.

Pecorino comes from the Barbagia.

Exploring the Nuraghe Santu Antine.

TRAVEL TIPS

SARDINIA

TRANSPORT

GETTING THERE AND GETTING AROUND

GETTING THERE

A potential problem in visiting Sardinia in the summer months is transport: high demand and a limited number of ferries if you plan to arrive by sea mean it is essential to book well in advance.

By Air

From Europe

You also need to book your flight in advance, especially for the hectic July–August period. British Airways provides a regular and dependable London Gatwick–Cagliari service in season. EasyJet has services to Cagliari from London Stansted, and to Olbia from Bristol (in season) and London Gatwick. Ryanair flies from London Stansted to Alghero.

In the past few years summer flights have increased because of greater demand. Many air companies of various countries schedule a large number of flights from/to European towns in July and August. Alitalia and Meridiana fly to Cagliari via some mainland Italian airports from London. Alitalia offers the best connections but sometimes not the best fares, and the route is usually via Rome (40 minutes from Cagliari) or Milan. During the summer there are many charter flights from all over Italy and some European cities to Tortolì-Arbatax Airport.

From the US

There are no direct flights to Sardinia from North America, although you can fly to Rome Fiumincino from New York and Toronto with Delta. Air Canada

and Alitalia also fly direct to Milan Malpensa and Venice Marco Polo. The main European hubs with connecting flights to Sardinia are Rome, London and Paris.

The largest airport, Cagliari-Elmas, is 10 minutes' drive away from the town centre, and there is a regular bus link (see page 225). The same is also true of the other two main airports on the island, Olbia and Alghero (Fertilia).

Airport Websites

Cagliari
www.sogaer.it
Alghero
www.algheroairport.com
Olbia
www.geasar.it

By Rail

The most direct route to Sardinia by rail from the UK begins by taking the Eurostar at St Pancras International in London, then involves a high-speed TGV journey from either Paris (swap stations from Gare du Nord to Gare de Lyon) or Lille, to Toulon or Marseille, where you can catch a ferry to Porto Torres. An alternative route is to take the sleeper service from Paris Gare de Bercy to Roma Termini, then another train to Civitavecchia to take the ferry to Cagliari or Arbatax.

By Sea

Advance reservation is vital for visiting Sardinia by boat in the summer season, especially if you are intending to take a car with you. Reservations cannot be accepted by navigation lines for deck seats (passaggio ponte) – the most inexpensive way of

travelling to Sardinia – unless all the cabin spaces have already been sold.

The most important ferry companies, with connections to the rest of Italy, are:
Moby Lines, tel: from Italy 199-303 040, from abroad +49-611-14020, www.moby.it
Sardinia-Corsica Ferries, tel: +33-4-9532 9595, www.corsica-ferries.co.uk
Tirrenia, from abroad and from mobiles tel: +39-039-689 9965, from Italy tel: 892 123, www.tirrenia.it
Grandi Navi Veloci, reservations tel: +39-010-209 4591, www.gnv.it
Saremar, from abroad tel: +39-02-3959 5016, from Italy tel: 199 11 88 77, www.saremar.it

There are daily connections between Cagliari and Civitavecchia (in Lazio, near Rome), Porto Torres and Genoa, Olbia and Civitavecchia. Other connections include: Cagliari with Naples and Palermo, Olbia with Genoa, Civitavecchia, Piombino and Livorno (Tuscany); and Golfo Aranci with Livorno. Crossing from all ports takes about 10 hours, but new high-speed ferries connect Olbia to Civitavecchia in approximately three hours.

Airline Numbers

Alitalia, tel: 892010 from Italy, +39-06-65649 from abroad, www.alitalia.ie
British Airways, tel: 0844-493 0787, www.ba.com
EasyJet, tel: 0905-821 0905, 0871-244 2366, www.easyjet.com
Meridiana from UK tel: 0844-482 2360, 39-0789 52682, www.meridiana.it
Ryanair, tel: 0871-246 0000 in the UK, www.ryanair.com

By Coach/Bus

Obviously, there are no bus or coach services to Sardinia from Europe, only ferries or flights. There are a few private companies that can provide transport for groups from mainland Europe, including Logudotours (www. logudorotours.it) and Turmo Travel (www.gruppoturmotravel.com).

By Road

From the UK the most direct road route is through France to Toulon, where there are ferry services to Porto Torres in the north of the island. The journey time is around 22 hours. Another more adventurous option for those with time on their hands is to drive through mainland Italy so as to visit other regions, before catching the ferry either at Genoa, Civitavecchia (in Lazio, near Rome), Piombino, Livorno or Naples.

GETTING AROUND

Rail travel in Italy and Sardinia is inexpensive and generally very reliable. However, Trenitalia services are generally limited to mainline stations (Orsitano, Ozieri and Sassari) on the island's principal Cagliari–Porto Torres line. The whole journey from south to northwest takes a little over four hours. Two branch lines connect other parts of the island: the first heads west from Decimommanu to Iglésias (40 mins), while the other heads eastwards from Ozieri-Chilivani to Golfo Aranci (90 mins).

Sardinia's road network is very good and, unlike mainland Italy's, does not suffer from intolerable traffic congestion. Improved sections of the SS 125 road are considerably shortening journey times to and from Cagliari and the onceisolated Ogliastra province.

To and from the Airport

From Cagliari International

Since 2013 a railway line connects the airport to the city centre 6km (4 miles) away. The journey time is about 5–7 minutes. The trains run every 20 minutes between 5am and 9pm (www.trenitalia.com). A taxi takes about 10 minutes.

From Alghero International

There is an ARST bus connection from the airport to the city 12km (7.5 miles) away. Journey time is approximately 30 minutes. The company also operates

bus services to Sassari and Bosa. For more information visit http://arst. sardegna.it. A taxi takes 15 minutes.

Logudoro Tours (www.logudorotours. it) run bus services to and from Cagliari, Oristano and Macomer. There are also buses to Nuoro operated by Redentours (www.redentours.com) and seasonal connections to Stintino (www.sardabus.it) and Santa Teresa Gallura (www.digitur.it).

From Olbia for the Costa Smeralda

Bus services 2 and 10 connect the airport with Olbia, 5km (3 miles) away (www.aspoolbia.it) and Sun Lines go to Costa Smeralda (www. sunlineseliteservice.com).

Public Transport

By Train

The main train station is in Cagliari; the main line is Cagliari–Oristano–Porto Torres. Travelling by train in Sardinia is sometimes slow, but worthwhile for the spectacular landscapes. For timetables and fares see www.trenitalia.com.

The tourist Trenino Verde, "The Little Green Train", runs from Sorgono to Isili or from Arbatax to Mandas through beautiful valleys and mountains (the locomotive is the same one that D.H. Lawrence took in 1921). There are also routes in the north – from Bosa to Macomer, and from Nulvi to Palau, through Tempio Pausania. The Trenino Verde route covers a total of 400km (248 miles). Contact: AFST tel: 070-26576; www.treninoverde.com. ARST SpA also operates train as well as bus services (www.arst.sardegna.it).

By Bus

There is an extensive and efficient network of buses and coaches with services run by both public and private companies. The most reliable companies in the area are: ARST (Azienda Regionale Sarda Trasporti, tel: 800-865 042, from Sardinia,

tel: 070-499 8324; www.arst. sarcegna.it), Autolinee Pani (a private company, tel: 070-913 8839; www.paniviaggieturismo.com), Turmo Travel (a private company, tel: 0789-21487; www.gruppoturmotravel.com).

It takes three hours to travel non-stop from one end of the island to the other (Cagliari–Sassari–Olbia).

There are a number of minibus services run by individuals and small companies. Local tourist offices have lists of these handy services.

By Boat

There are ferry services between Cagliari and Arbatax, and Olbia and Arbatax. Lots of other ferry services are available to, from and between the islands. Saremar (tel: 199-11 88 77, www.saremar.it) provides the following services: Calasetta–Carloforte, Porto Vesme–Carloforte, Santa Teresa di Ga lura–Bonifacio and Palau–La Maddalena. Delcomar (tel: 0781-857 123, www.delcomar.it) operates these routes: Carloforte–Calasetta, La Maddalena–Palau and Porto Torres–Asinara. Operator Moby Lines (www.mobylines.com) plies the waves between Palau and La Maddalena.

There are also lots of small operators who run ferry services and boat excursions around Sardinia's stunning coastline.

Taxis

Cagliari, tel: 070-400 101; www.cagliaritaxi.com
Sassari, tel: 079-25 39 39; www.cts.ss it
Alghero, tel: 079-973 9795; www.algherotaxi.it

Validating Tickets

It is important to remember to validate your bus or rail ticket before you travel. There are machines for date-stamping your rail ticket on station platforms and similar machines on buses.

Pedal power on the Bastione di San Remy, Cagliari.

Private Transport

By Car
Car insurance from most European countries is valid in Sardinia. The biggest danger to unwary visiting drivers is not poor roads but the haphazard driving habits of the locals. Petrol in Italy and Sardinia is usually not much more expensive than in the UK.

Driver's Licences
Members of the EU who have a national driver's licence may drive and hire cars; non-EU drivers should hold an International Driving Licence.

Car Hire
If you want to hire a car, there are a number of rental companies, both international and national, and their offices are located not only at the airports and ports but in towns and seaside resorts. It is advisable, once again, to book well in advance to ensure you get the vehicle you prefer (especially in August). Expect slightly higher prices than those in Britain and Northern Europe in general, but good deals can be obtained through travel agencies and flight carriers when purchasing package holidays. The following is a selection of the main car hire outlets, but there are many more.

Cagliari
Avis, Railway Station, tel: 070-674 903, Elmas Airport, tel: 070-240 081; www.avis.com.
Budget Rent-a-Car, Elmas Airport, tel: 070-240 081; www. budgetinternational.com.
Hertz Rent-a-Car, Elmas Airport, tel: 070-240 037; www.hertz.com.
Maggiore Rent-a-Car, Viale Monastir 116, tel: 070-273 692, Elmas Airport, tel: 070-240 818; www.maggiore.it.
Matta Autonoleggio, Elmas Airport, tel: 070-240 050; www. autonoleggiomatta.it.

Sassari
Avis, Via Predda Niedda 23/A, tel: 079-263 9011; www.avis.com.
Maggiore Rent-a-Car, Zona Ind.predda Niedda Strada 18 N. 38, tel: 079-260 409; www.maggiore.it.

Alghero
Avis, Fertilia Airport, tel: 079-935 064; www.avis.com.
Budget Rent-a-Car, Fertilia Airport, tel: 079-935 064; www. budgetinternational.com.
Maggiore Rent-a-Car, Fertilia Airport, tel: 079-935 045; www.maggiore.it.

Olbia
Avis, Olbia Costa Smeralda Airport, tel: 0789-6954Ctel: 0789-69540; www.avis.com.
Budget Rent-a-Car, Costa Smeralda Airport, tel: 0789-69605; www. budgetinternational.com.
Maggiore Rent-a-Car, Via Rudargia 84, tel: 0789-35840, Costa Smeralda Airport, tel: 0789-69457; www. maggiore.it.

Oristano
Avis, Via Liguria 17/19, tel: 0783-310 638; www.avis.com..
Sardinya Rent-a-Car, Via Cagliari 436, tel: 0783-779 106 ; www. autonoleggiosardinya.com.

Main Roads
The main road connecting the south of Sardinia with the north is the SS 131 (Carlo Felice), built in four lanes. It starts in Cagliari and reaches Porto Torres, passing by Oristano; near Abbasanta the road divides and a branch now reaches Olbia: the SS 131 dir. The other main road is the SS 125 going from Cagliari to Arzachena, following the coast; it is a slow road which usually takes longer than anticipated, often because of lorries or campers (during the summer) which don't allow overtaking. As mentioned earlier, ongoing improvements to the SS 125 – including new tunnels and flyovers – are shortening journey times.

Parking
Large towns like Cagliari have adopted "blue stripes" parking places: each parking place is marked with a blue line indicating that you must pay. Look for a car park attendant with a blue badge or buy a ticket from a parking machine. Always lock your car when parked; never leave anything valuable in the car or even risk hiding belongings in the boot.

Driving Information
Seat belts are compulsory.
The use of headlights is compulsory outside urban centres
Children should travel in the back seat. According to EU law child seats for smaller children are mandatory.
Maximum speed in built-up areas is 50kmh (30mph), in other areas it is 90kmh (55mph) on ordinary roads. The Carlo Felice may seem like a motorway but it is not; speed limits vary along it (maximum speed is 110kmh (68 miles) on dual carriageways).
Senso Unico means One Way.

Oristano farmer on his bike.

Cycling
Cycling is popular, especially outside Sardinia's main towns and cities. In recent years it has become a particularly popular destination for cycle touring. Specialist tour operators who organise bike tours include http://skedaddle.co.uk, www.dolcevitabiketours.com, www. sardiniacycling.com and www. sardiniagrandtour.com.

There is also an automated bike sharing system operating in numerous Italian cities, with several renting stations in Cagliari, Carbónia and Olbia in Sardinia. The first half an hour is free of charge, while the second half costs €0.50 and subsequent hours €1. For more information visit http://bicincitta.tobike.it.

On Foot
Many of Sardinia's towns are a joy to walk around, as they are compact with most of their main sights easily accessible on foot. Both Alghero and Oristano have small historic centres, while Sassari's medieval quarter can be explored in a few hours. Cagliari may sprawl up and down hills and along beaches and lakes, but its *centro storico* can be explored on foot – although some nifty legwork is needed to pack in all the sights in one day. Some streets around the Marina area (Via Sardegna, Via Concezione, Via Napoli and Via Barcellona) are pedestrian-only, which makes exploring the city even more enjoyable. The mountainous interior, especially around La Barbagia, Monti di Gennarentu and Golfo di Orosei, is wild country that attracts outdoor enthusiasts and climbers. Don't forget to bring sturdy walking boots and other kit if you are planning trekking adventures. Local walking guides are invaluable for the more challenging routes.

EATING OUT

BEST RESTAURANTS, BARS AND CAFÉS

WHAT TO EAT

Contrary to the assumption of many foreigners, the island's name has nothing to do with sardines. Sardinia is not traditionally a seafaring island although fish abound in the surrounding waters. Although meat is central to the island's cuisine, in many restaurants on or near the sea the menu is 80 percent fish-based. Popular seafood dishes include *anguille* (eels), *gamberi* (prawns), *calamari* (squid), *arselle* (clams) and, at the top end of the scale, *aragosta* (lobster), in season from March to the end of August. As fish is concerned, there is *orata* (gilthead bream), *tonno* (tuna), *sogliola* (sole), *spigola* (seabass), *cefalo* (grey mullet) and *pesce spada* (swordfish). They are either grilled, lightly fried, baked or served in a marinade or white wine sauce.

Nevertheless, typical Sard cuisine is rustic and hearty. Typical main course meats are roast pork, chicken, wild boar and lamb – the choice varies according to the season. Best known meat dish is *porchetto* (also called *porcetto* and *porceddu*) – suckling pig. A young pig is gently roasted on a spit, flavoured with myrtle, rosemary, laurel and sage, and served on cork trays with *pane carasau* (crisp flatbread) and myrtle leaves. *Capretto* (kid goat) is cooked in the same way, though it's not quite as popular. Another favourite is *agnello allo spiedo*, spit-roast lamb, best eaten in December. Vegetables come separately and are not a Sardinian strong point. Artichokes (sometimes served with peas), aubergines and asparagus are usually the best bets. Salads are invariably *verde* (green,

that is, lettuce only) or *misto* (mixed, with tomato).

The island is also well-known for its cheeses. Most of Italy's *pecorino* is produced here. Made from ewes' milk it comes in various forms, most commonly the *pecorino romano* and the stronger *pecorino sardo* which is matured for three to 12 months. Sardinia manufactures light wines, and around 20 of them boast a DOC status (Denominazione di Origine Controllata, indicating a quality wine). Only one Sardinian wine – Vermentino di Gallura – is classified as DOCG (Denominazione di Origine Controllata Garantita), which guarantees an even higher quality. House wine (*vino della casa*) is usually fine and reasonably priced. Wine by the glass is almost unheard of, so diners should be prepared for a full bottle. A good meal is often concluded with a glass of liqueur or a choice of *amari* (bitters).

WHERE TO EAT

Given the centrality of eating out to Sardinian social life and the pride taken in the preparation of meals, the standard of even moderately priced restaurants is high. Nearly all restaurants offer some local variations of typical Sardinian dishes, and few visitors will return home feeling dissatisfied. It is also worth noting that snacking in bars is much more part of daily life in Sardinia than in other European countries. As a consequence, there are numerous bars throughout the island which serve a variety of sandwiches and other snacks as well as drinks. Tourist centres and villages are usually quite small, so you will tend to find the

best bars in the main square or its surroundings.

Bars serve *panini* (rolls) and *tramezzini* (small sandwiches) with alcoholic and non-alcoholic drinks. Pay first and give the receipt to the barman with the order. Most people stand at the bar, as a charge is made for sitting at a table. *Paninotecche* are sandwich bars where you can pop in for a quick meal. A *ristorante* is traditionally a formal place to eat. A *trattoria* is generally less formal than a restaurant and serves local dishes – however, in recent years the distinction between *ristoranti* and *trattorie* has blurred somewhat, so many expensive eateries now have the word trattoria in their title.

Courses are served in this order: *un antipasto*: appetiser; *un primo*: first course (risotto, pasta or soup perhaps); *un secondo*: main course, usually meat or fish served with *contorni*: side dishes of vegetables, etc; *un dolce* is a dessert; and *il conto* is the bill.

Italian coffee is to many the best in the world.

CAGLIARI

Restaurants

Antica Hostaria
Via Cavour 60
Tel: 070-665 870
www.anticahostaria.it €€
One of Cagliari's oldest eateries –
opened in the 1850s – is renowned
for its seasonal and seafood menu
which might include risotto al
radicchio and pappardelle pasta with
salmon and prawns.

Crackers
Corso Vittorio Emanuele 195
Tel: 070-653 912 €€
A very original blend of Sardinian
and Piemontese cuisines – expect
risottos and stews alongside braised
meat and fish – with fresh seafood
and produce including lots of truffles
and mushrooms reminiscent of Le
Langhe.

Dal Corsaro
Viale Margherita 28
Tel: 070-664 318
www.dalcorsaro.com €€€
Elegance and refinement are
the watchwords here, from the
immaculate table settings in the
two pristine dining rooms to the
beautifully crafted cuisine. The classic
starter of thin escalopes of *pesce del
giorno* is typically followed by a risotto
and then a novel meat dish combo
or seafood main like sea bass with
saffron and potatoes.

Dal Corsaro al Mare
Porto Turistico di Marina Piccola
Tel: 070-370 295
www.dalcorsaroalmare.it €€€
A magical position on Poetto's Marina
Piccola, combined with classic fish
and seafood dishes make this perfect
for a special occasion. Good selection
of spaghetti, gnocchetti and ravioli
complements the menu.

Flora
Via Sassari 45
Tel: 070-664 735 €€
Antiques fill the spacious dining
rooms of this traditional trattoria.
They do a mighty tasty *linguine ai ricci*
(pasta with sea urchin eggs), stewed
cinghiale (wild boar) and San Pietro
(John Dory) with fresh tomatoes.

Lillicu
Via Sardegna 78
Tel: 070-652 970 €
A long-time favourite, famed for its
relaxed dining and seafood classics
like *fritto misto di mare* and *spaghetti
con arselle* (tiny clams). Amiable
waiters keep bringing the plates to
the white marble tables while regulars
slurp house wine from small battered
glasses and fire banter around the old

refectory-like dining hall. Revel in the
Cagliaritana spirit.

Lord Nelson
Via Tevere 2
Tel: 349-870 2215 €€
A popular seafood restaurant
showcasing pictures of Lord Nelson
and small replicas of HMS Victory. As
you can expect, the delicious menu is
very much fish-based.

Luigi Pomata
Viale Regina Margherita 14
Tel: 070-672 058
www.luigipomata.com €€
Luigi Pomata's team serve sushi-
inspired dishes, handmade pasta
and tasty grilled meat and fish, all
with a modern, often revelatory
twist. Standouts include the *tartare
di tonno* rosso (red tuna tartare)
with celery, green apple and lemon
purée. The business lunch (two
courses plus water for €15) is
superb value.

Martinelli's
Via Principe Amedeo 51
www.martinellis.it €€
Run by chef Roberto Raccis,
Martinelli's serves up inventive
seasonal dishes. Portions are
generous too. The only downside
is that the place is small, so book
ahead.

Pizzeria Federico Nansen
Corso Vittorio Emanuele 269
Tel: 070-651 444 €
Typical Italian family-run pizzeria with
fast counter service and plenty of
choice of delicious pizzas. Seating
is available, but the shop is usually
fully packed, so takeaway may be a
better idea.

Il Rifugio dei Sapori
Corso Vittorio Emanuele 445

Tel: 070-756 1995 €
Full of vegetarian tastes of Sardinia,
this eatery serves reasonably priced
dishes made of local and seasonal
ingredients.

Sa Domu Sarda
Via Sassari 51
Tel: 070-653 400 €€
A homely, rustic wood and
handicrafts-filled dining room makes
for an atmospheric and relaxed
setting for enjoying no-nonsense
Sardinian plates of *cinghiale*,
culurgiones (ravioli-type parcels) and
carasau (crispy thin bread).

Stella Marina di Montecristo
Via Sardegna 140
Tel: 347-578 8964 €
This authentic Sardinian fish
restaurant with a set menu is always
full (though be warned that very little
English is spoken here). Do try the
deep-fried squid, grilled seabass or
scallops in tomato sauce.

La Tana del Gusto
Via Pergolesi 1/B
Tel: 070-754 3153 €€
A popular restaurant specialising
in seafood and excellent service.
The decor is rather dull, but don't
worry the beautiful dishes will liven
things up.

Trattoria del Porto
Via Roma (Molo Dogana)
Tel: 070-659 613
www.trattoriadelporto.com €
Amid the portside bustle there's
atmosphere and good-value seafood
aplenty here. The fresh pasta
with lobster, mussels, shrimps or
scampi are some of the mariners'
favourites.

Trattoria Gennargentu
Via Sardegna 60

Enjoying lunch alfresco on the terrace of the Librarium Nostrum.

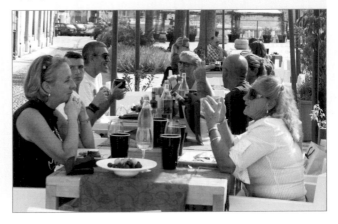

Tel: 070-658 247 €
Hearty Ogliastra cuisine including wild boar (in season) alongside seafood classics like *tonno alla Carlofortina* (tuna steak in a tomato salsa) are served in simple whitewashed surroundings.

Caffè-Bars, Pasticcerie and Gelaterie

Antico Caffe dal 1885
Piazza Costituzione 10/11
Tel: 070-658 206
www.anticocaffe1855.it €
Historic café once frequented by the likes of Grazia Deledda, D.H. Lawrence and Gabriele D'Annunzio, with a terrace overlooking the Bastione di San Remy. Sumptuous drinks, pastries, ice creams and dishes are served by dapper staff amid elegant interiors. Some original details remain – including railings forged by penal colony workers.

Caffè degli Spiriti
Bastione San Remy
Tel : 070-311 0373
www.caffedeglispiriti.com €€
Tucked below the Bastione San Remy's *molto*-chic terrace bar scene, this café has splendid views and serves Italian classics. At weekends DJs play music and the action moves outside.

Caffè Svizzero
Largo Carlo Felice 6/8
Tel: 070-653 784 €
Just up from the imposing town hall is this historic café with old wooden cabinets, brick arches and antique cash register. As well as doing a killer espresso, there are sweet *paste* to enjoy, and their savoury bites, beautifully displayed, are as tempting.

Emerson
Viale Poetto 4
Tel: 070-375 194
www.emersoncafe.it €

Pizza and beer for lunch.

The swankiest Poetto beach bar offers pasta dishes, salads and snacks, alongside the cocktails, DJ tunes and sun loungers.

Isola del Gelato
Piazza Yenne 35
Tel: 070-659 824
Amid the Piazza Yenne crowds is this long cavern-like space with a mini waterfall and hundreds of ice-cream flavours.

Libarium Nostrum
Via Santa Croce 33/35
€
There's a black cab that shuttles people to and from piazza Costituzione to this swanky bar-café. Cagliari's *bella gente* scoff *stuzzichini* (snacks), *gelati* and cocktails, listening to live music, while lounging on the Castello ramparts.

La Paillote
Cala Fighera
Tel: 070-371 584
www.lapaillote.it €
It's a bit of a hike but well worth the effort to reach the idyllic bay of Cala

Fighera, where you can lounge around the pool and pebbly beach, snacking on bar bites and sipping cool drinks. A bountiful buffet of pasta and seafood dishes is served in the evening as the sun sets.

Pasticceria Pirani
Via Pacinotti 11
Tel 070-493 378 €
Cagliaritani take time out from the nearby San Benedetto market to pick up pastries and coffee, as well as their famous party cakes and Christmas confections. Their savoury plates – salads, *frittate* and *pizzette* – also go down well.

Tramer
Piazza Martiri d'Italia 11
Te : 070-652 828 €
Established in 1857, Tramer has evocative reminders of its past, from the handsome old cabinets lined with sweet jars to period pieces. Delicious *cornetti* and brioche are perfect with their cappuccino. Their puff pastry pizzas and panini are fresh and filling.

CAGLIARI TO ARBATAX

Muravera

Centro Ippico Agriturismo del Sarrabus
Località S'Ollasteddu, Via Case Sparse
Tel: 070-999 078
€
This agriturismo and equestrian centre housed within a striking building is a good bet for hearty fare, including spit-roast pork, lamb and wild boar. There are wonderful grounds to explore too.

L'Escargot
Via Marco Polo 4, Località Costa Rei
Tel: 070-451 8150 €

The seaside location and large terrazza make this place special. Snail is on the menu alongside seafood classics like spaghetti with mussels, prawns and squid.

Marina Gio
Marina di San Giovanni
Tel: 333-986 0200
www.marinagio.it
€€
Right on the beach of San Giovanni with a suitably fishy menu that includes grilled *pescato del giorno* (catch of the day) and a crunchy *frittura di mare* (seafood medley).

They also have a pizza oven and a piano bar nearby.

Tortolí

Drago Rosso
Corso Umberto 75
Tel: 0782-623 579 €

PRICE CATEGORIES

Prices for a meal for two with a bottle of wine:
€ = under €40
€€ = €40–70
€€€ = over €70

TRANSPORT

EATING OUT

ACTIVITIES

A – Z

LANGUAGE

This café-restaurant is renowned for its excellent coffee, chocolate and snacks. In the evenings Tortolí's young things fill the place from *aperitivo* hour to midnight.

Ittiturismo La Peschiera
Peschiera San Giovanni, Arbatax
Tel: 0782-664 415
€€
A visit here may include a guided tour of the lagoon with the fishermen who run the local cooperative. The freshest sea bass, bream, red mullet, shellfish, crustaceans and *bottarga* (fish roe) are used in simple fishy dishes served in a rustic dining setting.

Spiedo d'Ogliastra
Via Zinnias 23
Tel: 0782-623 856 €€
This spacious restaurant serves classic Ogliastra fare, including *culugionis* (pasta pockets) served with a sauce of tomatoes and herbs,

cuts of meat (*bue rosso*) and fabulous artisan cheeses. Good selection of regional wines.

Villasimius
Carbonara
Via Umberto 60
Tel: 070-791 270 €€
A welcoming atmosphere and lots of simply prepared seafood dishes as well as hearty fare like lamb cutlets, local sausages and cheeses.

I Menhirs
Annunziata Castiadas,
Località Annunziata
Tel: 070-994 9272
www.imenhirs.it €€
This beguiling stone hotel development is a 20-minute drive inland from Villasimius towards the Sette Fratteli hills. It's all about simple, local country fare, from the antipasti *casu axedu* (fresh goat's cheese) and fried seasonal

vegetables, to *ravioli di ricotta*, roast piglet and grilled meats.

Mora Bianca
Via Roma 14
Tel: 331-399 5999€€
Whitewashed walls enclose the courtyard, where summer diners savour no-nonsense home-made cooking. Favourite dishes include freshly caught fish cooked in Vernaccia, penne with swordfish and aubergine. Evenings are popular with groups who come for decent pizza.

Il Moro
Località Villaggio dei Mandorli
Tel: 070-798 180€€
This amiable restaurant serves Sardinian specialities, including seafood classics like *aragosta* (lobster) and *insalata di mare* (seafood salad), meaty morsels of pork and beef, accompanied by roast vegetables, as well as long-time favourite pasta dishes.

GOLFO DI OROSEI TO OLBIA

Altopiano del Golgo
Ristorante Tipico Golgo
Golgo, Baunei
Tel: 0782-610 675
www.ristorantetipicogolgo.com
€€
This rustic retreat on the high limestone plain of Golgo is perfect after a day in the great outdoors. Book a table on the terrace or in the wood- and stone-filled dining area and order hearty mountain fare, including *tagliata di manzo* (cuts of meat) and *culurgiones* (pasta pockets with sweet tomato salsa).

Dorgali and Cala Gonone
Ispinigoli
Hotel Ispinigoli, Doragli

Decorative angel on a café.

Tel: 0784-95268
www.hotelispinigoli.it €€
The top-notch menu favours land produce, but there is room for seafood surprises here. Don't miss the chance to sample their speciality fresh pasta ravioli with cheese and mint filling, called *sos anzellotos*. Roast meats are popular, as is the grilled *pescato del giorno* (catch of the day). The terrace boasts superb panoramic views.

Su Recreu
Piazza Andrea Doria, Cala Gonone
Tel: 0784-93135 €
For top-quality food on the beach, right by the natural wonders of Cala Gonone, there is no competition. Snacks and various pasta dishes

make it an excellent spot for lunch between dips. Those needing to cool down have a tempting choice of *gelati*, *sorbetti* and *granite*. It's a magical spot by morning and at sunset.

Olbia
Barbagia
Via Galviani 94
Tel: 0789-51640
http://ristorantebarbagia.com €€
Traditional *cucina sarda* creations like *maccarones* and *cagliata acida* cheeses, alongside pizza in the evenings, are the mainstays of this reliable trattoria.

Bacchus
Via degli Astronauti 2
Tel: 0789-651 010 €€
Located in the Jazz Hotel, this swanky restaurant serves a vast selection of local dishes and wines. The staff are particularly attentive. Good value for money.

Café Nord Est
Viale A. Moro 183
Tel: 07895-53456 €
The owners of this café in the centre of town provide quality pastries as well as salads, cheese and cured meat platters. The evening buzz starts with an excellent *ora dell'aperitivo* (aperitif hour).

Oliena
Su Gologone
Su Gologone
Tel: 0784-287 512

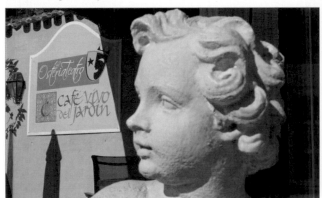

www.sugologone.it €€€
Su Gologone, a famous resort restaurant, delivers exquisite cuisine and atmosphere. Owner Pasqua Palimodde keeps an attentive eye on the standards, always adding new creations to the dizzying array of antipasti. Standouts include the *maharrones de punzu* (Oliena pasta dish) and roast meats (lamb, pork and goat).

Siniscola

Agriturismo Punta Lizzu
Ofricatu
Tel: 339-107 7654 €€
This farm stay does suitably hearty fare using the best local ingredients, including chunky wild mushrooms (*gardulas*), young, soft cheeses and homemade pasta. Roast meats (*s'arristu*) are cooked on spits and eaten outside.

Sometimes simple is best.

COSTA SMERALDA

Porto Cervo

Aruana Churrascaria
Località Liscia Di Vacca
Tel: 0789-906 085
www.aruana.it €€
Dine alfresco on a hearty Brazilian fare from all-you-can-eat buffet, including churrasco-style meat, while listening to live music. This trendy restaurant, which boasts a romantic garden setting with a small pool, is open from Easter to October. Unless you are a vegetarian it's a must when visiting Porto Cervo.

Aqua Lounge
Piazza Azzurra
Tel: 0789-902 294
www.aqualounge.it €€€
Somewhere so achingly trendy and glam-packed may dampen your appetite, but the portions in this bar-restaurant with its inventive and

truly international menu are small. The food is delicious, though. April to September all day.

La Briciola
Liscia di Vacca
Tel: 0789-91409 €
With wood-fired pizzas starting at €5 and grilled *manzo* (beef) served with rocket and Sardinian *pecorino* at €13, served by friendly sisters, this is a real find.

Café du Port
Molo Vecchio
Tel: 0789-92348
€
This historic café is in a fabulous position at the mouth of the marina. The prices are pretty decent too, despite its swanky location and jewel-encrusted clientele. The coffee is excellent, pastries adequate. A small selection of cold dishes is available

at lunch. Come the evening the crowd swells with *aperitivo* sippers.

Frati Rossi
Villa Della Pantogia, Arzachena
Tel: 0789-94395
www.fratirossi.it €€
For something special you don't need to blow the budget. Just 2km (1 mile) from the centre of Porto Cervo lies this rustic heaven for gourmands. Expect Sardinian classics with Ligurian and Tuscan culinary influences. Standout dishes include tuna carpaccio and vegetable *sformato* (kind of soufflé).

Lu Pasticciu
Liscia di Vacca
Tel: 0789-90060 €
Open every day from 9am until 11pm, you ll have plum position to people-watch here, especially outside on the terrace.

GALURA AND THE NORTH

Arzachena and environs

Le Café Prestige
Via Dettori 23
Tel: 0789-845 019 €€
This modern, gleaming café bar sells coffees and snacks, such as well-stuffed *tramezzini* and panini at all hours. Their *cornetto* with chocolate and cream filling is a knockout.

Il Fungo
Via La Marmora 21
Tel: 0789-83340 €€
A busy pizzeria that attracts families,

older couples, young lovers and tourists alike. The wood-fired pizzas are juicy and crisp at the same time, and you can take away if you prefer. Closed October to April.

Ristorante del Porto
Via Nazionale 94, Cannigione
Tel: 0789-88011
www.hoteldelporto.com €€
Located in the Hotel del Porto, this unpretentious place draws seafood lovers from distant shores, and with good reason.

La Vecchia Arzachena
Via Garibaldi 15
Tel: 0789-83105
www.lavecchiacosta.it
€€

PRICE CATEGORIES

Prices for a meal for two with a bottle of wine:
€ = under €40
€€ = €40–70
€€€ = over €70

Keeping it simple if a touch pricey, this vibrant long-time favourite is always buzzing.

La Maddalena

Il Rifugio dei Peccatori
Via Quarto 1
tel: 366-314 6855
www.rifugioceipeccatori.com €€€
This rustic Italian osteria only has a few tables, so make sure you book in advance if you want to savour their excellent Sardinian seafood.

Porto Torres

Il Mare
Via Galileo Galilei 28, Porto Torres
Tel: 0794-502 458
www.ristoranteilmare.it €€
For consistently good seafood dishes – such as *risotto pescatora* or *spaghetti ai frutti di mare* – this a good bet.

Da Ugo
Corso Italia 7, Lu Bagnu, Castelsardo
Tel: 0794-74124
www.ristorantedaugo.eu €€
Overlooking the sea, this is an ideal spot for those feeling romantic or just those who love fish, which you can

inspect before you commit to eat. Closed February.

Santa Teresa di Gallura

Saltara
Località Saltara
Tel: 0789-755 597
www.ristorantesaltara.it €€
A rural restaurant serving a set menu of homemade dishes in a picturesque setting. Portions are really huge, so you won't leave hungry. Despite the remote location, the restaurant is fully packed each night.

S'Andira
Via Orsa Minore 1, Santa Reparata
Tel: 0789-754 273
www.sandira.it €€€
Right on the top of a hill overlooking Santa Teresa di Gallura, this small restaurant mixes tradition and modernity. Their refined creations include gnocchi with ricotta cheese and cannellini beans with prawns. Closed October to early May.

Tempio Pausania

Bisson
Via San Luca 8

Tel: 079-632 876 €€
If you are after some innovative Sardinian cooking, this is a good bet. Expect some mouth-watering combinations, like melting slivers of pink beef oozing juices, served with orange slices and pan-fried potatoes.

Friend's Café
Viale Valentino 17
Tel: 0796-34021 €
A delightful mix of traditional with Italian gadgetry, this café is true to its name. This is a great place to unwind with a book or magazine (they have a small library for patrons) or to work in their computer corner.

Purgatorio
Via Garibaldi 9
Tel: 0796-34042
€€
A welcoming eatery in the *centro storico*. Ask for *assaggini di antipasti* (tasting selection) – including Oliena *salumi* and various cheeses. Their classic Sardinian dishes are beautifully executed, especially the *culurgiones* (potato-, cheese- and mint-filled pasta parcels).

SASSARI

L'Antica Hostaria
Via Cavour 55
Tel: 079-200 066 €€
An intimate setting to sample Sardinian cuisine bursting with originality and bold flavours. Imagine an antipasto of Ovinfort *pecorino* cheese *semifreddo* mousse accompanied by a hot *faro* (spelt) fritter with the whiff of wild fennel, followed by sea bass with broccoli salsa, then a *torrone semifreddo* dessert.

Ellas Snc
Via Usai 33
Tel: 079-9103 745 €

Classic Italian combination.

A slice of Greece in the heart of Sassari. It's small though, so takeaway is a good option. Moussaka eggplant rolls are exceptionally good, gyros and pita rank high too.

Fainè Sassu
Via Usai 17
Tel: 079-236 402 €€
Purveyor of *fainè*, that Genovese culinary import – a type of *farinata*, which takes a pizza-like form and is made of a batter mix of chickpea flour, olive oil and water. Served with savoury toppings like onions and sausages and washed down with beer.

Giamaranto
Via Alghero 69
Tel: 079-274 598 €
A well-established and reliable eatery that concentrates on seafood cuisine with the occasional inspired use of seasonal terra firma produce. Their plate of fresh *ricci* (sea urchins) combined with asparagus and wild mushrooms is sublime.

Gusta' Vinho's
Via Turritana 11
Tel: 079-200 250 €
Deep in the *centro storico*, this café-bar excels in its choice of regional wines (over 450 labels available), hot freshly made pastries, salads and cold dishes. Evenings they serve pasta and other simple dishes. They have a shop selling wines and Sassarese specialities nearby.

Liberty
Piazza N. Sauro 3
Tel: 079-232 681 €€€
Sumptuous, refined dining in elegant surroundings. Expect fresh seafood antipasti including oysters, scallops, tuna and prawns. Pasta dishes include spaghettini with scampi and sweet tomatoes. A typical main is catch of the day roasted and served with seasonal vegetables. Excellent wine list.

Fresh fish is not hard to find on the coast.

Al Vecchio Borgo
Largo Porta Utzeri 2
Tel: 339-808 9783
€€
This cosy yet elegant restaurant is one of the best in Cagliari. The seasonal menu concentrates on the freshest fish and seafood, all beautifully presented. Do try the tiramisu for dessert.
Il Vecchio Mulino
Via Figaglia 5
Tel: 079-4920 324
€€
Exciting, Sardinian cuisine served in the rustic setting of an old mill. Raviolis in all its guises. Appetisers and desserts are excellent too.

ALGHERO TO ORISTANO

Alghero

Andreini
Via Ardoino 45
Tel: 079-982 098
www.ristoranteandreini.it €€
An elegant and reliable choice deep in the heart of Alghero's atmospheric *centro storico*. The cuisine is a tad more inventive than traditional Alghero fare, with lots of wonderful local ingredients featuring like *pesce spada* (swordfish) carpaccio alongside some crazy combinations, including tuna steak served with red-pepper ice cream.
Caffè Costantino
Piazza Civica 30
Tel: 0799-76154 €
Bang-smack in the middle of Alghero on Piazza Civica, this bar within graceful Palazzo d'Alibis is the place to see and be seen. Eat tasty panini, *tramezzini* and *gelati* under the piazza foliage or amid the artworks and antiques inside.
Cavour
Via Cavour 110
Tel: 079-973 8762 €
Lots of Alghero atmosphere and characters fill this reasonably priced trattoria in the centre. Seafood favourites like sea bream bake and trusty *terra* dishes including *cinghiale* (wild boar). Excellent service and regional wine list too.

Bosa

Ristorante Chelo
Via Lungomare Mediterraneo
Tel: 0785-373013 €€€
This elegant restaurant on the waterfront specialises in seafood, but there are some good meat dishes on the menu too. For a romantic night out, have a sunset dinner on the terrace.

Sa Pischedda
Via Roma 8
Tel: 0785-373 065
www.hotelsapischedda.com
€
This fabulous hotel restaurant has a decent menu that favours seafood. Standout dishes include their fragrant pasta dish served with scorpion fish and basil. Lobster lovers will get their arthropod for a snip here. They also do a fabulous tiramisu.

Cabras

Agriturismo Pinuccia
Via Diaz 42
Tel: 0783-391 015
www.agriturismopinuccia.it €€
Hearty homemade Sardinian fare and unpretentious egalitarian seating at long tables make dining at this restaurant a unique cultural experience. Enjoyable food, wine and prices.

Cuglieri

Trattoria Desogos
Vico Cugia 6
Tel: 0785-39660 €€
A family-run trattoria with typical Sardinian cooking and cosy atmosphere attended by many a local. Superb selection of antipasti. The place is slightly off the beaten track, but you won't regret the effort to find it.

Macomer

Cubo Bar 90
Corso Umberto I 103
Tel: 0785-70677 €
Macomer's minimalist Cubo is a great place to start the day with one of their croissants. They also do superb panini.

Gulliver
Via Gramsci 42
Tel: 0785-226 001 €
Superb-value dining served here, enjoyed by Macomer's regulars and the odd tourist. Grilled meats are served with excellent fresh vegetable and lots of *funghi* dishes. The healthy choice of *contorni* (side dishes) make it a decent choice for veggies.

Magomadas

Riccardo
Via V. Emanuele 13
Tel: 0785-35631
www.recipesmediterranean.com €
Diners get superb seasonal dishes at an affordable price here. Classic seafood dishes include spaghetti *ai ricci* (sea urchin eggs), prawn and bean broth and grilled meats.

Oristano

Blac Ristorante
Via Mazzini 114
Tel: 0783-030 602
www.blac.it €€
A friendly restaurant with a brick interior, impeccable service and high-quality food. The menu features fish, seafood and meat dishes. The grilled vegetables are excellent.
Josto al Duomo
Via Vittorio Emanuele 34
Tel: 0783-778 061
www.hotelduomo.net €€€

PRICE CATEGORIES

Prices for a meal for two with a bottle of wine:
€ = under €40
€€ = €40–70
€€€ = over €70

Biscotti marmellata – traditional jam-filled biscuits – are a speciality of the region.

Run by chef Pierluigi Fais, this elegant hotel restaurant reinterprets traditional Sardinian dishes, focusing on seasonal specialities and local ingredients. All dishes are beautifully presented and the wine list is extensive.

Giovanni
Via Cristoforo Colombo 8, Torre Grande
Tel: 0783-22051 €
In recent years this old trattoria has undergone a gradual shift towards modern interpretations of *cucina oristanese* classics. A typical meal might kick off with a salad of *bottarga* (mullet roe) with artichokes, then fish-filled ravioli followed by catch of the day, often eel or bream.

THE SOUTHWEST

Carbónia

La Lanterna
Satta Sebastiano 67 ; Tel: 338-339 6223 €
This is a busy, no-frills ristorante-pizzeria. Don't be put off by how the place looks like from the outside – the food tastes just great.

Chia

Aquadulci
Domus de Maria
Tel: 070-923 0555
www.aquadulci.com €€€
Chef Angelo Biscotti combines tradition, innovation and stunning, arty plate presentation at this hotel restaurant amid Chia's dreamy dunes. After small but perfectly formed seafood and meat dishes, choose melt-in-your mouth nougat dessert. The superb wine list includes fruity and mellow white Nuvole di Ale from Gallura.

Iglésias

La Marmora
Piazza La Marmora €
A handsome peachy-hued 19th-century palazzo right on the piazza, with historic murals – including old adverts for Liquore Strega and Hallwood cash registers – make this café-*pasticceria* a splendid place for alfresco refreshments and pastries.

Isola di San Pietro – Carloforte

Nicolo
Corso Cavour 32
Tel: 0781-854 048
www.danicolo.net €€€
The reputation of the Pomatas (see Luigi Pomata review in Cagliari section) is built on a combination of Sardinian, Ligurian and even Arabic culinary influences, imagination and impeccable service. Locally caught tuna – sought out by the Japanese – is of the highest quality imaginable. Other menu mainstays include the chickpea *fainè*, couscous, *bottarga* (grey mullet roe) fish soup and *seadas* (a traditional sweet fritter pairing the sweetness of honey with the saltiness of *pecorino* cheese, making for an intriguing and intense flavour).

Osteria della tonnara
Corso Battellieri 36
Tel: 0781-855 734
www.ristorantedaandrea.it €€€
If you want tuna, this is the place to go. Also known as Ristorante Da Andrea, this highly-rated osteria is located on the Carloforte waterfront. Red tuna rules here, and Chef Andrea Rosso prepares it in myriad ways: tuna lasagne, tuna freselle, tuna tartar and tuna tagliata are just some of the options.

Isola di Sant'Antioco

Pasqualino
Via Regina Margherita 85, Calasetta
Tel: 0781-88473 €€
The bright dining room with its nautically themed photos matches the simple seafood fare served here. Don't miss the chance to sample the area's couscous, known as *cascà*. Grilled catch of the day and a fulsome fish soup are mainstays.

Rubiu Birrificio Artigianale
Via Bologna Senza Numero Civico, Sant'Antioco
Tel: 346-723 4605
www.rubiubirra.it €€
Prime-quality original pizzas with flavoured bases (basil or saffron), home-brewed beer and delicious desserts make this small, trendy place a must-do if you're in Sant'Antioco.

Nuxis

Letizia
Via San Pietro 12/14
Tel: 0781-957 021
www.letiziaristorante.it €€
Unpretentious eatery that prides itself on traditional Sardinian country cooking. Locally picked ingredients like wild herbs, mushrooms, fruits and vegetables add flavour and authenticity to classic dishes, including braised *cinghiale* (wild boar) with juniper berries. Those with a sweet tooth should try the creamy chocolate dessert with chilli.

Portoscuso

Ghinghetta
Via Cavour 26
Tel: 0781-508 143
www.laghinghetta.com €€€
A very posh setting and high-quality cuisine make this the perfect place for a special occasion. Starters include *affumicati* (smoked meats); a typical *primo* combines home-made pasta with seafood; among the mains are delicious local tuna and beef. The wine list comprises quality regional wines. Closed end of October to early April.

Pula

Su Nuraghe
Via Nora 57
Tel: 070-920 9144 €
The three Spano brothers who run this popular café produce some of the best ice cream in the southwest. Regional ingredients including Pula figs and strawberries from Arborea go into their delicious *gelati*. There's a good choice of savoury options too; the pleasant

terrace on the top floor is the place to go for snacks, salads and crêpes.

Zia Leunora
Via Trieste 19
Tel: 070-920 9559
www.ristorantezialeunorapula.com €€
Book a table in the intimate garden and enjoy bountiful portions of traditional Sardinian fare, including

chunks of tuna served in a herby tomato and onion salsa. *Malloreddus* pasta with punchy *pomodori* is another favourite.

Teulada

Trattoria da Gianni
Porto Budello
Tel: 070-928 3015

www.trattoria-dagianni.it €€
While eating the catch of the day (*pesce del giornata*) and fresh seafood pasta you can gaze out of the picture windows and admire the views of the Spanish watchtower and sparkling seascape. The *frittura di mare* (seafood medley) is especially good.

THE BARBAGIA

Aritzo

Hotel Sa Mavara
Località Fontana Rubia
Tel: 0784-629 336 €€
Take a table on the veranda overlooking lush pastures or in a spacious dining area, where you can feast on home-made pasta creations, grilled meats and cheeses.

Bitti and environs

Agriturismo Romanzesu
Località Romanzesu, Bitti
Tel: 0784-415 716
€€
Beyond the gnarly old olive trees and rustic stone facade you can sample hearty mountain fare from the farm, including lots of antipasti cold cuts and sausages, as well as roast meats and pasta dishes.

Agriturismo Testone
Località Sa Serra (Nùgoro/Nuoro)
Tel: 0784-230 539
www.agriturismotestone.com
€
Sitting on the Sa Terra table mountain, this farm takes some effort to get to, but its rustic charms and hearty food reward the intrepid. The friendly owners use their own products, which include lamb, cheese, honey, *pane carasau* and hams in traditional mountain dishes.

Enjoying an alfresco drink in Nuoro.

Fonni and Gavoi

Il Cinghialetto
Via Grazia Deledda, Fonni
Tel: 0784-57660
www.ilcinghialetto.it €€
Expect heaped helpings of roast meat dishes – including the occasional wild boar – at this relaxed hotel restaurant. Local mountain cheeses and cured meats are also strong here.

Santa Rughe
Via Carlo Felice 2, Gavoi
Tel: 0784-53774 €€
Gavoi is known for its subtly smoked Fiore Sardo cheese which compliments the robust local dishes here, which include *sa purpuza* (pork marinated in wine), home-made pasta and grilled meats.

Su Ninnieri
Località Bruncu Spina, Fonni
Tel: 0784-57729
www.suninnieri.com €
This rustic inn does excellent meat dishes and classic regional versions of *marraconis* and *culurgionis*. Their gooey *seadas* dessert made with local honey is worth the detour alone.

Nuoro

Caffè Tettamanzi
Corso Garibaldi 71 €
The decor is dedicated to local literary figure Sebastiano Satta, who used to enjoy the bar's excellent coffee and

cornetto al cioccolato. Good also for snacks and *aperitivi*, which come with *stuzzichini* (nibbles).

Ciusa
Viale Ciusa 55
Tel: 0784-257 052 €
Attentive service and a mix of traditional and creative elements makes Ciusa an excellent choice in Nouro. Grilled and fried meats and fish dominate the mains. The classic noodly Nuorese soup, *filindeu*, is a must.

Il Portico
Mons. Bua 13
Tel: 0784-217 641 €
This highly-rated restaurant serves superb, beautifully presented food in a friendly atmosphere. The menu focuses on seafood and fish, but there are lots of vegetarian options too.

Il Rifugio
Via A. Mereu 28
Tel: 0784-232 355
www.trattoriarifugio.com €
Mare and *terra* dishes are served in a cosy mountain refuge full of dark wood and delicious smells. Menu mainstays include cuttlefish and saffron risotto and spit-roast lamb with peas.

Seui-Ussassai

Ristoro Su Ponti 'E Irtzioni
SS 198, then turn off at Ponte sul Rio San Girolamo for Niala
Tel: 0782-55721 €
This welcoming rustic inn is immersed in dense wood and below towering *tacchi* outcrops, near the Trenino Verde stop of Niala. Simple local dishes like hardmade *culurgionis* pasta as well as *maialetto allo spiedo* (spit-roast piglet) are devoured by jolly crowds on long benches.

PRICE CATEGORIES

Prices for a meal for two with a bottle of wine:
€ = under €40
€€ = €40–70
€€€ = over €70

ACTIVITIES

THE ARTS, FESTIVALS, NIGHTLIFE, SHOPPING, OUTDOOR ACTIVITIES AND CHILDREN

THE ARTS

As well as thriving, state-funded arts venues in Cagliari and Sassari, there's lots going on all over the island, from a summer classical music festival in the buzzing seaside town of Alghero to theatrical performances in Cagliari and Sassari.

Music, Dance, Theatre and Ballet

Sardinia has some magical venues for concerts, gigs and theatrical events. Cagliari and Sassari may have the major auditoriums, but various festivals during the summer months bring world-class performances to provincial towns: see also Festivals.

Cagliari

Anfiteatro Romano
Viale Sant'Ignazio
Tel: 070-652 956
www.anfiteatroromano.it
Perhaps the most evocative venue hosts international acts like David Byrne and Brian Eno as well as musicals, classical concerts and dance events.

Fiera Campionaria
Viale Armando Diaz 221
Tel: 070-34961
www.fieradellasardegna.it
Cagliari's major exhibition centre hosts top Italian pop acts like Laura Pausini as well as jazz and classical.

Teatro Lirico and the Parco della Musica
Via Sant'Alenixedda
Tel: 070-40821
www.teatroliricodicagliari.it
Cagliari's top classical music venue stages traditional opera and ballet. Opened in 2011, Europe's biggest

piazza, Il Parco della Musica, stages outdoor cultural events in a grand amphitheatre. The park also boasts a musical fountain with lights and sounds chiming to the music of Händel.

Exmà
Via San Lucifero 71
Tel: 070-666 399
www.camuweb.it
A cultural centre that hosts the occasional jazz and chamber music concert.

Sassari

Teatro Civico
Corso Vittorio Emanuele II 39
Tel: 079-232 182
Stages plays, classical concerts and the occasional jazz gig.

Tempio Pausania
Teatro del Carmine, Piazza del Carmine
Tel: 079-671 580
Classical and operatic performances, and venue of the Festival d'Estate.

Museums

Cagliari's rich Neolithic and Nuraghic past makes it rich in archaeological finds. As well as the main collections at Cagliari's Museo Archeologico Nazionale and Sassari's Museo Nazionale G.A. Sanna, each small town seems to have an exhibition space dedicated to this fascinating past. Folk museums devoted to ancient pastoral lifestyles and crafts crop up all over the island as they dominate the island's history and culture. The opening times of these smaller museums and galleries especially are subject to change. It is advisable to telephone the museum beforehand to check, or contact the local tourist office.

FESTIVALS

With over 1,000 festivals taking place in Sardinia each year, there is no shortage of opportunities to sample heady rites that hail as far back as the Bronze Age. As well as *le sagre* which celebrate the harvest, each town honours its patron saint. In recent years many cultural events exploring musical and artistic themes have been added to the rich canon of traditional events. To check the latest events, consult: www.sardegna eventi24.it and www.giraitalia.it. Festivals range throughout the year from food and wine fairs to religious, cultural and musical festivals.

January–March

Lu Bogamarì (sea urchin festival), 1 Jan–early March; Alghero. For a month Alghero's restaurants have a sea urchin (*riccio di mare*)-based menu and there are lots of sea urchin-orientated events, especially at weekends. You can even hire a boat and go fishing with intrepid divers who plunge the depths for the spiky echinoderms. The orange salty eggs have a life-affirming taste of the sea, and are generally served unadorned with pasta.

Festa di Sant'Antonio Abate (16 and 17 January) marks the winter solstice and recalls pagan rites with bonfires and mask-wearing.

Carnevale happens the week before Ash Wednesday, with ghoulish parades in the Barbagia and masked horsemen stomping around the medieval streets of Oristano (Sa Sartiglia) and Santú Lussugiu (Sa Carrela è Nanti). The archaic ceremonies which take place during the masked parades in Mamoiada

The black carved mask of the Mamuthones.

and Ottana also present a fascinating spectacle, and there's a lively carnival in Bosa.

Easter

Sagra del Torrone (Nougat Fair), Easter weekend; Tonara.
This is the ideal time to see how the sweet Tonara version of *torrone* is made – from the intense initial mix of honey and dried fruit with *paioli in rame* (wooden paddles). Lots of music and cultural events are organised as the festival honours the town's celebrated tormented soul, the poet Peppinu Mereu (1872–1901), who loved to chew on things, both *dolce* and *amaro*.
Settimana Santa takes place in Easter week and is marked by silent processions which display Spanish and Catalan influences, including Alghero's Passion of Christ procession and the Lunissanti feast in Castelsardo. Impressive processions also take place in Sassari, Cagliari, Nuoro and Oliena.
Sa Festa Manna spans two weeks after Easter on the island of Sant'Antioco with parades and feasting to honour the Virgin Mary of Monserrato, the patron of Sulcis.

April

Sagra degli Agrumi (Citrus Fair), second Sunday before Easter; Muravera. This celebration of citrus fruit sees abundant markets full of fruits and lots of evocative folkloric dancing to the mournful sound of *launeddas*, an old wind instrument. Ox-drawn carts (*etnotraccas*) are paraded through town by traditionally dressed locals – some in masks hailing from all over the island.
Echi Lontani
A festival of chamber music – lots of Baroque – in evocative historical

places, Cagliari in April–June (www. echilontani.net).

May–June

Sant' Efisio on 1–4 May honours Cagliari's patron saint, who drove out the pestilence in the 17th century. Trying to get a room on 1 May in Cagliari is impossible. People dressed in ethnic and historical costumes come from all corners of the country to participate in the procession, beginning in Cagliari and finishing in Nora.
Cavalcata Sarda on the penultimate Sunday of May in Sassari involves costumed processions, horseracing and stunts.
Sant'Isidoro in Crosei is a celebration of agricultural life with traditionally dressed locals festooning their carts with flowers.
Girotonno (Tuna Fair), first week of June; Carloforte.
The Isola di San Pietro's world-famous tuna fair sees the main street turned into an open-air restaurant where international chefs compete in creating the prize *tonno* dish and versions of traditional plates of *tunnina*, *curzetti* and *cassuli*. The island's wonderful Tabarkine Ligurian-Tunisian cuisine is celebrated with tastings of *cashcà* (couscous) and breads focaccia and *farinata*.
Madonna dei Martiri (Monday after first Sunday of June) sees Fonni's residents carry a statue of the Virgin through the streets.
Here I Stay Festival (June)
Small indie music festival in Guspina, near Piscinas, with free camping (www.hereistay.com).
Sardinia International Music Festival This Italian classical musica festival is held in Sassari in late June–early July. Other festivals include: the
Tundimenta Seulesa (Sheep-

Shearing Festival) in Seulo; the **Cherry Fair** in Belvì; and the **Honey Fair** in Montevecchio.

July–August

Sagra dei Culurjones (Food Festival), early July. Tortoli.
The Ogliastra province's capital offers mountains of its *culurjones* pasta pockets (hearty type of ravioli filled with potatoes, cheese and onions) served with a tomato salsa. There's lots of music and wine-drinking all over the town's restaurants and piazzas.
Ardia (6 and 7 July) in Sedilo is a dust- and hair-raising, bareback stampede dedicated to San Costantino.
Notte dei Poeti (Night of Poets) Concerts and plays in the Roman theatre of Nora, Pula in July and August (www.lanottedeipoeti.it).
Estate Musicale Internazionale Alghero's classical music festival takes place in July and August (www.seratemusicalialghero.it).
La Sciampitta
The famous festival of folklore in Quartu S. Elena takes place every year in the first fortnight of July, with international and Sardinian folk groups (www.sciampitta.com).
Mondo Ichnusa Festival
A popular music festival featuring rock, folk-pop and hip-hop bands.
Is Fassonis at the end of July–early August involves the fishermen of Sinis race on *fassonis* rafts in the Stagno di Santa Giusta.
Cala Gonone Jazz Festival
CGJF features international jazz artists who wig out in Doragli's Parco Ticca (July–August; www.intermezzo nuoro it).
Time in Jazz
Annual festival in Berchidda attracts top jazz acts each August (www.time injazz.it).
Musica sulle Bocche
Summer Jazz festival in various jaw-dropping Santa Teresa Gallura venues including beach cliff-top, cloisters and piazza (www.musicasullebocche.it).
Sagra del Vermentino (Wine Fair), first Sunday of August. Monti. Up near the mountain of Limbara, this ancient vine, hailing from Portugal and Madeira, is the focus of much guzzling of the local wines accompanied by huge plates of *frittelle* (fritters) and local cheeses.
Santa Maria del Mare is a boat procession along the Temo river in Bosa followed by fireworks and feasting, on the first Sunday of August.
Li Candaleri on 14 August sees Sassari transformed by a vibrant procession of nine colossal candle towers.

TRANSPORT

EATING OUT

ACTIVITIES

A – Z

LANGUAGE

Le Palme Hotel on the Costa Smeralda.

Madonna Assunta on 15 August marks the cult of the "Risen Madonna" with traditionally dressed women parading a statue of the sleeping Virgin around various towns, including Cagliari and Orgoloso.
Corsa degli Scalzi is a bizarre barefoot race of white tunic-wearing young men carrying an effigy of Cabras's saint through the streets to the sanctuary of San Salvatore.
Festival Rocce Rosse and Blues Music festival usually in August, featuring performances by celebrated Italian songwriters like Baglioni and De Gregori as well as indie acts Subsonica and Sud Sound System (www.roccerosse.it) .
Other festivals include: **Vermentino** (wine) fair in Monti; and a **wild boar fair** in Domus de Maria.

September

Concordia Vocis–Festival Internazionale di cori polifonici (International festival of polyphonic choirs). From late August–October at various churches in Cagliari, Tortoli and Iglésias – including the Romanesque S. Saturnino and Cattedrale di Sant'Andrea (www.concordiavocis.it).
Cabudanne de sos Poetas Seneghe's is a festival of poetry at the end of August and comes with other cultural side dishes, including music concerts and culinary events (www.settembredeipoeti.it).
Villaggio Pescatori (Fish Festival). One week in early September. Giorgino, Cagliari.
Seafood specialities in the *marinaresca cagliaritana* tradition – *pruppu a schiscicnera* (octopus with garlic), *scabbecciu* (sweet and sour fishy dish), *lissa* (roast mullets) and *fritto misto* (fried seafood medley) – sizzle and are devoured by thousands all over town.

Mini football tournaments, concerts and culinary competitions add to the celebratory air.

October

Sagra delle Castagne e Nocciole (Chestnut and Hazelnut festival). Late October; Aritzo.
This humble nutty festival up in the wild Gennargentu mountains has been going strong since the early 1970s, and sees the mountain town of Aritzo swamped by foodies, who crunch the local nuts and sample lots of Barbagia's dishes and wines.

November–December

Festa del Vino Novello (all over Sardinia); November.
La vendemmia (grape harvest) is marked with festivals all over, including the Novello d'Oro (wine-tasting festival) held on the Trenino Verde, Arzana and similar events in Olbia and Milis.
Madonna dello Schiavo on 15 November involves a procession of a black Virgin through the streets of Carloforte.
Natale (Christmas) in Sardegna sees lots of presepi (Nativity scenes) created in churches and in people's homes.
Capo d'Any (New Year) Alghero, Cagiari, Sassari and Castelsardo are famed for their pyrotechnical displays to see in the New Year.

Festival Sardo: Cross-Pollination

A new strain of Sardinian festival has sprouted in recent years that pays tribute to folkloric traditions while emphasising new artistic expression and cross-pollination with

other cultures. Perhaps the most straightforward is La Sciampitta, a world-renowned festival of folklore, music and popular dance in Quartu S. Elena and other venues across the island in the first fortnight of July (www.sciampitta.com). As well as Sardinian folk groups, many international acts have appeared in recent years – from India, Bulgaria, Armenia, Portugal, Russia, Brazil, Senegal, Guatemala and Poland. Gavoi hosts Isola delle Storie in July, Sardinia's major literary gathering, where local and international writing talent come to read, chat and stroke chins (www.isoladellestorie.it).

NIGHTLIFE

Sardinians may meet up for an *apertivo* before a meal and then head out quite late in the evening to bars and clubs. Up-to-date information on concerts, theatre, nightclubs and discos can be found in the *L'Unione Sarda* and the *Nuova Sardegna*. During the summer they publish sections in English. Below are a few venues for a night out – bars and clubs change hands frequently so check details at your hotel or online before you set out.

Bars, Clubs and Music Venues

Cagliari

The swanky bars on the huge Bastione Saint Remy terrace are swelled with *la bella gente* at the weekends, who circulate and stretch out on outdoor sofas. In the summer Poetto's *baretti* (kiosks/bars) are the place to go.
Caffè De Candia
Via De Candia
A bar with a terrace on the bastions of S. Croce, open till 9pm.
Libarium Nostrum
Bastione S. Croce
Swanky American bar with music, situated in a 17th-century building. Their English cab taxies patrons to and from Piazza Costituzione.
Oasi Café
Viale Poetto
This Stylish bar on the Poetto beach has live music and DJ sets most summer nights.

Cagliari to Arbatax

El Peyote
Via Cagliari 17, Santa Maria, Villasimius
Dance, Eurohouse and hip-hop tunes are on the deep dish served at this club.

Golfo di Orosei to Olbia

Café Nord Est
Viale A. Moro 183, Olbia
Good food and snacks served here and a happening place at *l'ora di aperitivo* and beyond, open round the clock.

Southwest

Favola Disoteca
SS 126, 4km (2 miles) outside Sant'Antioco
A dressed-up crowd gyrate on three dance floors and sprawl out in the terrace gardens.

Alghero to Oristano

Alghero has some intimate bars in the Old Town and a popular club scene in the summer down by the waterfront. Oristano's *centro storico* has a lively bar scene.
El Trò
Via Lungomare Valencia, Alghero
Born in the mid-1970s, brought up on disco, rock and cheesy Italian pop, this seafront nightspot has developed into a sweaty live music venue and house music club.
Lola Mundo
Piazza Corrias 14, Oristano
This smart café by day is a great place to hang out during the earlier evening (closes at 10pm), as you can sit outside near the Antiquarium Arborese quaffing cocktails and eating *stuzzichini* snacks.
Ovest Club
Via Ghilarza 3, Oristano
Techno, *progressiva* and house club that attracts top DJs.
Il Ruscello
Località Angeli Custodi 57, Alghero
A long-established nightclub playing house and pop tunes.

Costa Smeralda, Gallura and the North

Porto Cervo has the dressed-up clubs with door policies and outrageous

bar prices. Unless you are a wannabe paparazzo or enjoy studying the tastes of the Porto Cervo set, clubs like Sottovento and Billionaire are best avoided.
Café du Port
Molo Vecchio, Porto Cervo
This historic café is not among the Costa Smeralda rip-off merchants, although it is still pricey compared to most Sardinian bars. It's the prime portside spot in Porto Cervo to enjoy cocktails and indulge in people-watching.
Bar Sport
Via Amisicora 32, Porto Torres
Fabulous food and drinks in this multi-level bar with outdoor seating. They show sport including Serie A football on the screens in one room.

Sassari

Sassari's university gives its café and bar scene an extra buzz. Via Roma and Via Torre Tonda are popular haunts.
Caffè Accademia
Via Torre Tonda 11, Sassari
Students' and professors' hangout by day and occasional night-time live music venue. Open until midnight.

SHOPPING

Where to Shop

Shopping areas n the island are generally situated on the main road of each town, leading to the main piazza. The exception is Cagliari, where shops are concentrated along the two pedestrian streets Via Manno and Via Garibaldi; here you will find mostly clothes and shoes. Alongside the usual big-label fashion outlets you find throughout Italy, there are a few interesting clothes shops with imaginative

tailoring and quirky designs including: 3C ci Trogu Abbigliamento (Via Trincea Dei Razzi 71; tel: 070-288 864) and Saloon (Piazza Martiri 14 ; tel: 070-666 421).
Alghero is famous for its jewellery shops, which are all concentrated in the old part of town.
Castelsardo is a centre for basket-weaving; women offer their products in front of their homes. Porto Cervo is the place to look for expensive fashions – all around the Piazzetta.

Crafts

Sardinia is famed for its craft goods – so much so that *L'Unione Sarda* once published a 16-volume series of lavishly produced books, *Costumi e gioielli della Sardegna* with exceptional photography exploring this rich heritage in costume- and jewellery-making.
A good place to start in Cagliari is Ente Bilaterale Artigianato Sardegnaat Via Goceano 8 (tel: 070-653 613). Tutto Artigianato in Castelsardo (Via Roma 50; tel: 079-471 266) stocks the town's famous handmade baskets. For anyone drawn to intricately patterned fabrics and carpets Tessuti Sardi at Via Sarrabus, Muravera is a must-visit. The Su Marmuri cooperative (Via Funtana Serì, Ulassai; tel: 0782-79076; www.sumarmuri.it) produces exquisite woven textiles for many domestic uses. Sardinia's artisan knife-makers have workshops and outlets in Arbus, Santu Lussurgiu, Tempio Pausania and Guispini. The most prized knife is the Pattada, which has a myrtle leaf-shaped blade folded into a horn handle. Piero Fogarizzu (Via Belvedere, Pattada; tel: 349-500 5194; www.fogarizzucoltelli.com) is one of the few craftsmen left. For something completely different – that will enchant kids and adults alike – enter the world of wooden marionette-makers Is Mascareddas, at their workshop/puppet theatre at Via XXXI Marzo 1943 no. 20, Monserrato; http://ismascareddas.it.
Mogoro is one of the leading centres for the weaving of carpets and tapestries in Sardinia. Every summer the town hosts an exhibition of old tapestry with a market for new products.
Dorgali is one of the most popular places for the production of handicrafts. An important centre for the artistic working of leather, it is also known for fabrics, filigree, pottery and wood objects.

Upmarket shopping in Porto Cervo, Costa Smeralda.

Local Food and Wine Producers and Shops

In most of the villages along the coast there are shops specialising in local food and wine products. Here are some other local producers and shops worth checking out:

Cagliari

While in Cagliari, a good place to see this rich tradition is to visit Sapori di Sardegna on Vico dei Mille 1 (www. saporidisardegna.com) which is full of cheese, wine, pasta, honey and sweets from around the island. Durke at Via Napoli 66 (www.durke.com) is famed for its pastries and sweet treats, which are free of artificial additives.

Cagliari to Arbatax

For the best cheeses of the Serrabus pop into family-run shop Sardaform, Formaggi di Muravera (SS 125 approaching Muravera; tel: 347-945 2664). Varieties include both mature and fresh *pecorino* as well as fresh ricotta and interesting creamy creations with added herbs. For fabulous wines Cannonau Doc Rosso and Rosato, go to the vineyard source at Cantina Perda Rubia, Cardedu (tel: 0784-328 32; www. perdarubia.it).

Golfo di Orosei to Olbia

Panificio Giullio Bulloni (Via Minerva 8, Bitti; tel: 0784-415 182; www. giuliobulloni.it) is an esteemed bakery, well worth visiting to sample traditional breads like *spianata*, *carasatu* and *pistoccu*. At Doragli you can taste lots of Cannonau wine at Cantina Sociale (Via Piemonte 11, Doragli; tel: 0784-96143; www. cantinadorgali.com), including all their DOC vintages from the robust Riserva to the light and fruity Rosato. Cooperativa Gruppo Pastori Budoni (Via Nazionale 150, Budoni; tel: 0784-844 543) is a fabulous place to pick up some big cheeses – including spicey sheep milk varieties *foggiano* and *Calcagno*, as well as soft ricotta and *muccarella*.

Gallura and the North

Ozieri is famed for its breathtaking desserts, including *sospiri* (sighs) made by Pasticceria Pinna Pietro (Via Pastorino 35, Ozieri; tel: 079-787 451) with almonds, chocolate, myrtle and sugar.

Sassari

Salumeria Mangatia at Via Università 68 is known for its selection of local *formaggi* and *panadus* pasta pockets (tel: 079-234 71; www.mangatia. com).

Alghero to Oristano

This area produces some fine wines including Tenute Sella and Mosca which can be bought at Località I Piani, Alghero (tel: 0799-97700). Bosa's Malvasia wine producers featured in the film documentary *Mondovino* (World of Wine). The wine produced in the Azienda Vitivinicola G. Battista Columbu in Fraus can be tasted and bought at a cellar in Bosa (Via Carmine 104, Bosa; tel: 339-5731 677). For sweet temptations head to Pasticceria Pietro Facella in Cabras (Via Tharros 21, tel: 0783-290 818; www. pasticceriafacella.it).

The Barbagia

The mountain villages of the Barbagia in the provinces of Nuoro and Ogliatra are alive with local producers. Make a detour to Belvì's Società Dolciaria Arancino Gian Luigi (Viale IV Novembre 70; tel: 0784-629 681) to try this baker's famous Caschettes mignon cakes, the so-called Sweet of the Bride. Tonara is famed for its myrtle-scented torrone, and Pili (Via Vittorio Emanuele 68; tel: 0784-63445; www.torronpili.it) is the place to get your teeth stuck into this special nougat.

Flea Markets

In Cagliari at the Bastione di San Remy there is a market of collectables held every Sunday morning from October to May and from Wednesday until Sunday 6.30pm–midnight in summer. Every third Sunday of the month there is also an antique and collectables market at the Piazza Matteotti in Olbia.

OUTDOOR ACTIVITIES

Sardinia is the ideal place for a wide range of sports and activities. Many hotels, holiday villages and campsites have their own private tennis courts, and there are some world-class golf courses as well. Sardinia's wild, largely unspoilt coastline and spectacular mountainous areas make it a prime destination for adrenalin junkies. For example, in the Ogliastra province you can go trekking on Punta La Marmora, the island's highest peak, in the morning, dabble in some canyoning or parachuting

in the afternoon, then head to Golfo di Orosei to climb limestone pillars overhanging the sea. If you have time and energy you could squeeze in some windsurfing, swimming or kayaking before the sun sets.

Surfboards, small sailing boats and motorboats are available for rent. Limpid waters around the offshore islands and the rocky coastlines offer snorkellers and scuba-divers ideal conditions. Information about sports activities is easily obtainable locally, so consult the local tourist office (see page 249), or just ask around, but the following information may be useful.

Birdwatching

The best places to see birds are the coastal marshes and lagoons all along the coast. The province of Oristano has the highest concentration and largest wetlands, followed by Cagliari, which has a greater variety of species. The most important lagoons/marshes near Oristano are:

Stagno di Sale e Porcus: 350 hectares (865 acres); interesting for the large number of birds stopping for the winter here, among which are

Grottoes

Beneath Sardinia a labyrinth of intriguing caves stretching under the island's mountains and along its coast. Guided tours are available. Here are some of the best:

Grotta di Su Marmuri
Ulassai (NU)
Tel: 0782-79859; www.ogliastraon theweb.it/sumarmuri.htm
Open from April to October.

Grotte di Su Mannau
Fluminimaggiore (CA)
Tel: 0781-580 189/347-541 3624; www.sumannau.it
Open from April to October, Nov–Mar by appointment.

Grotta di S. Barbara
Località San Giovanni, Iglésias (CA)
Tel: 0781-491 300

Grotte Is Zuddas
Santadi Carbonia, Iglesias
Tel: 0781-955 741; www.grotteis zuddas.com

Grotte di Nettuno
Capo Caccia, Alghero
Tel: 079-978 961; www.navisarda.it
or tel: 368-353 6824 www.grottedi nettuno.it (boat trip to the grotto)

Grotte del Bue Marino
Cala Gonone, Dorgali
Tel: 0784-96243

flamingos, black-winged stilts and shelducks.

Stagno di Cabras: simply the largest in Sardinia.

Stagno di Mistras: grey herons, little terns, marsh harriers, kingfishers.

Stagno di S. Giusta: mallards, little grebes.

Stagno di S'Ena Arrubia: purple herons, bitterns, purple gallinules.

Near Cagliari

Stagno di Molentargius: the most important on the island, with 187 different species of birds; it's also a nesting point for flamingos (Parco Naturale Regionale Molentargius-Saline; infopoint in Via La Palma, Cagliari; tel: 070-3791 9201; www.parcomolentargius.it; Mon–Fri 8.30am–5.30pm, Sat–Sun 9am–6pm).

Cagliari province

Stagni di Colostrai and Feraxi (Muravera area)

Oasi of Carloforte (Island of Carloforte): the most important nesting area of Eleonora's falcon. Organisation: LIPU; tel: 338-2776 307; www.lipu.it/sardegna.

Eastern coast

Foce del Cedrino (Orosei area): the last part of the Cedrino river.

Stagno di S. Teodoro: separated from the sea by a beautiful beach.

Canoe and Kayak

There are a few local organisations which offer canoe excursions or canoe rental to the Cedrino river, Lago del Liscia or the River Coghinas.

New Kayak
Valledoria (SS)
Tel: 338-125 8403
www.newkayaksardinia.com

Prima Sardegna
Viale Lungomare Palmasera 32, Cala Gonone, Nuoro
Tel: 0784-93367
www.primasardegna.com

You can also contact Federazione Italiana Canoa e Kayak, Viale Tiziano 70, Roma; www.federcanoa.it; or Federazione Italiana Canottaggio, Viale Tiziano 74, Roma; tel: 06-8797 4801, www.canottaggio.org.

For the more active types seeking a challenge, there are some wonderful excursions along Gallura's rivers: Cedrino river, Lago del Liscia or Coghinas river. Over the course of a few hours these rivers reveal varied landscapes from verdant rolling hills to dramatic canyons – all teeming with wildlife and scenic discoveries.

New Kayak Valledoria (SS), tel: 338-125 8403, www.newkayaksardinia.

Boat Excursions

Golfo di Orosei: Velamare Arbatax, tel: 338-422 8788; www.velamarearbatax.it. A day exploring the hidden grottoes and beaches is memorable – hire a *gommone* rubber-hulled speed boat or charter a ship with sails. Nuovo Consorzio Trasporti Marittimi Cala Gonone, (tel: 0784-93305; calagononecrociere.it) operates similar trips in the other direction.

La Maddalena (SS): to reach the islands of the archipelago (La Maddalena and Caprera) you have to take a ferry from Palau. The crossing takes only 20 minutes and ferries run every

com) offers memorable tailored tours along seldom-seen riverbanks.

Canyoning

Among the many outdoor activities you can take part in here is the relatively new sport of canyoning, which is basically following the path of a river, climbing over the rocks and wading and swimming through streams and waterfalls where necessary. **Barbagia No Limits** in Gavoi (tel: 0784-1820 373/347-173 6345, www.barbagianolimits.it) caters for most abilities. Get roped in for spectacular descents down gorges which reveal close-up views of nature's stunning work.

Caves and Caving

Sardinia has a large number of caves and several disused mines, some of which are open to the public. Detailed information about la speleogia – potholing or caving – can be found by contacting www.federazionespeleologicasarda.it.

Miniera Montevecchio
Piazza Rolandi, Guspini
Declared a Unesco World Heritage site. One of the largest mining complexes in Europe, with frescoes and machinery dating from 1900.
Tel: 369-164 3692/070-973 173, www.minieradimontevecchio.it.

Funtana Raminosa
Gadoni, Nuoro
Tel: 0781-491 300; www.igeaspa.it
Email: segr.pre@igeaspa.t

Porto Flavia
Località Masua (Iglesias)
Tel: 0781-491 300; www.igeaspa.it
Email: segr.pre@igeaspa.it

La Grotta di Su Marmuri
Ulassai, Nuoro
Tel: 0782-79859

15 minutes during the day. Costa tours (tel: 339-3877 196/328 6582 193; www.lamaddalenatrips.com) and Maggior Leggero Tour (tel: 345-3795 202; www.maggiorleggerotour.com) organise excursions to the other islands of the archipelago.

Alghero and Capo Caccia: Charter the Geir Jensen sailing boat (tel: 338-9708 139; www.ajsailing.com; includes lunch) to Capo Caccia and the thrilling Grotte di Nettuno.

Cheaper and less thrilling ferry trips are available with Traghetti Nav sarda, tel: 079-950 603; www.navisarda.it.

Climbing

Your instructor should have a licence called Abilitazione di Istruttore per Arrampicata Sportiva and should be part of the Italian Federation of Climbers (FASI, main office in Bologna, Via del Terrapieno 27, Bologna, tel: 051-601 4890, www.fedeclimb.it; Sardinian Delegation, tel: 070-666 680).

Cala Gonone is the most organised area for free climbing, with huge limestone pinnacles and small cliffs to suit most levels. See also Hiking and Trekking on page 242.

Cycling

A few organisations offer local tours:
Bike Tour Sardinia
Strada per Sanluri Stato km 1.4, Sanluri (VS)
Tel: 328-5458896, +44-20-352 93 237
www.biketoursardinia.com

Dolcevita Bike Tours
Via Cimarosa 18, Villa San Pietro (CA)
Tel: C70-9209 885
www.dolcevitabiketours.com

Sardinia Cycling
Via Donizetti 7a/b, Quartu Sant'Elena
www.sardiniacycling.com

Sardinia Cycling
Tel: 070-7966 157
www.sardiniagrandtour.com

For more information on cycling in Sardinia contact: Federazione Ciclistica Italiana, Via Sonnino 155, Cagliari 09127, tel: 070-663 231, www.federciclismo.it.

Diving

There are around 80 diving centres around the island, the highest concentration being on the northeast

Sailing Events

Maxi Yacht Rolex Cup
Porto Cervo (YCCS or Yacht Club
Costa Smeralda)
Tel: 0789-902 200; www.yccs.it
In the first week of September; this
is where you can see the largest
and most famous yachts.
Regata della Vela Latina
(Latin Sail Regatta), Stintino (SS);
at the end of August.
Sardinia Cup
Porto Cervo (YCCS); held
in September, this is the
Mediterranean alternative to the
Admiral's Cup.

coast. Activities range from night
diving to underwater photography. The
marine parks make Sardinia a great
natural aquarium. The parks are:
Capo Carbonara-Villasimius (Cagliari
province – CA); Golfo di Orosei
(Nuoro province – NU); Tavolara-
Capo Coca Cavallo (Sassari province
– SS); Arcipelago della Maddalena
(national park, Sassari province);
Isola Asinara (national park, Sassari
province); Capo Caccia-Porto Conte
(Sassari province); Sinis-Mal di Ventre
(Oristano province – OR).
Information on dive schools can
be obtained from the following: www.
anissub.com, www.fias.it, www.uisp.
it, www.padi.com, or from Comitato
Regionale FIPSAS, Via Pascoli 12,
Sinnai; tel: 340-9393 158; www.
fipsas.it.
Some of the well-established
schools listed below offer other
activities including kitesurfing,
windsurfing and sailing:
Palau, La Maddalena, Arzachena
Oyster Sub
c/o Camping Capo d'Orso, Golfo delle
Saline, Palau

Tel: 0789-702 070
www.oystersub.com
No Limits Diving
Via del Porto 16, Santa Teresa Gallura
Tel: 0789-759 026/348-800 2388
www.divingmediterraneo.it
Nautilus Diving Centre
Padi Gold Palm Resort #799044,
Piazza G. Fresi 8, Palau
Tel: 0789-709 058
www.divesardegna.com
Porto Rotondo, Golfo Aranci, Olbia,
San Teodoro
Centro Sub Tavolara
Via Molara 4, Porto S. Paolo
Tel: 340-8392 154
www.tavolaradiving.it
Aquarius Dive Center
Villaggio "Le Farfalle", Località Capo
Coda Cavallo, San Teodoro
Tel: 0784-834 124
www.diveaquarius.net
Argonauta Diving Club
Via dei Lecci 10, Cala Gonone (NU)
Tel: 0784-93046/ 347-5304 097
www.argonauta.it
Muravera, Villasimius, Quartu S.
Elena, Cagliari
Centro Immersioni Sardegna
Via delle Agavi, Località Costa Rei,
Muravera (CA)
Tel: 070-991 399/338-9797 979
www.sardiniadiving.com
Bosa Diving Centre
Piazza Paul Harris, Bosa
Tel: 335-818 9748
www.bosadiving.com
Adventure Diving Alghero
Via Aggius 14, Alghero (SS)
Tel: 079-9739 039/333-1847 750
www.adventurediving.it

Fishing

At Teulada, there's a fabulous
opportunity to experience
pescaturismo: a day out with
professional fishermen around the

bays of the Southwest. You'll get
hands-on fishing action, and the fresh
catch is cooked for lunch on deck
or on one of the gorgeous beaches.
(Pescaturismo Teulada Lucia Madre,
tel: 340-603 6978), tailors boat trips
for all ages – this is a great family
excursion.
You can also try www.sardiniafishing.it.

Hiking and Trekking

Sardinia offers an incredible variety of
different landscapes, ideal for hikers.
The following areas are of great
environmental interest: Sette Fratelli,
northwest of Cagliari; Monte Arcosu
and Monte Linas, west of Cagliari;
Giara di Gesturi and Gennargentu in
the centre of the island; and Limbara
in the northeast have already become
regional or national parks or natural
reserves.
The Supramonte in the Barbagia
is one of the best hiking areas on the
island. Hikes are also arranged by
trekking guides, who should belong
to the AIGAE (Associazione Italiana
Guide Ambientali Escursionistiche).
AIGAE Sardegna/Cooperativa Turistica
Sinis is a collaboration of numerous
operators with knowledgeable and
reliable guides. For information and
a guide contact the association: tel:
320-4816528; www.sardegnaguide.
org (regional site), www.aigae.
org (national site). The Sardinian
branch of the Italian Touring Club,
Alpino Italiani CAI, can also provide
information; tel: Cagliari 070-667
877, Nuoro 0784-34926 or Sassari
079-291 035; www.cai.it.
L'Altra Sardegna
Tel: 348-144 1820
www.laltrasardegna.it
Mariano Balbina takes guided treks
throughout the island as well as
organising motorbike, quad-bike and
horse-riding excursions.
Barbagia Insolita (Oliena)
Corso Vittorio Emanuele 48, Oliena (NU)
Tel: 0784-286 005
www.barbagiainsolita.it
All sorts of outdoor activities on foot,
road or 4x4.
Ogliastra Adventure
Villagrande Strisaili (Ogliastra)
Tel: 338-135 3707
www.ogliastraadventure.it
Amiable guides lead trekking,
climbing, parachute and quad-biking
adventures in the stunning Ogliastra
region.
Centro Escursioni In Sardegna
(Dorgali)
Viale Colombo, Cala Gonone (NU)
Tel: 349-672 7750
www.escursioniinsardegna.com

Fishing and tourism are combined in Santa Teresa di Gallura.

This outdoors centre at Cala Gonone has a full calendar of various outdoor activities led by experienced guides.

Coop. Goloritzè
Golgo di Baunei
Tel: 368-702 8980
www.coopgoloritze.com
Trekking, climbing, boat trips and other excursions organised from a beguiling *rifugio* base camp, which has accommodation.

Cooperativa Turistica Enis
Monte Maccioni, Oliena
Tel: 0784-288 363
www.coopenis.it
Trekking and climbing in the Supramonte.

Barbagia No Limits (Gavoi)
Tel: 0784-1820 373/347-173 6345
www.barbagianolimits.it
Trekking, canyoning, climbing, canoeing, caving, jeep tours and survival courses in the Barbagia.

Horse-Riding

Exploring Sardinia on horseback is a popular way to see the island. Programmes vary: you can take half-day excursions, expeditions lasting several days, or ones which traverse the entire island. Information is available at local tourist agencies and ANTE Sardegna (Riders' Association), Via Pasteur 4, Cagliari, tel: 070-305 816 or at Via Carso 35a, Sassari, tel: 079-299 889; http://sardegna.fitetrec-ante.it. The website www.sardegna cavalli.it also provides information. Don't forget to see one of the *Pariglie* (horse-riding competitions) which usually take place during the summer in central Sardinia.
Here are a few good horse-riding centres:

Horse Country
Strada Mare 24 no. 27, Arborea, Oristano
Tel: 0783-80500
www.horsecountry.it
A renowned equestrian centre which specialises in horse-riding excursions.

Il Maneggio di Giancarlo Cabras (Chia)
Tel: 070-923 6045/348-704 4447
www.cavalcareachia.it
Horse-riding along the sand dunes of Chia.

Sailing

The island has a rich tradition of sailing down through the millennia, and produces some of the finest yachtsmen in the world.

Sailing Schools
Almost all coastal resorts have sailing schools and equipment-hire facilities.

Further information from Federazione Italiana Vela, www.federvela.it or Lega Navale Italiana, www.leganavale.it.
Some of the most popular schools are listed below:

Centro Velico Caprera
Punta Coda, Caprera
Tel: 02-8645 2191 (office)
www.centrovelicccaprera.it
A renowned school with good residential courses that last from 1 to 2 weeks.

Velamare Club
Le Saline, Palau
Tel: 0789-702 163
www.velamare.it

Yacht Club
Marina Piccola, Cagliari
Tel: 070-370 350
www.yachtclubcagliari.it
The oldest club in Sardinia, with a long-term tradition of regattas.

Cruising Charter
Via Nanni 62, Olbia
Tel: 0789-25944
www.cruisingcharter.it

Protected Areas of Sardinia

Regional Parks include the following:
Parco del Limbara (Sassari province) is studded with spectacularly eroded granite peaks and is the home of a reintroduced deer subspecies, the *Cervus elaphus corsicanus* .
Parco del Monte Arci (Oristano province) is dominated by hard black volcanic rock that prehistoric Sardinians used to make arrowheads and knives. Prehistoric settlements include Bruncu'e S'Omu, Sa Domu Is Coambus, home of a mysterious ancient cult (www.parcomontearci. t).
Parco della Giara (between the three provinces of Cagliari, Oristano and Nuoro). Le Giare (Sa Jara Manna in Sarco) basalt rock high plains formed natural fortifications for Sardina's Nuraghic peoples, and they are lined with settlement remains. Look out for the *cavallini della Giara*, small horses (120cm/47ins on average) that are said to have been imported by the Phoenicians (www.parcodellagiara.it).
Parco del Linas-Marganai (Cagliari province) is famous for wild deer and royal eagles.
Parco dei Sette Fratelli, east of Cagliari takes its name from the seven mountain peaks dominating the region.
Parco del Sulcis (Cagliari province) is the largest Sardinian park, covering nearly 70,000 hectares (173,000 acres), and is home to

more than 300 wild deer.
Parco del Molentargius, located within the Sardinian capital, Cagliari. More than 1,000 pink flamingos are bred here each year (www.parcomolentargius.it).

National Parks

There are three national parks.
Parco Nazionale dell'Arcipelago di La Maddalena (www.la maddalenapark.it), in the northeast of the island, and the **Parco Nazionale dell'Asinara** (www.parccasinara.org) in the northwest are both geo-marine parks. Both have important seabird populations, while Asinara is famed for its mouflons and *asinelli bianchi* (little white donkeys). Parco nazionale del Golfo di Orosei e del Gennargentu (www.parco gennargentu.it) in the province of Nuoro includes the island's highest peak, Punta La Marmora.

Marine areas

Five marine protected areas have also been designated: Isola dell'Asinara, **Capo Caccia – Isola Piana, Tavolara – Punta Coda Cavallo, Penisola del Sinis – Isola Mal di Ventre and Capo Carbonara.** . Explore these areas by boat to glimpse the wildest Mediterranean ocean environments, rich in striking geology and creatures, above and below transparent waters.

Velamare Arbatax
Tel: 338-422 8788
www.velamarearbatax.it

Watersports

Watersports opportunities abound at Palau and the waters around. Paolo Silvestri, former Italian windsurfing champion, takes the adventurous route over the famous wind-whipped waters off the L'Isuledda Porto Pollo – some of the best windsurfing territory to be found anywhere in Europe. He also instructs and organises other adrenalin-fuelled marine activities, including kitesurfing, sailing and surfing, with diving to follow. Tel: 339-4293 300, www.silvestri.it.

Water skiing

Information regarding water skiing is available from Federazione Italiana Sci Nautico e Wakeboard (FISW), www.scinauticc.com.

Windsurfing and Kitesurfing

The favourite spot for windsurfers and kitesurfers has got to be the Isola Dei Gabbiani, with its 7km (4 miles) of beach and healthy gusts, in the northeastern province of Sassari. Paolo Silvestri, former Italian windsurfing champion (mentioned above), has been an instructor for over 30 years. He also coordinates kitesurfing, surfing and diving here.
Windsurfing Club
Via Marina Piccola, Cagliari
Tel: 070-372 694
www.windsurfingclubcagliari.org
This excellent club specialises in a range of courses and windsurfing regattas.

Sports

Football

Sardinia has an extraordinary passion for football, and the Cagliari Calcio football team is held in high esteem: Stadio San Elia; match tickets available at Cagliari Point, Viale La Playa 15; tel: 070-604 201; www.cagliaricalcio.net.

Specialist Guided Tours

A good local guide who can construct a tailored itinerary is often invaluable, especially as the wealth of Sardinia's charms can seem overwhelming at first. Piero Pirosu itel: 347-922 3804; email: pieropirosu@hotmail.com) is based in Cagliari and is an experienced and enthusiastic guide and travel specialist who speaks excellent English. As well as taking city tours he organises treks in the Barbagia and boat trips in the Golfo di Orosei.

One of the most interesting specialist tours available is with the family-run winemakers Argiolas (Via Roma 28–30, Serdiana, CA, tel: 070-740 606; www.argiolas.it), who not only show visitors around their vineyards, olive groves and grappa distillery, but also organise enogastronomico tasting events.

Most archaeological sites and some museums have a local guide, and the entrance fee includes a guided tour with a non-professional guide who often does not speak English. It is possible to hire English-speaking professional/licensed guides for a half- or full day for particular areas of interest.

Boats moored in Porto Cervo, Costa Smeralda.

Golf

Sardinia is home to some superb 18-hole golf courses, including the following championship-standard courses:
Is Molas Resort
Località Is Molas, Pula, Cagliari
Tel: 070-924 1006
www.ismolas.it
Pevero Golf Club
Cala di Volpe, Costa Smeralda
Tel: 0789-958 000
www.golfclubpevero.it
Other courses include:
Chia Golf
Via Belvedere, c/o Hotel Spartivento, Località Chia, Domus De Maria (CA)Tel: 070-651 819
www.chiasportingclub.it
Due Lune Resort Golf Spa Località Puntaldia, San Teodoro
Tel: 0784-864 075
www.duelune.com
Is Arenas
Pineta Is Arenas, Narbolia (OR)
Tel: 321-1851 130
www.isarenas.it

CHILDREN

Excursions

Children are welcomed in Sardinia, even in bars and restaurants. Many of the coastal hotels are ideal for family holidays, and lay on a variety of entertainment and activities for kids and parents. Many of Sardinia's historic festivals are full of colourful processions, strange costumes and high japes, which are sure to capture the imaginations of children (see Festivals, page 236).

Below are some ideas for child-oriented excursions.
Pescaturismo is a great way for families to enjoy a day out with fishermen with fresh catch cooked for lunch. Teulada Lucia Madre, tel: 340-603 6978, tailors boat trips for all ages.
Museo Naturalistico di Sa Corona Arrubia
Lunamatrona, Cagliari province
Tel: 070-9300 242
www.sacoronarrubia.it
Temporary exhibitions for children.
Il Trenino Turistico di Cagliari (The Little Train of Cagliari)
Tel: 070-655 549
www.trenino.it
The station is in Piazza Yenne.
Catalan small train, Alghero
Tel: 0336-691 836
Station in the port.
Parco Sardegna in miniatura (Sardinia in miniature), Via Michelangelo 6, Tuili
Tel: 070-936 1004
www.sardegnainminiatura.it
Boat trips, a Nuraghic village, planetarium and astronomy museum.
Aquadream (water park)
Baja Sardinia, Sassari
Tel: 0789-99511
www.aquadream.it
All kinds of fun water activities, slides, mini golf and eateries.
Small train, Porto Cervo
Station in bus parking lot.
Diverland
Località Cruxi Lilliu, Quartucciu
Tel: 070-829 9012
www.diverland.it
Sardinia's biggest water park is a whirl of high slides, pools and playgrounds, a few miles east of Cagliari off the SS 125.

A – Z

A HANDY SUMMARY
OF PRACTICAL INFORMATION

A

Accommodation

Sardinia has a wide range of accommodation available: hotels, tourist villages, holiday homes/flats for rental, camping and caravan sites, youth hostels, the rapidly expanding field of *agriturismo* (farm holidays) and, more recently, B&Bs.

Ever since the 1960s development boom on the Costa Smeralda, many Sardinian coastlines have seen luxury resorts appear. Luckily, swanky complexes and tasteless hotel buildings have not been allowed to spoil many sections of the coast and there are plenty of family-run small businesses for those after more traditional Sardinian hospitality.

It's best to decide exactly what kind of holiday you want and, if possible, make reservations well in advance – especially during the high season.

Hotel Categories

The Italian star rating system for hotels is somewhat eccentric, to put it mildly, and is not a reliable criterion for choosing where to stay. Facilities – however old – are what gives a hotel

Passports at the Ready

Upon checking in at a hotel you will be asked to hand over your passport or national ID, which according to Italian law must be photocopied. This is also the case when using the internet in some cafés. Don't forget to pick up your passports before you leave for home!

its rating, which means that some extremely tired establishments with appalling service parade themselves as stellar lodgings. In actual fact it is often the smaller hotels, B&Bs and *agriturismi* accommodation which provide the most gracious service and imaginative living spaces.

Bed and Breakfast

This is a new form of hospitality that is quickly spreading on the island, with a network of families renting out rooms in their own homes. It provides a great opportunity to be in close contact with locals and every-day island life.
Associazione Sarda Operatori Bed & Breakfast
Tel: 348-297 3461; www.bedand breakfastsardegra.it.

Apartments and Villas

For those after flexibility, renting an apartment or villa is often the best option. There are a number of agencies which act as brokers. Here are just a few:
James Villas, tel: +44-1622-655 900 or 0800-074 0122; www.jamesvillas.co.uk
Rent Sardinia, tel: 070-684 545; www.rent-sardinia.com
Soleya Vacanza, tel: 070-208 5095; www.soleyavacanze.it

Agriturismo

An increasing number of farms are converting to *agriturismo*, whereby visitors are offered lodging and meals in farmhouses; the advantages are a taste of excellent Sardinian food, genuine Sardinian hospitality and year-round availability. The following websites will give you an idea of what is on offer: www.agriturismo.net, www.agriturismo.it, www.agriturismo.com, www.agriturist.it, www.

agriturismodisardegna.it and www.agriturismi.it.

The majority need booking far in advance: you can either book online or telephone the farm directly.

Camping

There are at least 200 campsites in Sardinia, with amenities ranging from basic to excellent. As well as space for tents and camper-vans, most of them have small furnished bungalows for rent and static caravans. Information can also be obtained from Faita Sardegna, www.faitasardegna.org. Another useful website is www.camping.it.

Youth Hostels

There are only a handful of youth hostels in Sardinia belonging to Hostelling International. For more detailed information visit the Italian Youth Hostel Association's website www.aighostels.it.

Post your cards here.

Admission Charges

Museum and gallery entrance fees vary between €2–12. Some sponsored exhibitions may be free. Most state-run and civic galleries offer free entrance or special rates to EU citizens under the age of 18 or over 65, or in full-time education.

B

Budgeting for Your Trip

Prices generally match those in the rest of Italy, although they really fluctuate according to where and when you visit. If you avoid July and August and the main resorts on the Costa Smeralda you can find good value. Generally, the cost of eating out and food shopping in local markets is more akin to southern Italy rather than oft-overpriced northern Italy. A beer (*birra media*: 40cl) or a glass of house wine costs on average €3.50. A typical main course in a budget restaurant will cost €4–8, while in a moderately priced eatery expect to pay €10–15.

A double room in a budget B&B in Cagliari costs around €80, while a comfortable hotel with good facilities in the city is priced at €150. Luxury hotels are concentrated in coastal resorts: in the Costa Smeralda expect to pay at least €400, while in Chia the tariff is typically €300 for a double in high season.

Taxi journey to and from Cagliari-Elmas Airport: €15–20 each way. In Cagliari a single bus ticket is €1.20, a one-day pass €3 (www.ctmcagliari.it).

C

Children

Sardinians are very welcoming of children and families in general. Under-18s are usually given free or reduced admission to many state-run attractions.

Climate

Summer lasts for seven months in Sardinia, thanks to its southern location and the fact that it is an island. Average temperatures on the coast are 19°C (66°F) in autumn, 10°C (5C°F) in winter, 12°C (54°F) in spring and 22°C (72°F) in summer. Sea temperatures reach 26°C (79°F) in July and August. Do remember that these are average temperatures and

CLIMATE CHART

- ☐ Maximum temperature
- ☐ Minimum temperature
- — Rainfall

that in reality temperatures during the day are much higher and that during the night they often drop, even in the summer. You will be surprised to find that after a very hot day you may need a pullover in the evening if you are sitting outside.

A constant presence in Sardinia is wind, notably the *maestrale*, a strong wind from the northwest. During the summer two hot winds blow: from the southwest the moist *libeccio* and from the southeast the *scirocco*. There is no best time of year to visit Sardinia – it depends what kind of holiday you are looking for – but in certain respects the most enjoyable period is mid-September/early October because the weather is still warm and there are relatively few tourists.

What to Bring

Bring practical clothes, and comfortable shoes or sandals. In summer, particularly at noon, the heat can be unbearable, so it is sensible

Mural on a bar in Orgosolo.

to equip yourself with a sunhat and wear loose cotton clothing. If you are planning some adventures in the mountains, some sturdy hiking boots with ankle support and other kit are invaluable. Aqua shoes that protect your feet on rocks and pebbly beaches make boat trips – especially along the Golfo di Orosei – more comfortable.

Crime and Security

There are no special problems in Sardinia as far as personal security and safety are concerned, and no specific areas where tourists are targeted. The main problem for tourists is petty crime: pickpocketing, bag-snatching and theft from cars. As when travelling anywhere, common sense should prevail: bags, cameras and other valuables should never be left unattended in cars, on beaches or anywhere else. Leave money and valuables, including airline tickets, in the hotel safe. Hitchhiking and walking are as safe as anywhere.

Customs Regulations

Goods brought in and exported within the EU incur no additional taxes or duty, provided they are for personal use or consumption.

D

Disabled Travellers

Like the rest of Italy, Sardinia remains a difficult place to get around for disabled travellers. Some trains and buses have access arrangements and places reserved for disabled passengers, but the churches and museums of Italy have been slow to offer improved access. SATH (http://sath.org) and Accessible Italy (http://accessibleitaly.com) are good online resources. The Italian State Tourism Board (ENIT) dispenses some information for disabled travellers; www.enit.it.

Electricity

230 volts – you will need an adaptor to operate British appliances, and a transformer to use 100–120-volt appliances.

Embassies and Consulates

British Embassy and Consulate Rome
Via XX Settembre 80/a Tel: 06-4220 0001 , 06-4220 2431
Other nationals should also contact their embassies or consulates in Rome.

Italian Embassies Abroad

Australia
12 Grey Street, DEAKIN, ACT 2600
Tel: 02-6273 3333
Canada
275 Slater St, Ottawa, Ontario K1P 5H9
Tel: 613-232 2401
UK
No. 14, Three Kings' Yard, London W1Y 2EH
Tel: 0207-312 2000
US
3000 Whitehaven Street, NW Washington DC
Tel: 202-612 4400

Environmental Organisations

Lega Ambiente
Via Nuoro 43, Cagliari
Tel: 070-659 740
www.legambiente.it
World Wildlife Fund
Via dei Mille 13, Cagliari
Tel: 070-670 308
www.wwf.it
Amici della Terra
Via Cocco Ort ù 32, Cagliari
Tel: 070-490 904
www.amicidellaterra.it

G

Gay and Lesbian Travellers

Outside Cagliari and Sassari there isn't much of a gay scene. For detailed information about the latest events, check out the following:
www.movimentomosessualesardo.org, www.arcigay.it, www.associazionearc.eu

Emergency Numbers

General emergency number, tel: 112
Police, tel: 113
Ambulance *(Ambulanza)*, tel: 118
Fire Brigade *(Vigili del Fuoco)*, tel: 115
Roadside Assistance, tel: 116
Corpo Forestale (environment), tel: 1515
Coastguard *(Soccorso del mare)*, tel: 1530
Road conditions, tel: 1518
Minor first aid (eg sunburn) can be obtained free from the *Pronto Soccorso* (Med cal Standby/First Aid) in all hospitals or *Guardie Mediche*.

H

Health and Medical Care

The main health issues for tourists in the summer months arise from over-exposure to the sun. Stay out of the sun during the hottest hours, and at other times cover up or use plenty of sunscreen, and wear a hat. It is also very important to drink plenty of water to avoid dehydration. If you need urgent medical treatment, call the first aid number *(Pronto Soccorso)* at one of the main hospitals, or call 112 for emergencies. Most areas have a *Guardia Medica Turistica* (emergency medical service for tourists). A list of duty pharmacists is usually published in local newspapers, and each hotel should have information about local medical care.

Insurance

EU residents are entitled to free or reduced healthcare that becomes necessary during your visit, but you will need a European Health Insurance Card (EHIC). Apply for a card online at www.ehic.org.uk (delivery in 7 days), or by calling 0845-606 2030 (delivery in 10 days); or pick up an application pack from the Post Office (delivery in 21 days). The EHIC does not cover you for repatriation in case of illness, so you should consider taking out additional travel insurance.

Illness

Vaccinations are not required, although cholera and typhoid jabs are a wise precaution if you intend to travel on to North Africa. The worst that's likely to happen to you health-wise is suffering from the extreme heat in the height of summer or

getting an upset stomach – shellfish is usually to blame. Tap water is safe to drink in Sardinia, unless there is a sign saying *acqua non potabile.*

Pharmacies

Italian pharmacists are well qualified to give you advice on minor ailments. There's usually one open all night in the bigger towns. They work on a rota system, and to find the one open, check the listings posted on pharmacy doors, or in the local paper.

Dental Treatment

This is not covered by the health service, and is very expensive; your medical insurance may include dentists' fees.

I

Internet

Internet cafés are common in towns and tourist spots, and many hotels have Wi-Fi. Ask for *un punto internet.*

M

Maps

Road maps may be obtained from the Sardinian Tourist Offices. For specialised maps (archaeological routes, biking or trekking itineraries), contact the local tourist information office, called *pro loco*, in the nearest village.

Media

Newspapers

It is possible to find foreign newspapers all year round in Cagliari and Sassari –

Chemists can give advice too.

usually a day late. In summer you can find daily international newspapers and other publications in the tourist centres. The London-based *Guardian* publishes a special European edition. There are two daily Sardinian newspapers; the best-selling is *L'Unione Sarda*, based in Cagliari, with a circulation of nearly 100,000 copies (www.unionesarda.it); *La Nuova Sardegna*, which mainly serves the northern part of Sardinia (http://lanuovasardegna.gelocal.it), is the regional version of the national *La Repubblica*. Both newspapers are useful if you know a little Italian, because they run listings sections. All the national Italian newspapers are available in Sardinia, and the major ones are printed daily in both Cagliari and Sassari.

Television

In addition to the three main national radio and television broadcasting channels run by RAI (Italian Radio and Television), there are numerous others. There are news bulletins *(Telegiornali)* almost every hour of the day, although the most popular are between 1 and 2pm and from 7 to 8.30pm. Cable television and Euro-channels are also available, as well as satellite TV.

Radio

Numerous private radio stations operate, as well as the three main national public stations (RAI Radio 1, 2, and 3). Most are broadcast on stereo FM. There are hourly traffic and weather bulletins on the RAI channels, in cooperation with ACI (Italian Automobile Association). In the summer bulletins are broadcast in English, German and French.

Money

The unit of currency in Sardinia, as in the rest of Italy, is the euro. The use of credit cards has become common in

Discussing the news.

Sardinia, and the major international credit cards are accepted almost everywhere. They are particularly useful for settling bills in hotels or campsites, for purchasing expensive items in the bigger shops, or buying petrol. It is, however, advisable to travel with some money already changed into euros. Eurocheques and traveller's cheques can be exchanged in any Sardinian bank, and they represent the safest way of bringing money into the island, although a commission fee is usually charged by the bank. A number of banks in the major cities and tourist resorts are equipped with debit/credit card outlets (ATMs), with instructions in several languages.

Tipping

As a general rule tipping is not a Sardinian custom, although tips are, of course, readily accepted. Most restaurants add a service charge to the bill (usually 10–15 percent), so choosing to leave a tip *(la mancia)* depends on your personal judgement. Your final bill will also include a small cover charge per person, irrespective of consumption.

Taxi drivers do not expect a tip, but taxis are relatively expensive. Tariffs are fixed and metered, so there is no room for haggling.

O

Opening Hours

Banks are open Monday to Friday 8.30am–1.30pm and (usually) 3–4.30pm.
Shops are usually open from 9am–1pm and 5–8pm, but bear in mind that opening hours do change from spring to summer and some may stay open late, or all day in the main cities.

Public Holidays

1 January New Year's Day
6 January Epiphany
March/April Easter Sunday and Monday
25 April Liberation Day
1 May Labour Day
15 August Assumption Day
1 November All Saints' Day
8 December Immaculate Conception
25 December Christmas Day
26 December Santo Stefano

P

Postal Services

Post offices are open Monday to Saturday 8am–1pm. Some main post offices are also open in the afternoon, 3–6pm.

Stamps *(francobolli)* are available from tobacconists and newsagents displaying a black-and-white T-sign which reads *Valori Bollati*.

R

Religious Services

Italy is a Catholic country. The hours of Mass *(messa)* and services vary from town to village. Mass is generally held on Saturday afternoon and Sunday: timetables are pinned inside the main door of churches. Other denominations may practise their faith here – some have their own services in both Cagliari and Sassari.

S

Smoking

Smoking is not allowed in places that can be defined as "public", or in restaurants and bars, unless they have a separate air-conditioned area for smokers. Smoking in prohibited areas risks a fine of anything between €25 and €250.

T

Tax

Non-EU residents can claim back VAT (or IVA: *Imposta sul Valore Aggiunto*) on purchases made in Italy provided that: the goods are intended for personal or familiar

Crowned Madonna in a Sassari church.

use and are personally carried in the baggage; the overall value of goods exceeds €154,94 (VAT included); and the purchase is certified by an invoice. For official details of how to claim back this tax, consult: www. agenziadoganemonopoli.gov.it.

Telephones

The local telephone code must be used in front of every dialled number.

Public phone booths, and phones in public places, are no longer common because of the spread of mobile (cell) phones. When available, they are bright orange and are operated by Telecom (the national phone company). Most are operated with a *carta telefonica* (phone card) sold most commonly in units of €5 and €10. The cards can be bought at *edicole* (newsagents), bars, tobacconists and, of course, Telecom centres, from which lengthy long-distance calls may also be made. Sardinia has good mobile phone coverage. For travellers who own an "unlocked" GSM phone, planning to make a lot of calls while in Italy, it's advisable to buy a SIM card from an Italian mobile phone shop. Local mobile network operators include Tre (www.tre.it), Vodafone (www.vodafone. it) and Wind (www.wind.it). Bring your ID or passport along as there is some bureaucracy involved.

Enquiries

12 for directory enquiries
4176 for international directory enquiries
170 for operator-assisted calls

Time Zone

Greenwich Mean Time plus 1 hour. Daylight Savings Time from the end of March to the beginning of October.

International dialling codes:
Dial **00**, then the country code
Australia **61**
Canada and US **1**
Ireland **353**
New Zealand **64**
South Africa **27**
UK **44**

Toilets

Restaurants, motorway service stations, bars and cafés provide toilet facilities, by Italian law. Some of them are not well maintained, and expect still to find quite a few squat toilets.

Tourist Information

Sardinian state-run tourist information is a bureaucratic mess with a lack of decent customer service. Often the most helpful and enthusiastic staff in the smaller tourist offices are students or volunteers. Official website of the region is www.sardegnaturismo.it.

Tourist Information for Each Province

Cagliari
Palazzo Communale, Via Roma 145, Cagliari and Piazza Costituzione, Cagliari
Tel: 070-677 7397
www.cagliariturismo.it
Carbonia/Iglésias
Via Mazzini 39, Carbonia
Tel: 0781-672 61
www.su cisig esiente.eu
Medio Campidano
Via Carlo Felice 267, Sanluri
Tel: 070-935 6700,
www.provincia.mediocampidano.it
Ogliastra
Via Mameli 22, Tortolí
Tel: 0782-600 900
www.turismo.ogliastra.it
Oristano
Piazza Eleonora 18, Oristano
Tel: 0783-368 3210

www.gooristano.com
Olbia e Tempio
Via Dante 1, Olbia
Tel: 0789-522 06
www.olbiaturismo.it
Sassari
Palazzo di Città, Via Sebastiano Satta 13, Sassari
Tel: 079-200 8072
www.ccmune.sassari.it

Tourist Offices Abroad

The Italian State Tourist Board (www. enit.it) has offices in most major capitals:
Canada
110 Yonge Street, Suite 503, Toronto Tel: 416-925 4882
Italy
Via Marghera 2/6, Rome
Tel: 039-064 9711
UK
1 Princes Street, London W1B 8AY
Tel: 020-7399 3560
www.italiantouristboard.co.uk
US
630 Fifth Avenue, Suite 1965, New York, NY 10111
Tel: 212-245 5618

V

Visas and Passports

Citizens from the EU, US and Canada can enter Sardinia with a valid passport or identity card. You only need a visa if staying for more than three months. Entry regulations for citizens coming from other countries apply as for the rest of Italy, and visas can be obtained through Italian embassies. Tourists visiting Sardinia with cats or dogs must present proof at customs of their animals' inoculation against rabies. The vaccination must be given at least 20 days before arrival.

Weights and Measures

Metric–Imperial
1 centimetre = 0.4in
1 metre = 3ft 3ins
1 kilometre = 0.62 mile
1 gram = 0.04 ounce
1 kilogram = 2.2 pounds
1 litre = 1.76 UK pints
Imperial–Metric
1 inch = 2.54 centimetres
1 foot = 30 centimetres
1 ounce = 28 grams
1 pound = 0.45 kilogram
1 pint = 0.57 litre
1 UK gallon = 4.55 litres
1 US gallon = 3.78 litres

TRANSPORT · EATING OUT · ACTIVITIES · A – Z · LANGUAGE

LANGUAGE

UNDERSTANDING THE LANGUAGE

BASIC COMMUNICATION

Yes *Sì*
No *No*
Thank you *Grazie*
Many thanks *Mille grazie/Tante grazie/Molte grazie*
You're welcome *Prego*
All right/Okay/That's fine *Va bene*
Please *Per favore or per cortesia*
Excuse me (to get attention) *Scusi* (singular), *Scusate* (plural)
Excuse me (to get through a crowd) *Permesso*
Excuse me (to attract attention, eg of a waiter) *Senta!*
Excuse me (sorry) *Mi scusi* (singular), *Scusatemi* (plural)
Wait a minute! (informal) *Aspetta!* (formal) *Aspetti!*
Could you help me? (formal) *Potrebbe aiutarmi?*
Certainly *Ma certo*
Can I help you? (formal) *Posso aiutarLa?*
Can you show me...? (formal) *Può indicarmi...?*
Can you help me? (formal) *Può aiutarmi, per cortesia?*
I need... *Ho bisogno di...*
I'm lost *Mi sono perso*
I'm sorry *Mi dispiace*
I don't know *Non lo so*
I don't understand *Non capisco*
Do you speak English/French/German? *Parla inglese/francese/tedesco?*
Could you speak more slowly, please? *Può parlare piú lentamente, per favore?*
Could you repeat that please? (formal) *Può ripetere, per piacere?*
here/there *qui/lá*
What? *Cosa?*
When/Why/Where? *Quando/Perchè/Dov'è?*
Where is the lavatory? *Dov'è il bagno?*

GREETINGS

Hello (Good day) *Buon giorno*
Good afternoon/evening *Buona sera*
Good night *Buona notte*
Goodbye *Arrivederci*
Hello/Hi/Goodbye (familiar) *Ciao*
Mr/Mrs/Miss *Signor/Signora/Signorina*
Pleased to meet you (formal) *Piacere di conoscerLa*
I am English/American *Sono inglese/americano*
Irish/Scottish/Welsh *irlandese/scozzese/gallese*
Canadian/Australian *canadese/australiano*
Do you speak English? (formal) *Parla inglese?*
I'm here on holiday *Sono qui in vacanza*
Do you like it here? (formal) *Si trova bene qui?*
How are you? (formal/informal) *Come sta/Come stai?*
Fine thanks *Bene, grazie*
See you later *A più tardi*
See you soon *A presto*
Take care (formal) *Stia bene*, (informal) *Stammi bene*

TELEPHONE CALLS

the area code *il prefisso telefonico*
I'd like to make a reverse charges call *Vorrei fare una telefonata a carico del destinatario*
May I use your telephone, please? *Posso usare il telefono?*

Hello (on the telephone) *Pronto*
My name's *Mi chiamo/Sono*
Could I speak to...? *Posso parlare con...?*
Sorry, he/she isn't in *Mi dispiace, è fuori*
Can he call you back? *Può richiamarla?*
I'll try again later *Riproverò più tardi*
Can I leave a message? *Posso lasciare un messaggio?*
Please tell him I called *Gli dica, per favore, che ho telefonato*
Hold on *Un attimo, per favore*
A local call *una telefonata locale*
Can you speak up, please? (formal) *Può parlare più forte, per favore?*

IN THE HOTEL

Do you have any vacant rooms? *Avete camere libere?*

Emergencies

Help! *Aiuto!*
Stop! *Fermate!*
I've had an accident *Ho avuto un incidente*
Watch out! *Attenzione!*
Call a doctor *Per favore, chiami un medico*
Call an ambulance *Chiami un'ambulanza*
Call the police *Chiami la Polizia/i Carabinieri*
Call the fire brigade *Chiami I pompieri*
Where is the telephone? *Dov'è il telefono?*
Where is the nearest hospital? *Dov'è l'ospedale più vicino?*
I would like to report a theft *Voglio denunciare un furto*

Days and Dates

morning/afternoon/evening la mattina/il pomeriggio/la sera
yesterday/today/tomorrow ieri/oggi/domani
the day after tomorrow dopodomani
now/early/late adesso/presto/ritardo
a minute un minuto
an hour un'ora
half an hour un mezz'ora
a day un giorno
a week una settimana
Monday lunedì
Tuesday martedì
Wednesday mercoledì
Thursday giovedì
Friday venerdì
Saturday sabato
Sunday domenica
first il primo/la prima
second il secondo/la seconda
third il terzo/la terza

I have a reservation Ho fatto una prenotazione
I'd like... Vorrei...
a single/double room (with a double bed) una camera singola/doppia (con letto matrimoniale)
a room with twin beds una camera a due letti
a room with a bath/shower una camera con bagno/doccia
for one night per una notte
for two nights per due notti
We have one with a double bed Ne abbiamo una matrimoniale
Could you show me another room please? Potrebbe mostrarmi un'altra camera?
How much is it? Quanto costa?
on the first floor al primo piano
Is breakfast included? É compresa la prima colazione?
Is everything included? É tutto compreso?
half/full board mezza pensione/pensione completa
It's expensive É caro
Do you have a room with a balcony/view of the sea? C'è una camera con balcone/con vista sul mare?
a room overlooking the park/the street/the back una camera con vista sul parco/che dà sulla strada/sul retro
Is it a quiet room? É una stanza tranquilla?
The room is too hot/cold/noisy/small La camera è troppo calda/fredda/rumorosa/piccola
Can I see the room? Posso vedere la camera?

What time does the hotel close? A che ora chiude l'albergo?
I'll take it La prendo
big/small grande/piccola
What time is breakfast? A che ora è la prima colazione?
Please give me a call at... Mi può chiamare alle...
Come in! Avanti!
Can I have the bill, please? Posso avere il conto, per favore?
Can you call me a taxi please? Può chiamarmi un taxi, per favore?
dining room la sala da pranzo
key la chiave
lift l'ascensore
towel l'asciugamano
toilet paper la carta igienica
pull/push tirare/spingere

EATING OUT

Bar Snacks and Drinks

I'd like... Vorrei...
coffee un caffè (espresso: small, strong and black)
un cappuccino (with hot, frothy milk)
un caffelatte (like café au lait in France)
un caffè lungo (weak)
un corretto (laced with alcohol – usually brandy or grappa. You should specify)
tea un tè
lemon tea un tè al limone
herbal tea una tisana
hot chocolate una cioccolata calda
orange/lemon juice (bottled) un succo d'arancia/di limone
fresh orange/lemon juice una spremuta di arancia/di limone
orangeade un'aranciata

Pronunciation and Grammar Tips

Italian-speakers claim that pronunciation is straightforward: you pronounce it as it is written. This is approximately true, but there are a couple of important rules for English-speakers to bear in mind: c before e or i is pronounced "ch", eg ciao, mi dispiace, la cirghiale. Ch before i or e is pronounced as "k", eg la chiesa. Likewise, sci or sce are pronounced as in "sheep" or "shed" respectively. Gn in Italian is rather like the sound in "onion", while gl is softened to resemble the sound in "bullion".

Nouns are either masculine (il, plural i) or feminine (la, plural le). Plurals of nouns are most often formed by changing an o to an i and an a to an e, eg il panino, i panini; la chiesa, le chiese.

Words are stressed on the penultimate syllable unless an accent indicates otherwise.

Like many languages, Italian has formal and informal words for "You". In the singular, Tu is informal while Lei is more polite. Confusingly, in some parts of Italy or in some circumstances, you will also hear Voi used as a singular polite form. (In general, Voi is reserved for "You" plural, however.) For visitors, it is simplest and most respectful to use the formal form unless invited to do otherwise.

There is, of course, rather more to the language than that, but you can get a surprisingly long way towards making friends with a mastery of a few basic phrases.

water (mineral) acqua (minerale)
fizzy/still mineral water acqua minerale gasata/naturale
a glass of mineral water un bicchiere di minerale
with/without ice con/senza ghiaccio
red/white wine vino rosso/bianco
beer (draught) una birra (alla spina)
a gin and tonic un gin tonic
a bitter (Vermouth, etc.) un amaro
milk latte
a (half) litre un (mezzo) litro
bottle una bottiglia
ice cream un gelato
cone un cono
pastry una pasta
sandwich un tramezzino
roll un panino
Anything else? Desidera qualcos'altro?
Cheers Salute
Let me pay Offro io
That's very kind of you Grazie, molto gentile

In a Restaurant

I'd like to book a table Vorrei riservare un tavolo
Have you got a table for... Avete un tavolo per...
I have a reservation Ho fatto una prenotazione
lunch/supper il pranzo/la cena
We do not want a full meal Non desideriamo un pasto completo
Could we have another table? Potremmo spostarci?
I'm a vegetarian Sono vegetariano/a
Is there a vegetarian dish? C'è un piatto vegetariano?
May we have the menu? Ci dà il menu, per favore?

wine list *la lista dei vini*
What would you like? *Che cosa prende?*
What would you recommend? *Che cosa ci raccomanda?*
home-made *fatto in casa*
What would you like as a main course/dessert? *Che cosa prende di secondo/di dolce?*
What would you like to drink? *Che cosa desidera da bere?*
a carafe of red/white wine *una caraffa di vino rosso/bianco*
fixed price menu *il menu a prezzo fisso*
the dish of the day *il piatto del giorno*
VAT (sales tax) *iva*
cover charge *il coperto/pane e coperto*
That's enough; no more, thanks *Basta (così)*
The bill, please *Il conto, per favore*
Is service included? *Il servizio è incluso?*
Where is the lavatory? *Dov'è il bagno?*
Keep the change *Va bene così*
I've enjoyed the meal *Mi è piaciuto molto*

MENU DECODER

Antipasti (Hors d'Oeuvres)

antipasto misto **mixed hors d'oeuvres** (including cold cuts, possibly cheeses and roast vegetables – ask, however)
buffet freddo **cold buffet** (often excellent)
caponata **mixed aubergine, olives and tomatoes**
insalata caprese **tomato and mozzarella salad**
insalata di mare **seafood salad**
insalata mista/verde **mixed/green salad**
melanzane alla parmigiana **fried or baked aubergine** (with parmesan cheese and tomato)
mortadella/salame **salami**
pancetta **bacon**
peperonata **vegetable stew** (made with peppers, onions, tomatoes and sometimes some aubergines)

Primi (First Courses)

Typical first courses in Sardinia include soup or numerous varieties of pasta in a wide range of delicious sauces. Risotto and gnocchi are more common in the north of Italy than here.
il brodetto **fish soup**
il brodo **consommé**
i crespolini **savoury pancakes**

Bar Notices

Prezzo in terrazza. Terrace price often double what you pay standing at the bar.
Si prende lo scontrino alla cassa. Pay at the cash desk, then take the receipt to the bar to be served.

gli gnocchi **potato dumplings**
la minestra **soup**
il minestrone **thick vegetable soup**
pasta e fagioli **pasta and bean soup**
il prosciutto (cotto/crudo) **ham** (cooked/cured)
i supplí **rice croquettes**
i tartufi **truffles**
la zuppa **soup**

Secondi (Main Courses)

Typical main courses are fish-, seafood- or meat-based, with accompaniments *(contorni)* that vary greatly from region to region.

La Carne (Meat)

allo spiedo **on the spit**
arrosto **roast meat**
i ferri **grilled**
al forno **baked**
al girarrosto **spit-roasted**
alla griglia **grilled**
involtini **skewered veal, ham, etc.**
stagionato **hung, well-aged**
stufato **braised, stewed**
ben cotto **well done** (steak, etc.)
al puntino **medium** (steak, etc.)
al sangue **rare** (steak, etc.)
l'agnello **lamb**
la bistecca **steak**
a bresaola **dried salted beef**
il capriolo/cervo **venison**
il carpaccio **lean beef fillet**
il cinghiale **wild boar**
il coniglio **rabbit**
il controfiletto **sirloin steak**
le cotolette **cutlets**
il fagiano **pheasant**
il fegato **liver**
il filetto **fillet**
la lepre **hare**
il maiale **pork**
il manzo **beef**
l'ossobuco **shin of veal**
il pollo **chicken**
le polpette **meatballs**
il polpettone **meat loaf**
la porchetta **roast suckling pig**
la salsiccia **sausage**
saltimbocca (alla romana) **veal escalopes with ham**
le scaloppine **escalopes**
lo stufato **stew**
il sugo **sauce**
il tacchino **turkey**

la trippa **tripe**
il vitello **veal**

Frutti di Mare (Seafood)

Beware the word *surgelati*, meaning frozen rather than fresh.
affumicato **smoked**
alle brace **charcoal grilled/ barbecued**
alla griglia **grilled**
fritto **fried**
ripieno **stuffed**
al vapore **steamed**
le acciughe **anchovies**
l'anguilla **eel**
l'aragosta **lobster**
il baccalà **dried salted cod**
i bianchetti **whitebait**
il branzino **sea bass**
i calamaretti **baby squid**
i calamari **squid**
la carpa **carp**
i crostacei **shellfish**
le cozze **mussels**
il fritto misto **mixed fried fish**
i gamberetti **shrimps**
i gamberi **prawns**

Numbers

0 *zero*
1 *uno*
2 *due*
3 *tre*
4 *quattro*
5 *cinque*
6 *sei*
7 *sette*
8 *otto*
9 *nove*
10 *dieci*
11 *undici*
12 *dodici*
13 *tredici*
14 *quattordici*
15 *quindici*
16 *sedici*
17 *diciassette*
18 *diciotto*
19 *diciannove*
20 *venti*
30 *trenta*
40 *quaranta*
50 *cinquanta*
60 *sessanta*
70 *settanta*
80 *ottanta*
90 *novanta*
100 *cento*
200 *duecento*
500 *cinquecento*
1,000 *mille*
2,000 *duemila*
5,000 *cinquemila*
50,000 *cinquantamila*
1 million *un milione*

Pasta Dishes

Common Pasta Shapes
cannelloni (large stuffed tubes of pasta); *farfalle* (bow- or butterfly-shaped pasta); *tagliatelle* (flat noodles, similar to *fettuccine*); *tortellini* and *ravioli* (different types of stuffed pasta packets); *penne* (quill-shaped tubes, smaller than *rigatoni*).

Typical Pasta Sauces
pomodoro (tomato); *pesto* (with basil and pine nuts); *matriciana* (bacon and tomato); *arrabbiata* (spicy tomato); *panna* (cream); *ragù* (meat sauce); *aglio e olio* (garlic and olive oil); *burro e salvia* (butter and sage).

il granchio **crab**
il merluzzo **cod**
le moleche **soft-shelled crabs**
le ostriche **oysters**
il pesce **fish**
il pesce spada **swordfish**
il polipo **octopus**
il risotto di mare **seafood risotto**
le sarde **sardines**
la sogliola **sole**
le seppie **cuttlefish**
la triglia **red mullet**
la trota **trout**
il tonno **tuna**
le vongole **clams**

I Legumi/La Verdura (Vegetables)

a scelta **of your choice**
i contorni **accompaniments**
ripieno **stuffed**
gli asparagi **asparagus**
i carciofini **artichoke hearts**
il carciofo **artichoke**
le carote **carrots**
il cavolo **cabbage**
la cicoria **chicory**
la cipolla **onion**
i funghi **mushrooms**
i fagioli **beans**
i fagiolini **French (green) beans**
le fave **broad beans**
il finocchio **fennel**
l'indivia **endive/chicory**
l'insalata mista **mixed salad**
l'insalata verde **green salad**
la melanzana **aubergine**
le patate **potatoes**
le patatine fritte **chips/French fries**
i peperoni **peppers**
i piselli **peas**
i pomodori **tomatoes**
le primizie **spring vegetables**
il radicchio **red, slightly bitter lettuce**
la rughetta **rocket**
i ravanelli **radishes**
gli spinaci **spinach**

la verdura **green vegetables**
la zucca **pumpkin/squash**
gli zucchini **courgettes**

I Dolci (Desserts)

al carrello **(desserts) from the trolley**
un semifreddo **semi-frozen dessert (many types)**
la bavarese **mousse**
la cassata **Sicilian ice cream with candied peel**
le frittelle **fritters**
un gelato (di lampone/limone) **(raspberry/lemon) ice cream**
una granita **water ice**
una macedonia di frutta **fruit salad**
il tartufo (nero) **(chocolate) ice cream dessert**
il tiramisù **cold, creamy cheese and coffee dessert**
la torta **cake/tart**
lo zabaglione **sweet dessert made with eggs and Marsala wine**
la zuppa inglese **trifle**

La Frutta (Fruit)

le albicocche **apricots**
le arance **oranges**
le banane **bananas**
le ciliegie **cherries**
il cocomero **watermelon**
i fichi **figs**
le fragole **strawberries**
i frutti di bosco **fruits of the forest**
i lamponi **raspberries**
la mela **apple**
il melone **melon**
la pesca **peach**
la pera **pear**
il pompelmo **grapefruit**
l'uva **grapes**

Basic Foods

l'aceto **vinegar**
l'aglio **garlic**
il burro **butter**
il formaggio **cheese**
la focaccia **oven-baked snack**
la frittata **omelette**
il grana **hard grating cheese, similar to parmesan**
i grissini **bread sticks**
l'olio **oil**
la marmellata **jam**
il pane **bread**
il pane integrale **wholemeal bread**
il parmigiano **parmesan cheese**
il pepe **pepper**
il riso **rice**
il sale **salt**
la senape **mustard**
le uova **eggs**
lo yogurt **yoghurt**
lo zucchero **sugar**

SIGHTSEEING

Si può visitare? **Can one visit?**
il custode **custodian**
Suonare il campanello **ring the bell**
aperto/a **open**
chiuso/a **closed**
chiuso per la festa **closed for the festival**
chiuso per ferie **closed for the holidays**
chiuso per restauro **closed for restoration**
Is it possible to see the church? *É possibile visitare la chiesa?*
Entrata/uscita **Entrance/exit**
Where can I find the custodian/sacristan/key? *Dove posso trovare il custode/il sacrestano/la chiave?*

AT THE SHOPS

What time do you open/close? *A che ora apre/chiude?*
Closed for the holidays (typical sign) *Chiuso per ferie*
Pull/Push (sign on doors) *Tirare/Spingere*
Entrance/exit *Entrata/uscita*
Can I help you? (formal) *Posso aiutarla?*
What would you like? *Che cosa desidera?*
I'm just looking *Sto soltanto guardando*
How much does it cost? *Quant'è, per favore?*
How much is this? *Quanto viene?*
Do you take credit cards? *Accettate carte di credito?*
I'd like... *Vorrei...*
this one/that one *questo/quello*
I'd like that one, please *Vorrei quello lì, per cortesia*
Have you got...? *Avete...?*
We haven't got (any)... *Non (ne) abbiamo...*
Can I try it on? *Posso provare?*
the size (for clothes) *la taglia*
What size do you take? *Qual'é la sua taglia?*
the size (for shoes) *il numero*

Coffee Italian-Style

Espresso: small, black and strong
Cappuccino: with hot, frothy milk
Caffè lungo: espresso watered down
Caffè macchiato: espresso with a drop of milk
Caffè corretto: espresso with a shot of alcohol
Caffè latte: half milk half coffee in large cup or glass

TRANSPORT
EATING OUT
ACTIVITIES
A – Z
LANGUAGE

Is there/do you have...? *C'è...?*
Yes, of course *Sì, certo*
No, we don't (there isn't) *No, non c'è*
That's too expensive *É troppo caro*
Please write it down for me *Me lo scriva, per favore*
cheap *economico*
Don't you have anything cheaper? *Ha niente che costa di meno?*
It's too small/big *É troppo piccolo/grande*
brown/blue/black *marrone/blu/nero*
green/red/white/yellow *verde/rosso/bianco/giallo*
pink/grey/gold/silver *rosa/grigio/oro/argento*
No thank you, I don't like it *Grazie, ma non è di mio gusto*
I (don't) like it *(Non) mi piace*
I'll take it/I'll leave it *Lo prendo/Lo lascio Una ruberia*
This is faulty. Can I have a replacement/refund? *C'è un difetto. Me lo potrebbe cambiare/rimborsare?*
Anything else? Altro?
The cash desk is over there *Si accomodi alla cassa*
Give me some of those *Mi dia alcuni di quelli lì*
a (half) kilo *un (mezzo) chilo*
100 grams *un etto*
200 grams *due etti*
more/less *più/meno*
with/without *con/senza*
a little *un pochino*
That's enough/No more *Basta così*

Types of Shops

antique dealer *l'antiquario*
bakery *pasticceria*
bank *la banca*
bookshop *la libreria*
boutique/clothes shop *il negozio di moda*
bureau de change *il cambio*
butcher *la macelleria*
chemist *la farmacia*
delicatessen *la salumeria*
department store *il grande magazzino*
dry cleaner *la tintoria*
fishmonger *la pescheria*
food shop *l'alimentari*
florist *il fioraio*
grocer *l'alimentari*
greengrocer *il fruttivendolo*
hairdresser (women) *il parrucchiere*
ice-cream parlour *la gelateria*
jeweller *il gioielliere*
leather shop *la pelletteria*
market *il mercato*
news-stand *l'edicola*

post office *l'ufficio postale*
shoe shop *il negozio di scarpe*
stationer *la cartoleria*
supermarket *il supermercato*
tobacconist *il tabaccaio* (also usually sells travel tickets, stamps, phone cards)
travel agency *l'agenzia di viaggi* (also usually books train tickets for domestic and international journeys)

TRAVELLING

Transport

airport *l'aeroporto*
arrivals/departures *arrivi/partenze*
boat *la barca*
bus *l'autobus/il pullman*
bus station *l'autostazione*
car *la macchina*
connection *la coincidenza*
ferry *il traghetto*
ferry terminal *la stazione marittima*
first/second class *la prima/seconda classe*
flight *il volo*
left luggage office *il deposito bagagli*
motorway *l'autostrada*
no smoking *vietato fumare*
platform *il binario*
porter *il facchino*
railway station *la stazione (ferroviaria)*
return ticket *un biglietto di andata e ritorno*
single ticket *un biglietto di andata sola*
sleeping car *la carrozza letti/il vagone letto*
smokers/non-smokers *fumatori/non-fumatori*
stop *la fermata*
taxi *il taxi*
ticket office *la biglietteria*
train *il treno*
WC *la toilette*

Road Signs

Accendere le luci in galleria **Lights on in tunnel**
Alt **Stop**
Autostrada **Motorway**
Attenzione **Caution**
Avanti **Go/walk**
Caduta massi **Danger of falling rocks**
Casello **Toll gate**
Dare la precedenza **Give way**
Deviazione **Diversion**
Divieto di campeggio **No camping allowed**
Divieto di sosta/Sosta vietata **No parking**

Divieto di passaggio/Senso vietato **No entry**
Dogana **Customs**
Entrata **Entrance**
Galleria **Tunnel**
Guasto **Out of order** (eg phone box)
Incrocio **Crossroads**
Limite di velocità **Speed limit**
Non toccare **Don't touch**
Passaggio a livello **Railway crossing**
Parcheggio **Parking**
Pedaggio **Toll road**
Pericolo **Danger**
Pronto Soccorso **First aid**
Rallentare **Slow down**
Rimozione forzata **Parked cars will be towed away**
Semaforo **Traffic lights**
Senso unico **One way street**
Sentiero **Footpath**
Solo uscita **No entry**
Strada interrotta **Road blocked**
Strada chiusa **Road closed**
Strada senza uscita/Vicolo cieco **Dead end**
Tangenziale **Ring road/bypass**
Traffico di transito **Through traffic**
Uscita **Exit**
Uscita (autocarri) **Exit for lorries**
Vietato il sorpasso **No overtaking**
Vietato il transito **No thoroughfare**

At the Airport

I'd like to book a flight to Venice *Vorrei prenotare un volo per Venezia*
When is the next flight to...? *Quando parte il prossimo aereo per...?*
Are there any seats available? *Ci sono ancora posti liberi?*
Have you got any hand luggage? *Ha bagagli a mano?*
My suitcase has got lost *La mia valigia è andata persa*
My suitcase has been damaged *La mia valigia è rovinata*
The flight has been delayed *Il volo è rimandato*
The flight has been cancelled *Il volo è stato cancellato*

At the Station

Can you help me please? *Mi può aiutare, per favore?*
Where can I buy tickets? *Dov'è posso fare i biglietti?*
What time does the train leave? *A che ora arriva/parte il treno?*
What time does the train arrive/depart? *A che ora il treno?*
Can I book a seat? *Posso prenotare un posto?*
Is this seat free/taken? *É libero/occupato questo posto?*
You'll have to pay a supplement *Deve pagare un supplemento*

Do I have to change? *Devo cambiare?*
Where does it stop? *Dove si ferma?*
Which platform does the train leave from? *Da quale binario parte il treno?*
The train leaves from platform one *Il treno parte dal binario uno*
How long will it take to get there? *Quanto tempo ci vuole per arrivare?*
Will we arrive on time? *Arriveremo puntuali?*
Next stop please *La prossima fermata per favore*
Is this the right stop? *É la fermata giusta?*
The train is late *Il treno è in ritardo*
Can you tell me where to get off? *Mi può dire dove devo scendere?*

Directions

right/left *a destra/a sinistra*
first left/second right *la prima a sinistra/la seconda a destra*
Turn to the right/left *Gira a destra/sinistra*
Go straight on *Va sempre diritto*
Go straight on until the traffic lights *Va sempre diritto fino al semaforo*
Is it far away/nearby? *É lontano/vicino?*
It's five minutes' walk *Cinque minuti a piedi*
It's 10 minutes by car *Dieci minuti con la macchina*
opposite/next to *di fronte/accanto a*
up/down *su/giú*
traffic lights *il semaforo*
junction *l'incrocio, il bivio*
building *il palazzo*
Where is...? *Dov'è...?*
Where are...? *Dove sono...?*
Where is the nearest bank/petrol station/bus stop/hotel/garage? *Dov'è la banca/il benzinaio/la fermata di autobus/l'albergo/l'officina più vicino/a?*
How do I get there? *Come si può andare? (or: Come faccio per arrivare a...?)*
Can you show me where I am on the map? *Può indicarmi sulla cartina dove mi trovo?*

On the Road

Where can I rent a car? *Dove posso noleggiare una macchina?*
Is comprehensive insurance included? *É completamente assicurata?*
Is it insured for another driver? *É assicurata per un altro guidatore?*
By what time must I return it? *A che ora devo consegnarla?*
underground car park *il garage sotterraneo*
driving licence *la patente (di guida)*
petrol *la benzina*
petrol station/garage *la stazione di servizio*
oil *l'olio*
Fill it up please *Faccia il pieno, per favore*
lead free/unleaded/diesel *senza piombo/benzina verde/diesel*
My car won't start *La mia macchina non s'accende*
My car has broken down *La mia macchina è guasta*
How long will it take to repair? *Quanto tempo ci vorrà per la riparazione?*
The engine is overheating *Il motore si surriscalda*
There's something wrong (with/in the)... *C'è un difetto (nel/nella/nei/nelle)...*
accelerator *l'acceleratore*
brakes *i freni*
engine *il motore*
exhaust *lo scarico/scappamento*
fanbelt *la cinghia del ventilatore*
gearbox *la scatola del cambio*
headlights *le luci*
radiator *il radiatore*
spark plugs *le candele*
tyre(s) *la gomma (le gomme)*
windscreen *il parabrezza*

Tourist Signs

Most regions in Italy have handy signs indicating the key tourist sights in any given area:
Abbazia (Badia) **Abbey**
Basilica **Church**
Belvedere **Viewpoint**
Biblioteca **Library**
Castello **Castle**
Centro storico **Old town/historic centre**
Chiesa **Church**
Duomo/Cattedrale **Cathedral**
Fiume **River**
Giardino **Garden**
Lago **Lake**
Mercato **Market**
Monastero **Monastery**
Monumenti **Monuments**
Museo **Museum**
Parco **Park**
Pinacoteca **Art gallery**
Ponte **Bridge**
Ruderi **Ruins**
Scavi **Excavations/archaeological site**
Spiaggia **Beach**
Tempio **Temple**
Torre **Tower**
Ufficio turistico **Tourist office**

HEALTH

Is there a chemist nearby? *C'è una farmacia qui vicino?*
Which chemist is open at night? *Quale farmacia fa il turno di notte?*
I don't feel well *Non mi sento bene*
I feel ill *Sto male/Mi sento male*
Where does it hurt? *Dove Le fa male?*
It hurts here *Ho dolore qui*
I suffer from... *Soffro di...*
I have a headache *Ho mal di testa*
I have a sore throat *Ho mal di gola*
I have a stomach ache *Ho mal di pancia*
Have you got something for air sickness? *Ha/Avete qualcosa contro il mal d'aria?*
Have you got something for sea sickness? *Ha/Avete qualcosa contro il mal di mare?*
antiseptic *crema la crema antisettica*
sunburn *scottatura da sole*
sunburn cream *la crema antisolare*
sticking plaster *il cerotto*
tissues *i fazzoletti di carta*
toothpaste *il dentifricio*
upset stomach pills *le pillole per mal di stomaco*
insect repellent *l'insettifugo*
mosquitoes *le zanzare*
wasps *le vespe*

TRANSPORT

EATING OUT

ACTIVITIES

A – Z

LANGUAGE

FURTHER READING

GENERAL READING

The Advocate: A Sardinian Mystery by Marcello Fois. A lyrical and sometimes haunting noir novel based in Nuoro.
Bandit at the Billiard Table by Alan Ross. The late, former editor of *The London Magazine* describes his journey around Sardinia in the 1950s. The 1954 account of a summer journey is now also available as an e-book.
Death in Sardinia by Marco Vichi. Contemporary Italian crime fiction, the popular Inspector Bordelli series.
Reeds in the Wind *(Canne al Vento)* by Grazia Deledda. Originally published in 1913, the Nobel laureate's most famous work describes the decline of a noble family.
A Sardinian Cookbook by Giovanni Pilu and Roberta Muir. A passionately written introduction to the cuisine of Sardinia, full of tasty recipes.
The Sardinian Cookbook: The Cooking and Culture of a Mediterranean Island by Viktorija Todorovska. A broad spectrum of authentic regional recipes, beautifully presented with full-colour photos.
Sardinian Chronicles by Bernard Lortat-Jacob (translated by Teresa L. Fagan). Rural Sardinia is brought to life through its music, dance and family portraits. The book includes black-and-white photographs and a CD of Sardinian music.
Sea and Sardinia by D.H. Lawrence. Lawrence recalls his journey to Sardinia in 1921. His observations cover the island in all its dimensions, including the people, politics and landscape.
Sweet Myrtle and Bitter Honey: The Mediterranean Flavors of Sardinia by Efisio Farris. Sardinia's famous chef takes readers on a culinary tour. Includes recipes.

OTHER INSIGHT GUIDES

Insight Guides cover nearly 200 destinations, providing information on culture and all the top sights, as well as superb photography and detailed maps. Other Insight Guides to destinations in the region include Italy, Italian Lakes, Tuscany and Sicily. Italian destinations in Insight's detailed and colourful **City Guides** series include Rome, Florence and Siena, and Venice.

The itinerary-based **Insight Explore Guides**, written by local hosts, come complete with a pull out map. Titles include Naples and the Amalfi Coast, the Italian Lakes, Sicily, Venice, Florence and Rome.

Send Us Your Thoughts

We do our best to ensure the information in our books is as accurate and up-to-date as possible. The books are updated on a regular basis using local contacts, who painstakingly add, amend and correct as required. However, some details (such as telephone numbers and opening times) are liable to change, and we are ultimately reliant on our readers to put us in the picture.

We welcome your feedback, especially your experience of using the book "on the road". Maybe we recommended a hotel that you liked (or another that you didn't), or you came across a great bar or new attraction we missed.

We will acknowledge all contributions, and we'll offer an Insight Guide to the best letters received.

Please write to us at:
  Insight Guides
  PO Box 7910
  London SE1 1WE
Or email us at:
  hello@insightguides.com

CREDITS

258

Insight Guide Credits

Distribution
UK
Dorling Kindersley Ltd
A Penguin Group company
80 Strand, London, WC2R 0RL
sales@uk.dk.com

United States
Ingram Publisher Services
1 Ingram Boulevard, PO Box 3006,
La Vergne, TN 37086-1986
ips@ingramcontent.com

Australia and New Zealand
Woodslane
10 Apollo St, Warriewood,
NSW 2102, Australia
info@woodslane.com.au

Worldwide
Apa Publications (Singapore) Pte
7030 Ang Mo Kio Avenue 5
08-65 Northstar @ AMK
Singapore 569880
apasin@singnet.com.sg

Printing
CTPS-China

All Rights Reserved
© 2015 Apa Digital (CH) AG and
Apa Publications (UK) Ltd

First Edition 1991
Fifth Edition 2015

No part of this book may be reproduced, stored in a retrieval system or transmitted in any form or means electronic, mechanical, photocopying, recording or otherwise, without prior written permission from Apa Publications. Every effort has been made to provide accurate information in this publication, but changes are inevitable. The publisher cannot be responsible for any resulting loss, inconvenience or injury. We would appreciate it if readers would call our attention to any errors or outdated information. We also welcome your suggestions; please contact us at: hello@insightguides.com

www.insightguides.com

Editor: Carine Tracanelli
Author: Nick Bruno
Updater: Katarzyna Marcinkowska
Head of Production: Rebeka Davies
Update Production: AM Services
Picture editor: Tom Smyth
Cartography: original cartography Berndtson & Berndtson, updated by Carte

---

Contributors

This new edition of Insight Guide Sardinia builds on a previous edition updated by Nick Bruno, an experienced travel writer with a special fondness for all things Italian; Nick has written and contributed to numerous guidebooks on Italy, and Sardinia in particular.

About Insight Guides

Insight Guides have more than 40 years' experience of publishing high-quality, visual travel guides. We produce 400 full-colour titles, in both print and digital form, covering more than 200 destinations across the globe, in a variety of formats to meet your different needs.
  Insight Guides are written by local authors who use their on-the-ground experience to provide the very latest information; their local expertise is evident in the extensive historical and cultural background features. All the reviews in **Insight Guides** are independent; we strive to maintain an impartial view. Our reviews are carefully selected to guide you to the best places to eat, go out and shop, so you can be confident that when we say a place is special, we really mean it.

Legend
City maps
Freeway/Highway/Motorway
Divided Highway
Main Roads
Minor Roads
Pedestrian Roads
Steps
Footpath
Railway
Funicular Railway
Cable Car
Tunnel
City Wall
Important Building
Built Up Area
Other Land
Transport Hub
Park
Pedestrian Area
Bus Station
Tourist Information
Main Post Office
Cathedral/Church
Mosque
Synagogue
Statue/Monument
Beach
Airport

Regional maps
Freeway/Highway/Motorway (with junction)
Freeway/Highway/Motorway (under construction)
Divided Highway
Main Road
Secondary Road
Minor Road
Track
Footpath
International Boundary
State/Province Boundary
National Park/Reserve
Marine Park
Ferry Route
Marshland/Swamp
Glacier   Salt Lake
Airport/Airfield
Ancient Site
Border Control
Cable Car
Castle/Castle Ruins
Cave
Chateau/Stately Home
Church/Church Ruins
Crater
Lighthouse
Mountain Peak
Place of Interest
Viewpoint

INDEX

Main references are in bold type